Progress
and Poverty

Henry George

Progress
and Poverty

**Why there are recessions
and poverty amid plenty
— and what to do about it!**

Edited and abridged
for modern readers by Bob Drake

Robert Schalkenbach Foundation

Henry George

Progress and Poverty

Why there are recessions, and poverty amid plenty
— and what to do about it!

Edited and abridged for modern readers by Bob Drake

Book design by Lindy Davies
Cover design by Vajramati

ISBN   0-911312-98-6

Library of Congress Control Number: 2006928337

Second printing, 2010

Dedicated to the memory of Bob Drake (1948 – 2009)

Printed in the USA by John S. Swift Print of New Jersey, Inc.

Contents

Fourth Part: The Effect of Material Progress on the Distribution of Wealth

Fifth Part: The Problem Solved

Sixth Part: The Remedy

Seventh Part: Justice of the Remedy

Eighth Part: Application of the Remedy

Ninth Part: Effects of the Remedy

Tenth Part: The Law of Human Progress

Publisher's Foreword

WE OWE Bob Drake a debt of gratitude for this meticulous condensation and modernization of Henry George's great work. The original version had an elegance that evoked a passion for social justice among millions of readers in the nineteenth and early twentieth centuries. However, by the beginning of the twenty-first century, George's complex prose stood in the way of that intention for large numbers of people. Now his ideas can once again be widely accessible.

What were those ideas and why are they still important today? When *Progress and Poverty* was published in 1879, it was aimed in part at discrediting Social Darwinism, the idea that "survival of the fittest" should serve as a social philosophy. That ideology, developed by Herbert Spencer, William Graham Sumner, and others, provided the intellectual basis for 1) American imperialism against Mexico and the Philippines, 2) tax policies designed to reduce burdens on the rich by shifting them onto the poor and middle class, 3) the ascendancy of the concept of absolute property rights, unmitigated by any social claims on property, 4) welfare programs that treat the poor as failures and misfits, 5) racial segregation in education and housing, and 6) eugenics programs to promote the "superior" race. The intellectual defense of racism is in abeyance, but the economic and political instruments of domination have changed little. The renewed defense of taxing wages and consumer goods rather than property holdings, expanded intellectual property rights, and vast imperial ambitions are indications that Social Darwinism is back in full force.

The revival of Social Darwinism continues to justify social disparities on the basis of natural superiority or fitness. *Progress and Poverty*, by contrast, reveals that those disparities derive from special privileges. Many economists and politicians foster the illusion that great fortunes and poverty stem from the presence or absence of individual skill and risk-taking. Henry George, by contrast, showed that the wealth gap occurs because a few people are allowed to monopolize natural opportunities and deny them to others. If we deprived social elites of those monopolies, the whole facade of their greater "fitness" would come tumbling down. George did not advocate equality of income, the forcible redistribution of wealth, or government management of the economy. He simply believed that in a society not burdened by the demands of a privileged elite, a full and satisfying life would be attainable by everyone.

Henry George is best remembered as an advocate of the "single tax" on location values. (I say "location" rather than "land" to avoid the common confusion that George was primarily interested in rural land. In fact his attention was focused on the tens of trillions of dollars worth of urban land that derives its value from location.) Yet, for George, wise tax policy was merely a vehicle to break the stranglehold of speculative ownership that effectively limits the opportunity to earn a decent living and participate in public life.

Perhaps the image that best captures George's ultimate intention is the final scene in a popular science fiction film, when the hero is able to restore the oxygen supply to the surface of a planet so that people will no longer be enslaved by the man holding the oxygen monopoly. Freeing people from the oppression of monopoly power in any form was Henry George's great dream. Those who have conceived of George as being concerned only with tax policy should closely read the last third of *Progress and Poverty*, which reveals his larger vision of justice and genuine freedom.

Progress and Poverty stands the test of time. It contains profound economic analysis, penetrating social philosophy, and a practical guide to public policy. Those who read it today will find in George's work a great source of vision and inspiration.

Cliff Cobb
Robert Schalkenbach Foundation

Editor's Preface

THOSE WHO FIRST pick up this book are likely to share some concern about the problem of poverty; those who finish it may also find some cause for hope. For the great gift that Henry George gave the world was a systematic explanation—logical and consistent—of why wealth is not distributed fairly among those who produce it. But he did not stop there—he also gave us a simple yet far-reaching plan for a cure. It was, and still is, a plan for peace, prosperity, equality, and justice.

Progress and Poverty is an enduring classic. It has been translated into dozens of languages; millions of copies have been distributed worldwide.

Why, then, the need for a modern edition, and an abridged one at that? Simply put, Henry George, like many late-19th century authors, wrote in a style that modern readers may find unduly complex. As editor, I have endeavored to break long and intricate sentences into shorter ones, creating what I call a "thought-by-thought translation."

Furthermore, references to history, mythology, and literature that do not advance the central argument have been removed. Gender-balanced language has also been incorporated. However, I have not attempted to update financial statistics or technological examples.

I prepared this edition in two distinct stages: modernization and condensation. I have sought to ensure that nothing of substance was left out.

In modernizing the text, I reduced the average sentence length and increased the number of sentences. Sentences were shortened by about one-third. For example, one passage showed a decline in average sentence length from twenty-eight words to nineteen words. By comparison, the average sentence in *Time* magazine was fifteen words in 1974, perhaps fewer today.

By simplifying language, I reduced the number of syllables per hundred words by about ten percent, to about 1.7 syllables per word. The number of sentences per hundred words was increased by fifty percent.

The combined effect of these changes transformed the text from one comprehensible to only a small fraction of the population to one that can be easily read by a high-school senior. An early test I performed showed that students were able to read the modernized text about twenty-five percent faster than the original, even before condensation. Although no formal testing for comprehension was done, anecdotal reports indicate that comprehension was greatly improved.

In the second stage, I condensed the modernized text by rewriting sentences using simpler language, removing multiple examples where one would suffice, and generally editing for brevity. Although I occasionally rearranged sentences for clarity and continuity, keeping George's original thesis intact was of utmost importance. In doing this, I followed the exposition as Henry George presented it. I endeavored to remove what is excessive and retain what is essential. In the end, this edition is less than half the size of the original.

This project has been a collective endeavor. Many people contributed to the various drafts, starting with those teachers and students at the Henry George Schools in Chicago, New York, and Philadelphia who provided suggestions and encouragement.

Many thanks to Terry Topczewski, Bob Jene, the late Roy Corr, and Chuck Metalitz for their help and encouragement at various stages; Wyn Achenbaum, Herb Barry, Cliff Cobb, George Collins, Josh Farley, Damon Gross, Heather Remoff, and Tom Smith of the Robert Schalkenbach Foundation board for their editorial reviews; and George M. Menninger, Jr., John Kuchta, Scott Walton, Sue Walton, Bruce Oatman, and Steve Zarlenga for their moral support. Particular thanks to Lindy Davies and Mark Sullivan for their assistance in the final stages of editing and text preparation. Thanks also to the Robert Schalkenbach Foundation and the Center for the Study of Economics for institutional support.

Finally, special thanks must go to my wife (and great jazz singer) Spider Saloff. Without her love and support, none of the rest would have mattered.

Bob Drake
Henry George School of Chicago
April 15, 2006

Preface to the Fourth Edition

IN 1871, I FIRST PUBLISHED these ideas in a pamphlet entitled *Our Land and Land Policy*. Over time, I became even more convinced of their truth. Seeing that many misconceptions blocked their recognition, a fuller explanation seemed necessary. Still, it was impossible to answer all the questions as fully as they deserve. I have tried to establish general principles, trusting readers to extend their application.

While this book may be best appreciated by those familiar with economics, no previous study is needed to understand its argument or to judge its conclusions. I have relied upon facts of common knowledge and common observation, which readers can verify for themselves. They can also decide whether the reasoning is valid.

I set out to discover why wages tend to a bare minimum despite increasing productive power. The current theory of wages, I found, is based on a misconception [namely, that wages are paid from capital]. In truth, wages are produced by the labor for which they are paid. Therefore, other things being equal, wages should increase with the number of laborers.

This immediately confronts the influential Malthusian doctrine that population tends to increase faster than subsistence. Examination shows that this theory has no real support. When brought to a decisive test, it is utterly disproved.

Since these theories cannot explain the connection between progress and poverty, the solution must lie in the three laws governing the distribution of wealth. These laws should correlate with each other, yet economists fail to show this. An examination of terminology reveals the confusion of thought that permits this discrepancy.

To work out these laws, I first take up the law of rent. Although economists correctly understand this law, they fail to appreciate its implications. For whatever determines the part of production that goes to landowners must necessarily determine what is left over for labor and capital.

Nonetheless, I independently deduce the law of interest and the law of wages. Investigation shows that interest and wages rise together when rent falls, and fall together when rent rises. Therefore, rent, wages, and interest are all determined by the margin of production, the point in production where rent begins. I also point out a source of much confusion: mistaking the profits of monopoly for the legitimate earnings of capital.

The laws of distribution are thus brought into harmony. The fact that rent always increases with material progress explains why wages and interest do not.

The question is, what causes rent to increase? Population growth not only lowers the margin of production, it also increases productivity. Both factors increase the proportion of income taken by rent, reducing the proportion of wages and interest. Yet, technological and organizational improvements lead to the same results. Even with a constant population, these alone would produce all the effects Malthus attributes to population growth—as long as land is held as private property.

Further, progress inevitably causes a continuous, speculative increase in land values if land is private property.

This drives rent up and wages down. It also produces periodic industrial depressions.

This analysis points to a remedy, although a radical one. But is there any other? Examining other measures advocated to raise wages merely proves our conclusion. Nothing short of making land common property can permanently relieve poverty.

The question of justice naturally arises, so I next examine the nature and basis of property. There is a fundamental and irreconcilable difference between property in the products of labor and property in land. One has a natural basis, the other none. Recognizing property in land inherently denies the right to property produced by labor.

Landowners have no claim to compensation if society chooses to resume its natural rights. Private property in land always has led—and always must lead—to the enslavement of workers as development proceeds. In the United States, we are already beginning to feel the effects of accepting this erroneous and destructive principle.

As a practical matter, private ownership of land is not necessary for its use or improvement. In fact, it entails enormous waste. Recognizing the common right to land does not require any shock or dispossession. It can be reached by the simple and easy method of taxing only land values. The principles of taxation show that this is the best means of raising revenue.

What would be the effects of this proposed change? It would enormously increase production. It would secure justice in distribution. It would benefit all classes. And it would make possible a higher and nobler civilization.

The inquiry now rises to a wider field. My conclusions assert certain laws. If these are really natural laws, they must be apparent in universal history. As a final test, therefore, I must work out the law of human progress.

Investigation reveals that differences in civilization are not due to differences in individuals or races, but rather to differences in social organization. Progress is always kindled by association. And civilization always declines as inequality develops.

Even now, in modern civilization, the causes that have destroyed all previous civilizations are beginning to appear. Political democracy, without economic opportunity, will devolve into anarchy and despotism.

But the law of social life agrees with the great moral law of justice. This shows how decline may be prevented and a grander advance begun.

If I have correctly solved the great problems I set out to investigate, my conclusions completely change the character of political economy. They give it the coherence and certainty of a true science. And they bring it into sympathy with the aspirations of humanity, from which it has long been estranged.

What I have done in this book is to unite the truth perceived by Smith and Ricardo with the truth perceived by Proudhon and Lassalle.* I have shown that laissez faire—in its full, true meaning—opens the way for us to realize the noble dreams of socialism.

This work was written between August, 1877, and March, 1879. Since its publication, events have shown these views to be correct. The Irish land movement, especially, shows the pressing nature of the problem.

---

* Adam Smith (1723-1790), David Ricardo (1772-1823), Pierre-Joseph Proudhon (1809-1865), and Ferdinand Lassalle (1825-1864). The first two were classical economists; the latter two were socialist reformers.

There has been nothing in the criticisms received to induce me to change or modify these views. In fact, I have yet to see an objection that was not already answered in the book itself. Except for correcting some verbal errors and adding this preface, this edition is the same as the previous ones.*

Henry George
New York, November, 1880
Modernized and abridged, 2006

---

* George subsequently made one modification, regarding patents and copyrights. See page 228.

To those who, seeing the vice and misery that spring from the unequal distribution of wealth and privilege, feel the possibility of a higher social state and would strive for its attainment.

San Francisco, March, 1879

The Problem of Poverty Amid Progress

THE NINETEENTH CENTURY saw an enormous increase in the ability to produce wealth. Steam and electricity, mechanization, specialization, and new business methods greatly increased the power of labor.

Who could have foreseen the steamship, the railroad, the tractor? Or factories weaving cloth faster than hundreds of weavers? Who could have heard the throb of engines more powerful than all the beasts of burden combined? Or envisioned the immense effort saved by improvements in transportation, communication, and commerce?

Surely, these new powers would elevate society from its foundations, lifting the poorest above worry for the material needs of life. Imagine these new machines relieving human toil, muscles of iron making the poorest worker's life a holiday, giving our nobler impulses room to grow. Given such bountiful material conditions, surely we could anticipate the golden age long dreamed of. How could there be greed when everyone had enough? How could things that arise from poverty—crime, ignorance, brutality—exist when poverty had vanished? Such were the dreams born of this wonderful century of progress.

True, there were disappointments. Discovery upon discovery, invention after invention still did not lessen the toil of those who most need relief or bring plenty to the poor. But it seemed there were so many things that could be blamed for this failure that our faith has hardly weakened. Surely we would overcome these difficulties in time.

Yet we must now face facts we cannot mistake. All over the world, we hear complaints of industrial depression: labor condemned to involuntary idleness; capital going to waste; fear and hardship haunting workers. All this dull, deadening pain, this keen, maddening anguish, is summed up in the familiar phrase "hard times."

This situation can hardly be accounted for by local causes. It is common to communities with widely differing circumstances, political institutions, financial systems, population densities, and social organization. There is economic distress under tyrannies, but also where power is in the hands of the people. Distress where protective tariffs hamper trade, but also where trade is nearly free. Distress in countries with paper money, and in countries with gold and silver currencies.

Beneath all this, we can infer a common cause. It is either what we call material progress, or something closely connected with it. What we call an industrial depression is merely an intensification of phenomena that always accompany material progress. They show themselves more clearly and more strongly as progress goes on.

Where do we find the deepest poverty, the hardest struggle for existence, the greatest enforced idleness? Why, wherever material progress is most advanced. That is to say, where population is densest, wealth greatest, and production and exchange most highly developed. In older countries, destitution is found amid the greatest abundance.

Conversely, workers emigrate to newer countries seeking higher wages. Capital also flows there seeking higher interest. They go where material progress is still in earlier stages. The older countries, where material progress has reached its later stages, is where poverty occurs.

Go to a new community where the race of progress is just beginning, where production and exchange are still rude and inefficient. The best house may be only a log cabin; the richest person must work every day. There is not enough wealth to enable any class to live in ease and luxury. No one makes an easy living, or even a very good one—yet everyone can make a living. While you won't find wealth and all its effects, neither will you find beggars. No one willing and able to work lives in fear of want. Though there is no luxury, there is no poverty.

But just when they start to achieve the conditions civilized communities strive for, poverty takes a darker turn. This occurs as savings in production and exchange are made possible by denser settlement, closer connection with the rest of the world, and labor-saving machinery. It occurs just as wealth consequently increases. (And wealth increases not only in the aggregate, but in proportion to population.)

Now, some will find living better and easier—but others will find it hard to get a living at all. Beggars and prisons are the mark of progress as surely as elegant mansions, bulging warehouses, and magnificent churches.

Unpleasant as it may be to admit, it is at last becoming evident that progress has no tendency to reduce poverty. The great fact is, poverty, with all its ills, appears whenever progress reaches a certain stage. Poverty is, in some way, produced by progress itself.

Progress simply widens the gulf between rich and poor. It makes the struggle for existence more intense. Wherever these forces are at work, large classes are maintained on charity.

Yes, in certain ways, the poorest now enjoy what the richest could not a century ago. But this does not demonstrate an improvement—not so long as the ability to obtain the necessities of life has not increased. A beggar in the city may enjoy many things that a backwoods farmer cannot. But the condition of the beggar is not better than that of an independent farmer. What we call progress does not improve the condition of the lowest class in the essentials of healthy, happy human life. In fact, it tends to depress their condition even more.

These new forces do not act on society from underneath. Rather, it is as though an immense wedge is being driven through the middle. Those above it are elevated, but those below are crushed.

Where the poor have long existed, this effect is no longer obvious. When the lowest class can barely live, it is impossible to get any lower: the next step is out of existence altogether. This has been the case for a long time in many parts of Europe. But where new settlements advance to the condition of older ones, we see that material progress not only fails to relieve poverty, it actually produces it.

In the United States, it is obvious that squalor and misery increase as villages grow into cities. Poverty is most apparent in older and richer regions. If poverty is less deep in San Francisco than New York, is it not because it lags behind? Who can doubt that when it reaches the point where New York is now, there will also be ragged children in the streets?

So long as the increased wealth that progress brings goes to building great fortunes and increasing luxury, progress is not real. When the contrast between the haves and have-nots grows ever sharper, progress cannot be permanent. To educate people condemned to poverty only makes them restless. To base a state with glaring social inequalities on political institutions where people are supposed to be equal is to stand a pyramid on its head. Eventually, it will fall.

This relation of poverty to progress is the great question of our time. It is the riddle that the Sphinx* of Fate puts to us. If we do not answer correctly, we will be destroyed.

As important as this question is, we have no answer that accounts for the facts or provides a cure.

Experts break into an anarchy of opinion, and people accept misguided ideas. They are led to believe that there is a necessary conflict between capital and labor; that machinery is an evil; that competition must be restrained; or that it is the duty of government to provide capital or furnish work. Such ideas are fraught with danger, for they allow charlatans and demagogues to control the masses.

But these ideas cannot be successfully challenged until political economy gives some answer to the great question.

Political economy is not a set of dogmas. It is the explanation of a certain set of facts and their mutual relationships. Its deductions follow from premises we all recognize. In fact, we base the reasoning and actions of everyday life on them. These premises can be reduced to

---

* The Sphinx was a creature in Greek mythology who challenged travelers with a riddle. If they could not answer correctly, it devoured them.

an expression as simple and basic as the physical law that says: motion follows the line of least resistance.

Political economy proceeds from the following simple axiom:

People seek to satisfy their desires with the least exertion.

The process then consists simply of identification and separation. In this sense it is as exact a science as geometry. Its conclusions, when valid, should be just as apparent.

Now, in political economy we cannot test theories by artificially producing combinations or conditions, as other sciences can. Yet we can apply tests that are no less conclusive. This can be done by comparing societies in which different conditions exist. Or, we can test various theories in our imagination—by separating, combining, adding, or eliminating forces or factors of known direction.

Properly done, such an investigation should yield a conclusion that will correlate with every other truth. Every effect has a cause; every fact implies a preceding fact.

In the following pages, I will use these methods to discover what law connects poverty with progress. I believe this law will also explain the recurring cycles of industrial and commercial depression, which now seem so unexplainable.

Current political economy cannot explain why poverty persists in the midst of increasing wealth. It teaches only unrelated and disjointed theories. It seems to me, this is not due to any inability of the science. Rather, there must be some false step in its premises, or some overlooked factor in its estimates.

Such mistakes are generally concealed by respect paid

to authority. Therefore, I will take nothing for granted. Accepted theories will be tested; established facts will be freshly questioned. I will not shrink from any conclusion, but promise to follow the truth wherever it may lead.

What the outcome proves to be is not our affair. If the conclusions we reach run counter to our prejudices, let us not flinch. If they challenge institutions that have long been regarded as wise and natural, let us not turn back.

First Part:
Wages and Capital

Chapter 1:
Why Traditional Theories of Wages are Wrong

First, let's clearly define the problem we are investigating and review how currently accepted theories attempt to explain it. We want to discover why poverty persists despite increasing wealth. It is universally recognized that wages tend toward a minimum level. Whatever causes this must also cause the persistence of poverty. So let's frame our inquiry like this:

Why do wages tend to decrease to subsistence level, even as productive power increases?

Current theory erroneously attempts to explains it thus: (a) wages are set by the ratio between the number of workers and the amount of capital available for labor; (b) population is presumed to increase faster than the increase in capital; (c) therefore, wages always move toward the lowest level workers will tolerate. That is, wages are equal to capital divided by population. Increasing population is held in check only by the limitations of wages, so even if capital increases toward infinity, there will be no improvement.

In plain English, current theory incorrectly claims that wages cannot rise faster than the population among which capital must be divided. Only low wages will slow the population growth of workers.

This doctrine, though false, is virtually undisputed; it is endorsed by noted economists and taught in great universities. It is popular among those not clever enough to have theories of their own, as may be seen daily in newspaper columns and legislative debates. The general public holds even cruder forms. Why—despite obvious inconsistencies and fallacies—do people cling to protectionist views? They accept the mistaken belief that each community has only a fixed amount of wages available, and that this would be further divided among "foreign competition." This misconception is the basis of most other failed attempts to increase the workers' share, such as restricting competition or abolishing interest.

Yet, despite being so widely held, this theory simply does not fit the facts.

If wages are set by the ratio between labor and capital, then the relative abundance of one must mean a lack of the other. Now, if capital is not used for wages, it can be invested elsewhere. So the current interest rate is a relatively good measure of whether capital is scarce or abundant.

According to this theory, then, high wages (scarce labor) must be accompanied by low interest (abundant capital). In the reverse case, low wages (abundant labor) must be accompanied by high interest (scarce capital).

But we can see that, in fact, the opposite is true: Interest is high when wages are high. Interest is low when wages are low. Wherever labor goes seeking higher wages, capital also flows seeking higher interest. Whenever there has been a general rise or fall in wages, there has been a similar rise or fall in interest at the same time.

Wages are usually higher in new countries (where capital is relatively scarce) than in old countries (where capital is relatively abundant). Both wages and interest have been higher in the United States than in England, and in the Pacific rather than in the Atlantic States. In California, when wages were higher than anywhere else in the world, interest was also higher. Later, wages and interest in California went down together.

Consider the economics of "good times" and "hard times." A brisk demand for labor (and good wages) is always accompanied by a brisk demand for capital (and high interest rates). However, when jobs are scarce and wages slump, there is always an accumulation of capital seeking investment at low rates.

It is true that rates may be high during commercial panics. However, this is not properly called a high rate of interest. Rather, it is a rate of insurance against risk.

The present depression (1879) has seen unemployment and lower wages. It has also seen the accumulation of unused capital in all the great cities, with nominal interest on safe investments.

These are all well-known facts. They do point to a relationship between wages and interest—but it is a relation of conjunction, not of opposition. There is no explanation of these conditions that is consistent with current theory.

How, then, could such a theory arise? Why was it accepted by economists from Adam Smith to the present? If we examine the reasoning supporting this theory, it becomes clear that it is not an induction from observed facts. Rather, it is a deduction from a previously assumed theory.

Specifically, it has already been assumed that wages are drawn from capital.

If capital is the source of wages, it logically follows that total wages must be limited by the capital devoted to wages. Hence, the amount individual laborers can receive must be determined by the ratio between their number and the amount of capital available.

This reasoning process is logically valid. However, as we have seen, the conclusion drawn from it does not fit the observed facts. Therefore, the problem must be in the premise.

I am aware that the idea that wages are drawn from capital is one of the most fundamental and widely accepted theorems of current political economy, accepted as axiomatic by all the great economists. Nevertheless, I think I can demonstrate that this is a fundamental error. It forms the basis of a long series of errors that distort the practical conclusions drawn from them.

The proposition I intend to prove is this:

Wages are not drawn from capital. On the contrary, wages are drawn from the product of the labor for which they are paid. *

Now, while current theory says wages are drawn from capital, it also says capital is reimbursed from production.

---

* For simplicity, George restricts his analysis here to the production of physical wealth. Wages for services, the use of labor to satisfy desires directly, are not advanced from capital, but from wealth devoted to consumption (see page 33).

So at first glance this may appear to be a distinction without a difference. If this were merely a change in terminology, any discussion would only add to the meaningless petty arguments that comprise so much of economics. But it will become apparent that this is much more than a formal distinction. Indeed, all the current theories regarding the relation between capital and labor are built on this difference. Doctrines deduced from it are regarded as axiomatic; they limit and direct the ablest minds in discussing issues of momentous importance.

Among the beliefs based on the assumption that wages are drawn directly from capital—not from the product of labor—are the following: industry is limited by capital; labor can only be employed as capital is accumulated; every increase of capital enables additional employment; conversion of circulating capital into fixed capital reduces the fund available to labor; more laborers can be employed at low wages than at high wages; profits are high when wages are low; profits are low when wages are high.

In short, almost all the important theories of current political economy are based on the erroneous assumption that labor is paid out of existing capital before any product is produced. I maintain, on the contrary, that wages are drawn directly from the product of labor. They do not—even temporarily—come close to relying on existing capital.

If I can prove this, then all those other theories are left without any support and must be discarded—including all theories based on the belief that the supply of wages is fixed. For such reasoning holds that as the number of workers increases, the share to each must diminish.

On this foundation, current economists have built a

vast superstructure of related theories. But in truth, this foundation has merely been taken for granted. Not the slightest attempt has been made to distinguish whether or not it is based on fact.

It is inferred that wages are drawn from preexisting capital because wages are generally paid in money. In many cases, wages are paid before the product is fully completed or useful. From this it is concluded that industry is limited by capital. That is, that labor cannot be employed until capital has been accumulated; and then, only to the extent of such capital.

Yet in the same books holding these theories, we find the contradiction. First they claim, without reservation, that capital limits labor. Then they state that capital is stored up or accumulated labor. If we substitute this definition for the word capital, the proposition refutes itself. That is, it says labor cannot be employed until the results of labor have been accumulated. This is patently absurd. But we cannot end the argument with this *reductio ad absurdum* alone, for other explanations are likely to be tried. Perhaps Divine Providence provided the capital that allowed the first labor to begin? More likely, the proposition would be said to refer to more advanced societies where complex production methods are used.

However, there is a fundamental truth in all economic reasoning that we must firmly grasp and never let go of. Modern society, though highly developed, is only an elaboration of the simplest society. Principles that are obvious in simple relationships are not reversed or abolished in more complex ones. The same principles are merely disguised by the use of sophisticated tools and the division of labor.

The modern grist mill, with all its complicated machinery, is only a means of grinding corn. Factory workers may run machines, print labels, or keep books. Yet, they are really devoting their labor to the same task: preparing food. The modern mill serves the same purpose as an ancient stone mortar unearthed by archeologists. Both the ancient and modern workers are attempting to satisfy their desires by exerting labor on natural resources.

Modern economy is a vast and intricate network of production and exchange, with complex operations infinitely subdivided into specialized functions. Yet looking at production as a whole, we see it is the cooperation of all to satisfy the desires of each. Keeping this in mind, we see clearly that the reward each obtains, though engaged in diverse tasks, comes truly and directly from nature as the result of that particular exertion. It is no different from the efforts of the very first human.

Consider the example of a primitive fishing village. Under the simplest conditions, they all catch their own fish and dig their own bait. Soon, they realize the advantage of a division of labor. So now one person digs bait while the others go out fishing. It is obvious at this point that the one who digs bait is, in reality, doing as much toward catching fish as those who actually take in the catch.

Next the advantages of canoes are discovered. Instead of each person building a canoe, only one stays behind to make and repair canoes for the others. In reality, the canoe-maker is devoting labor to catching fish as much as those actually fishing. The fish eaten each night are as much a product of the labor of the canoe-maker as they are of the labor of those fishing. As the division of labor continues, we find that one group fishes, another hunts, a third picks berries, a fourth gathers fruit, a fifth makes tools, a sixth builds huts, and a seventh prepares clothing.

Division of labor, when fairly established, benefits all by common pursuit. It is used instead of individuals attempting to satisfy all of their wants by directly resorting to nature on their own. As they exchange with each other the product of their labor for the products of others' labor, they are really applying their own labor to the production of the things they use—just as if each person had made each item alone. They are, in effect, satisfying their own particular desires by the exertion of their own individual powers. That is to say, they genuinely produce whatever they receive.

These principles are obvious in simple society. If we follow them through the complexities of what we call civilization, we can clearly see the same principles. In every case where labor is exchanged for commodities, production actually precedes enjoyment. Such wages are not the advance of capital.

Someone's labor has contributed to the general stock of wealth. He receives in return a draft against this general stock. He may use that draft in any particular form that will best satisfy his desires. Though the money itself may have been printed before his labor, it is really an exchange of the products of his labor for the products of others' labor. The important point is that neither the money, nor the particular items he chooses to buy, are advances of capital. On the contrary, money is merely a draft that represents the wealth his labor has already added to the general stock.

Keeping these principles in mind, we can see the same truth in a variety of examples. An engineer cooped up in some dingy office drawing plans for a great turbine is, in reality, devoting her labor to the production of bread and meat. She is doing so just as truly as if she were harvesting grain in California or swinging a lariat on the pampas of Argentina. She is as truly making her own clothes as if she were shearing sheep in Australia or weaving cloth in a factory. She is effectively producing the wine for her dinner just as though she had gathered the grapes in France.

A miner, digging silver ore thousands of feet underground, is, by virtue of a thousand exchanges, in effect harvesting crops in the valley or fishing in the arctic; picking coffee in Honduras and cutting sugar in Hawaii; gathering cotton from Georgia and weaving it in Manchester; or plucking fruit in the orchards of California.

The wages he receives for the week are merely certificates to show the world that he has done these things. The money he receives in return for his labor is only the first in a long series of exchanges. These transmute his labor into those particular things for which he has really been laboring.

All this is clear when we look at it this way. But the fallacy remains firmly entrenched in many hiding places. To reveal it, we must now change our investigation from the deductive to the inductive. Our conclusions have been obvious when we began with general principles and deduced specific examples. Let us now see if we arrive at the same conclusions inductively—that is, by examining specific facts and tracing their relations into general principles.

Chapter 2
Defining Terms

BEFORE PROCEEDING FURTHER, we must define our terms so that each meaning remains consistent. Otherwise, our reasoning will be vague and ambiguous. Many eminent authors have stressed the importance of clear and precise definitions. I cannot add to this, except to point out the many examples of these same authors falling into the very trap they warn against.

Certain words—such as *wealth, capital, rent,* and *wages*—require a much more specific meaning in economic reasoning than they do in everyday speech. Unfortunately, even among economists, there is no agreement on the meaning of these terms. Different writers give different meanings to the same term. Even worse, one author will use the same term in different senses. Nothing shows the importance of precise language like the spectacle of the brightest thinkers basing important conclusions on the same word used in different senses.

I will strive to state clearly what I mean by any term of importance—and to use it only in that sense. Further, I will conform to common usage as much as possible, rather than assign arbitrary meanings or coin new terms. The reader should keep these definitions in mind, for otherwise I cannot be properly understood. My desire is to fix the meaning plainly enough to express my thoughts clearly.

Now, we had been discussing whether wages are, in fact, drawn from capital. So let's start by defining wages and capital. Economists have given a sufficiently definite meaning to wages. However, capital will require a detailed explanation, since it has been used ambiguously by many economists.

In common conversation, wages mean compensation paid to someone hired to render services. The habit of applying it solely to compensation paid for manual labor further narrows its use. We do not speak of the wages of professionals or managers, but of their fees, commissions, or salaries. So, the common meaning of wages is compensation for manual labor.

But in political economy, the word wages has a much wider meaning. Economists speak of three factors of production: land, labor, and capital. Labor includes all human exertion in the production of wealth. Wages are the portion of production that goes to labor. Therefore, the term wages includes all rewards for such exertion.

In the economic sense of the term, none of the distinctions of common speech apply. It does not matter what kind of labor it is. Nor does it matter whether the reward for labor is received from an employer or not. Wages, in the economic sense, simply means the return for the exertion of labor. It is distinguished from the return for the use of capital (interest), and from the return for the use of land (rent).

The wages of hunters are the game they kill; the wages of fishermen, the fish they catch. Farmers get wages from their crops. In addition, if they use their own capital and their own land, part of the crop will be considered interest, part rent. Gold panned by self-employed prospectors is as much their wages as money paid to hired miners.

And, as Adam Smith noted, the high profits of retail store-keepers are in large part wages—that is, compensation for their labor, not just for their capital.

In short, whatever is received as the result or reward of exertion is wages. This is all we need to know for now, but it is important to keep it in mind. In standard economics texts, this term is used more or less clearly—at first. Sadly, this clear definition is frequently ignored later on.

The idea of capital, on the other hand, is so beset with ambiguities that it is difficult to determine a precise use of the term. In general discourse, all sorts of things that have a value, or will yield a return, are vaguely spoken of as capital. Economists themselves use the term in so many senses that it hardly has any fixed meaning.*

I could go on for pages citing contradictory—and self-contradictory—definitions from other authors, but this would only bore the reader. You can find further illustration of the confusion among economists and learned professors in any library, where their works are arranged side by side.

What name we call something is not the issue here. The point is to use it to always mean the same thing—and nothing else. Most people, in fact, understand what capital is well enough—until they begin to define it. Even economists use the term in the same sense—in every case except in their own definitions and the reasoning based on them. They apply their particular definition to set up the premise of their reasoning. But when conclusions are drawn, capital is always used—or at least always understood—in one particular sense.

This commonly understood sense separates capital from

---

* Curious readers may find examples in the original text, pp. 33-36.

land and labor, the other factors of production. It also separates it from similar things used for gratification. The common meaning of capital is, simply put, wealth devoted to producing more wealth. Adam Smith correctly expresses this common idea when he says: "That part of a man's stock which be expects to afford him revenue is called his capital." The capital of a community is therefore the sum of such individual stocks. Said another way, it is the part of the aggregate stock that is expected to procure more wealth.

Political and social writers are even more striking than economic ones in their failure to use capital as an exact term. Their difficulties arise from two facts. First, there are certain things that—to an individual—are equivalent to possessing capital. However, they are not part of the capital of the community. Second, things of the same kind may—or may not—be capital, depending on what they are used for.

Keeping these points in mind, we can use the term capital in a clear and constant manner, without any ambiguity or confusion. Our definition will enable us to say what things are capital and what are not. The three factors of production are land, labor, and capital. The term capital is used in contradistinction to land and labor. Therefore, nothing properly included as either land or labor can be called capital.

The term land does not simply mean the surface of the earth as distinguished from air and water—it includes all natural materials, forces, and opportunities. It is the whole material universe outside of humans themselves. Only by access to land, from which their very bodies are drawn, can people use or come in contact with nature.

Therefore, nothing freely supplied by nature can be

properly classed as capital.

Consider a fertile field, a rich vein of ore, or a falling stream, which can supply power. These may give the owner advantages that are equivalent to possessing capital. However, calling them capital would end the distinction between land and capital. It would make the terms meaningless in relation to each other.

Similarly, the term labor includes all human exertion. So human powers can never be properly classed as capital. This, of course, applies whether they are natural or acquired powers. In common parlance, we often speak of someone's knowledge, skill, or industry as his or her capital. This language is obviously metaphorical. We cannot use it in reasoning that requires exactness. Such qualities may increase income, just as capital would. The community may increase its production by increases in knowledge, skill, or industry.

The effect may be the same as an increase of capital. However, the increase in production is due to the increased power of labor, not capital. Increased velocity may give the impact of a cannon ball the same effect as increased weight. Nevertheless, weight is one thing and velocity another.

Therefore, capital must exclude everything that may be included as land or labor. This leaves only things that are neither land nor labor. These things have resulted from the union of the two original factors of production. In other words, nothing can be capital that is not wealth.

Many of the ambiguities about capital derive from ambiguities in the use of the inclusive term wealth. In common use, wealth means anything having an exchange value. When used as an economic term, however, it must be limited to a much more definite meaning.

If we take into account the concept of collective or general wealth, we see that many things we commonly call wealth are not so at all. Instead, they represent the *power to obtain wealth* in transactions between individuals (or groups). That is, they have an exchange value. However, their increase or decrease does not affect the sum of wealth in the community. Therefore, they are not truly wealth.

Some examples are stocks, bonds, mortgages, promissory notes, or other certificates for transferring wealth. Neither can slaves be considered wealth. Their economic value merely represents the power of one class to appropriate the earnings of another. Lands or other natural opportunities obtain exchange value only from consent to an exclusive right to use them. This merely represents the power given to landowners to demand a share of the wealth produced by those who use them.

Increase in the amount of bonds, mortgages, or notes cannot increase the wealth of the community, since that community includes those who pay as well as those who receive. Slavery does not increase the wealth of a people, for what the masters gain the enslaved lose. Rising land values do not increase the common wealth, as whatever landowners gain by higher prices, tenants or purchasers lose in paying them.

All this relative wealth is undistinguished from actual wealth in legislation and law, as well as common thought and speech. Yet with the destruction of nothing more than a few drops of ink and a piece of paper, all this "wealth" could be utterly annihilated. By an act of law, debts may be canceled, slaves emancipated, land made common property. Yet the aggregate wealth would not be diminished at all—for what some would lose others would gain. Wealth was not created when Queen Elizabeth graced her favorite courtiers with profitable monopolies, nor when Boris Godunov declared Russian peasants to be property.

The term wealth, when used in political economy, does not include all things having an exchange value. It includes only those things that increase the aggregate wealth when produced or decrease it when destroyed. If we consider what these things are and what their nature is, we will have no difficulty defining wealth.

We speak of a community increasing its wealth. For instance, we say that England increased its wealth under Queen Victoria, or that California is wealthier than when it belonged to Mexico. By saying this, we do not mean there is more land or natural resources. We do not mean some people owe more debts to others. Nor do we mean there are more people. To express that idea, we speak of an increase in population—not wealth.

What we really mean is there was an increase of certain tangible goods—things that have an actual, not merely a relative, value. We mean buildings, cattle, tools, machinery, agricultural and mineral products, manufactured goods, ships, wagons, furniture, and the like. More of such things is an increase in wealth; less of them is a decrease in wealth. We would say the community with the most of such things, in proportion to its population, is the wealthiest.

What is the common characteristic of these things? They all consist of natural substances that have been adapted by human labor for human use. Wealth, then, may be defined as natural products that have been secured, moved, combined, separated, or in other ways modified by human exertion to fit them for the gratification of human desires.

Their value depends on the amount of labor that, on average, would be required to produce things of like kind. In other words, it is labor impressed upon matter so as to store up the power of human labor to satisfy human desires, as the heat of the sun is stored in coal.

Wealth is not the sole object of labor, for labor is also expended to directly satisfy human desires. Wealth is the result of what we may call productive labor—that is, labor that gives value to material things. Wealth does not include anything nature supplies without human labor. Yet the result of labor is not wealth unless it produces a tangible product that satisfies human desires.

Capital is wealth devoted to a certain purpose. Therefore, nothing can be considered capital that does not fit within the definition of wealth.

But though all capital is wealth, all wealth is not capital. Capital is only a particular part of wealth—that part devoted to aid production. We must draw a line between wealth that is capital and wealth that is not capital. If we keep this in mind, we can eliminate misconceptions that have led even gifted thinkers into a maze of contradiction.

The problem, it seems to me, is that the idea of what capital *is* has been deduced from some preconceived idea of what capital *does*. Logic would dictate first determining what something is, then observing what it does. Instead, the functions of capital have first been assumed. Then a definition is fitted to include everything that does, or may perform, those functions.

Let us adopt the natural order and ascertain what capital is before declaring what it does. The term in general is well understood; we need only make the edges sharp and clear. If actual articles of wealth were shown to a dozen intelligent people who had never read a line of economics, it is doubtful that they would disagree at all about what was capital or not.

No one would think of counting as capital someone's wig, or the cigar in the mouth of a smoker, or the toy a child plays with. But we would count, without hesitation, a wig for sale in a store, the stock of a tobacconist, or the goods in the toy store. A coat made for sale would be accounted capital; but not the coat a tailor made to wear. Food used in a restaurant would be capital; but not food in a pantry. Part of a crop held for seed or sale, or given as wages, would be capital; the part used by the farmer's family would not.

I think we would agree with Adam Smith that capital is "that part of a man's stock which he expects to yield him a revenue." As examples, he lists:

- ♦ machines and instruments of trade that aid or lessen labor;
- ♦ buildings used in trade, such as shops, farmhouses, etc. (but not dwellings);
- ♦ improvements of land for agricultural purposes;
- ♦ goods for sale, from which producers and dealers expect to derive a profit;
- ♦ raw materials and partially manufactured articles still in the hands of producers or dealers;
- ♦ completed articles still in the hands of producers or dealers.*

If we look for what distinguishes capital in this list, we will not find it among the character or capabilities of the

---

*Smith's original list included two items that do not fit under George's definition of capital. See original text, p. 47.

items (though vain attempts have been made to do so).

The key, it seems to me, is whether or not the item is in the possession of the consumer. Wealth yet to be exchanged is capital. Wealth in the hands of the consumer is not.

Hence, we can define capital as wealth in the course of exchange. We must understand here that exchange does not mean merely passing from hand to hand—it also includes the increase in wealth from the reproductive or transformative forces of nature. Using this definition, we can include all the things that capital properly includes, and eliminate all it does not.

This definition includes all tools that are really capital. For what makes a tool capital is whether its uses or services are to be exchanged or not. Thus, the lathe used to make things for exchange is capital; one kept as a hobby is not. Wealth used in the construction of a railroad, a theater, or a hotel is wealth in the course of exchange. The exchange does not occur all at once, but little by little, with an indefinite number of people—yet there is an exchange. The consumers are not the owners, but rather the patrons who use these facilities.

This definition is consistent with the idea that capital is that part of wealth devoted to production of more wealth. But to say production is merely "making things" is too narrow an understanding of the term. Production also includes bringing things to the consumer. Storekeepers are as much producers as farmers or manufacturers. The stock in a store is capital, and it is as much devoted to production as the capital of the others.

We are not yet concerned with the functions of capital. That will be easier to determine later. Nor is the definition itself important. I am not writing a textbook;

I am trying to discover the laws governing a great social problem. My purpose here has been to help the reader form a clear idea of what things are meant when we speak of capital.

In ending this chapter, let me note what is often forgotten. Terms like wealth, capital, and wages, as used in political economy, are abstract terms. Nothing can be stated or denied about them unless it applies to the whole class of things they represent. The idea of wealth involves the idea of exchangeability. To possess a given amount of wealth is potentially to possess any or all types of wealth that would be equivalent to it in exchange. Of course, the same is true of capital.

The failure to bear this in mind has allowed fallacies, which otherwise would be transparent lies, to pass for obvious truths.

Chapter 3

Wages Are Produced By Labor, Not Drawn From Capital

THE IMPORTANCE of defining our terms can be seen at once in this chapter. When people say wages are drawn from capital, they are obviously using wages in the everyday sense, forgetting the economic meaning.

When workers take their reward directly from the product of their labor, their wages clearly are not drawn from capital. If I go out and pick wild berries, the wages for my labor are the berries. Surely no one will argue that wages are drawn from capital in such a case—there is no capital involved!

If I work a piece of leather into a pair of shoes, those shoes are my wages, the result of my labor. They are not drawn from capital, my own or anyone else's. They are brought into existence by my effort, and my capital is not lessened at all—not even for a moment. At the start, my capital consists of leather, thread, and so on. As I work, value is steadily added. When the shoes are finished, I still have my capital, plus the difference in value between the original material and the shoes. This additional value becomes my wages.

Adam Smith recognized that wages are the product of labor in such simple cases. His chapter on wages begins: "The produce of labor constitutes the natural recompense

or wages of labor. In that original state of things which precedes both the appropriation of land and the accumulation
of stock, the whole produce of labor belongs to the laborer.
He has neither landlord nor master to share with him."

If Smith had traced this obvious truth through more
complicated forms of production—recognizing wages as
the product of labor, with landlord and master merely
sharers—political economy would be very different today,
not a mess of contradictions and absurdities. Instead, he
recognized it only momentarily and abandoned it immediately—restarting his inquiry from the point of view of
the business owner providing wages from her capital.

Let us pick up the clue where Adam Smith dropped
it. Proceeding step by step, we will see whether these relationships, obvious in simple examples, still hold true in
the most complex forms of production.

In the "original state of things," as we have seen, the
entire product of labor belongs to the worker. Next in simplicity are cases where wages are paid in kind. That is to
say, workers' wages come from the things produced by their
labor, even though they may be working for another or
using the capital of another. Clearly, these wages are drawn
from the product of the labor, not from capital. Let's say I
hire workers to pick berries or make shoes. I then pay them
from the berries or shoes. There can be no question that
the source of their wages is the same labor for which they
are being paid.

Take the next step where wages are estimated in kind,
but paid in an equivalent value of something else. For instance, the custom on American whaling ships is to pay
each crew member a proportion of the catch. At the end
of a successful cruise, a ship carries the wages of her crew

in her hold, along with the owner's profits and reimbursement for stores used during the voyage. The oil and bone the crew have caught are their wages. Can anything be clearer than that these have not been drawn from capital? They are the product of their labor.

This fact is not changed or obscured in the least when the crew is paid in cash. This is simply a matter of convenience: the value of each share is estimated at market price, instead of dividing the actual oil and bone. Money is just the equivalent of their real wages: the oil and bone. In no way is there any advance of capital in such payment. The obligation to pay the whalers does not accrue until the value of the catch, from which wages are to be paid, is brought into port. When the owner takes money from her capital to pay the crew, she adds the oil and bone to her capital.

So far, there can be no dispute. Let us now take another step: the usual method of employing labor by paying wages. A company hires workers to stay on an island gathering eggs, which are sent to San Francisco every few days to be sold. At the end of the season, the workers are paid a set wage in cash. Now, the owners could pay them a portion of the eggs, as is done in other hatcheries. They probably would, if there were uncertainty about the outcome. But since they know so many eggs will be gathered by so much labor, it is more convenient to pay fixed wages. This cash merely represents the eggs—for the sale of eggs produces the cash to pay the wages. These wages are the product of the labor for which they are paid—just as the eggs would be to workers who gathered them for themselves without the intervention of an employer.

In these cases, we see that wages in money are the

same as wages in kind. Is this not true of all cases in which wages are paid for productive labor? Isn't the fund created by labor really the fund from which wages are paid?

Now, the argument may be made that those working for themselves get nothing if some disaster spoils the work; but those working for an employer get their wages anyhow. This is not a real distinction, however. Generally, any disaster that prevents an employer from benefiting from labor also prevents the employer from paying wages. On the whole, labor done for fixed wages produces more than the amount of the wages. Otherwise, employers could not make any profit.

Production is the source of wages. Wages come from the fruits of labor—not the advance of capital. Labor *always* precedes wages. This is true whether wages are received from an employer, or wages are taken directly from the efforts of the workers. Wages paid by an employer imply the previous rendering of labor by the employee for the benefit of the employer. This is true whether paid by the day, week, or month, or even by the piece.

Though it is obvious the way I have explained it, many important deductions are based on the opposite position. How can it be considered plausible that wages are drawn from capital? It begins with the assertion that labor cannot operate unless capital supplies it with maintenance. The unwary reader agrees that labor must have food and clothing in order to work. Having been told that such items are capital, the reader then accepts the conclusion that capital is required before labor can be applied. From this misdirection, it appears to be an obvious deduction that industry is limited by capital. That is to say, that the demand for labor depends on the supply of capital. Hence, it appears to follow that wages are set by the ratio between the number of laborers looking for employment and the amount of capital available to hire them.

A fallacy exists in this reasoning that has entangled some of the brightest minds in a web of their own spinning. But I think our discussion in the previous chapter will enable us to spot the error. It is the use of the term capital in two different senses.

The primary proposition is that capital is required for labor. Here "capital" is understood as including all food, clothing, shelter, and so on. Whereas in the deductions drawn from it, capital is used in its common and legitimate meaning. That is: wealth devoted to procuring more wealth. This does not include wealth used for the immediate gratification of desire. It means wealth in the hands of employers as distinguished from laborers.

So to say that workers cannot work without food and clothing does not mean that only those who first receive breakfast and clothes from an employer may work. The fact is that laborers generally furnish their own breakfasts and their own clothes. Further, capitalists are never compelled to make advances to labor before work begins (though in exceptional cases they may choose to do so). Of all the unemployed labor in the world today, there is probably not a single one who could not be hired without paying wages in advance. Many would gladly wait until the end of the month to be paid, many more until the end of the week, as most workers usually do. The precise time is immaterial. The essential point is that wages are paid after the performance of labor.

Wages always imply the previous rendering of labor. And what does "rendering of labor" imply? The production of wealth. If this wealth is to be used in exchange or in production, then it is capital. Therefore, the payment of capital in wages presupposes some production of capital—by the very labor for which those wages are paid.

Since the employer generally makes a profit in this transaction, paying wages is merely returning part of the capital received from labor. The employee gets part of the capital labor has produced.

How can it be said that wages are advanced by capital or drawn from preexisting capital? The value paid in wages is an exchange for value created by labor. And the employer always gets the capital created by labor before paying out capital in wages. At what point, then, is capital lessened, even temporarily?

Note that I refer to labor as producing capital for simplicity's sake. Labor always produces either wealth (which may or may not be capital) or services. Only in an exceptional case of misadventure is nothing produced. Now, sometimes labor is performed simply for the satisfaction of the employer. For example, getting one's shoes shined. Such wages are not paid from capital, but from wealth devoted to consumption. Even if such funds were once considered capital, they no longer are. By the very act, they pass from the category of capital to that of wealth used for gratification. It is the same as when a tobacconist takes cigars from the stock for sale and pockets them for personal use.

Let's test our reasoning against the facts. Consider a manufacturer who produces finished products from raw materials, say cloth from cotton. The company pays its workers weekly, as is the custom. Before work begins on Monday morning, we take an inventory of their capital. It consists of buildings, machinery, raw materials, money on hand, and finished products in stock. After work has ended for the week and wages paid, we take a new inventory. For the sake of simplicity, we will assume that nothing was bought or sold during that week.

Let us look at their capital now. There will be less money, since some was paid out in wages. There will be less raw material, less coal, and so on. A deduction for wear and tear must be made from the value of the buildings and machinery. But if the business is profitable, as most are, the items of finished products will more than compensate for these costs. There will be a net increase of capital.

Obviously, then, wages were not drawn from capital. They came from the value created by labor itself. There was no more an advance of capital than if someone hired workers to dig clams and paid them with the clams they dug. Their wages were truly the product of their labor. The same as, in Adam Smith's words, "before the appropriation of land and the accumulation of stock."

This situation is similar to that of bank depositors: After they have put money in, they can take money out. By withdrawing what they have previously put in, the bank depositors do not lessen the capital of the bank. Likewise, by receiving wages, the worker does not lessen, even temporarily, the capital of the employer. Nor does the worker lessen the total capital of the community.

It is true workers generally are not paid in the same kind of wealth they have created. Likewise, banks do not give depositors the same bills or coins they deposited—instead, they receive it in an equivalent form. We rightly say the bank gives depositors the money they paid in. So we are justified in saying workers receive in wages the wealth they created with their labor.

This universal truth is often obscured because we confuse wealth with money, due to our habit of estimating capital in terms of money. Money is a general medium of exchange, the common flow through which wealth is transformed from one form to another.

Difficulties in exchanging wealth generally show up on the side of reducing wealth to money. Money may easily be exchanged for any other form of wealth. Yet sometimes it is more difficult to exchange a particular form of wealth for money. The reason is simple: there are more who want to make *some* exchange of wealth than there are those who want to make a particular exchange.

Employers who pay wages in money sometimes find it difficult to turn their products back into money quickly. They are spoken of as "having exhausted" or "advanced" their capital in wages. Yet the money paid out in wages has, in fact, been exchanged for an increase in the value of their products. (Only in exceptional cases is the value created by the labor less than wages paid.)

The capital they had before in money, they now have in goods. It has been changed in form—but not lessened.

Now, in some cases production may require months or years, during which no return is received. Meanwhile, wages must be paid. Such cases—where wages are paid before the desired results are completed—are always given as examples of wages advanced from capital. Well, let us see.

In agriculture, for instance, harvesting must be preceded by several months of plowing and sowing. Similarly, in the construction of buildings, ships, railroads, and so on, owners cannot expect an immediate return. They must wait, sometimes for many years. In these cases, it is easy to jump to the conclusion that wages are advanced by capital—if fundamental principles are forgotten. But if I have made myself clear, the reader will not be fooled. A simple analysis will show that such instances are no exception to the rule. The fundamental principle is clear whether the product is finished before or after wages are paid.

Let's say I go to a broker to exchange silver for gold. As I give them my silver, they hand me the equivalent in gold (minus commission). Does the broker advance any capital? Certainly not! What they had before in gold, they now have in silver (plus profit!). Since they received the silver before paying out the gold, they did not—even for an instant—advance any capital.

The operation of the broker is exactly analogous to the cases we are considering. Labor is rendered and value is created before wages are paid. Creating value does not depend on finishing the product—it takes place at every stage of the process. It is the immediate result of the application of labor. No matter how long the process, labor always adds capital before it takes it in wages. The owner merely exchanges one form of capital for another.

Consider a blacksmith hired to make simple pickaxes. Clearly, the smith adds picks to the employer's capital before taking money from that capital in wages. But what about a boilermaker working on a great ship? One may be completed in a few minutes, the other not for years. Yet both are items of wealth, articles of production. Each day's work produces wealth and adds capital. In the steamship as in the pick, it is not the last blow (any more than the first) that creates the value of the finished product. Value is created continuously—it is the immediate result of the exertion of labor.

We see this quite clearly when different parts of the process are carried out by different producers. Here we customarily estimate the value of labor in various preparatory stages. A moment's reflection will show this to be the case in the vast majority of products. Take a building, a book, or a loaf of bread. The finished products were not produced in one operation or by one set of producers. In clearly defined steps, we can easily distinguish the different stages of creation and the value of materials. At each step, we habitually estimate the creation of value and the addition to capital.

The bread from the baker's oven has a certain value. But this is composed, in part, of the value of the flour from which the dough was made. This, again, is composed of the value of the wheat and the value given by milling. And so on.

Production is not complete until the finished product is in the hands of the consumer. Not, for example, when a crop of cotton is gathered; nor when it is ginned; nor made into yarn; nor even into cloth. The process is finished only when the consumer receives the finished coat or shirt or dress. Yet at each step, it is clear there is the creation of value—an addition to capital.

It may take years to build a ship—but value is created day by day, hour by hour, from the very start. The value of the finished ship is the sum of these increments. No capital is advanced in paying wages during the building, because labor produces more capital than is paid back. Clearly, if someone asked to buy a partially completed ship, the owner would expect to make a profit at any stage of construction. Likewise, a company's stock does not lose value as capital in one form (wages paid) is gradually changed into capital in another form (the ship). On the contrary, on average its value probably increases as work progresses.

This is obvious in agriculture also. Value is not created all at once, but step by step during the whole process. A plowed field will bring more than an unplowed one; a sown field more than one merely plowed. The harvest is merely the conclusion. Orchards and vineyards bring prices proportionate to their age, even though too new to bear fruit. Likewise, horses and cattle increase in value as they mature. We do not always discern this increase in value, except at the usual points of exchange. Yet it most definitely takes place every time labor is exerted.

Hence, whenever labor is rendered before wages are paid, the advance of capital is really made by the worker—not the owner. The advance is from the worker to the employer—not from the employer to the employed.

Yet, you may protest, "Surely in the cases we have considered, capital is required!" Certainly. I do not dispute that. But it is not needed to make advances to labor. It is required for quite another purpose, as we shall see.

Suppose I hire workers to cut wood. If I pay in kind, with a portion of the wood, it is clear no capital is required to pay wages. But it is often easier and more profitable to sell one large pile than several smaller ones. So for mutual convenience, I pay wages in cash instead of wood. If I can exchange the wood for money before wages are due, I still do not need any capital.

It is only when I must wait to accumulate a particular quantity of wood that any capital is required. Such quantity might be needed before I can make any exchange; or merely before I can get the terms I want. Even then, I will not need capital if I can make a partial or tentative exchange by borrowing against the wood.

I will need capital only if I cannot—or choose to not—sell the wood or borrow against it. In other words, I will need capital only if I insist on accumulating a large stock of wood. Clearly, I need this capital only to accumulate a stock of product—not for paying wages.

Consider something more complicated, like cutting a tunnel. If the workmen could be paid in pieces of tunnel, no capital for wages would be required. Indeed, this could be done easily by paying them in stock of the company. It is only when the backers wish to accumulate capital in the form of a completed tunnel that they need capital.

Let's return to our initial example of a metals broker. Surely they cannot carry on their business without capital. But they do not need it to make any advance of capital to me when they take my silver and hand me back gold. They need it because the nature of their business requires keeping a certain amount of capital on hand, so they are prepared to make the type of exchange the customer desires.

We shall find it the same in every type of production. Capital is required only when production is stored up. Producers never need capital to employ labor. When they need capital, it is as merchants or speculators in the products of labor. That is, in order to accumulate such products.

To recapitulate: People who work for themselves get their wages in the things they produce, as they produce them. They exchange this value into other forms whenever they sell these products.

The people who work for another and are paid in money, work under a contract of exchange. They, too, create their wages as they render their labor. But they only collect them at stated times, in stated amounts, and in a different form. In performing the labor, they are advancing on this exchange. When they get their wages, the exchange is completed. During the time they are earning wages, the workers are advancing capital to their employer. At no time (unless wages are paid before work is started) is the employer advancing capital to them.

Whether the employer chooses to exchange the output immediately or to keep it for awhile in no way alters the character of the transaction. It matters no more than the final disposition of the product by the ultimate consumer, who may be somewhere on another continent at the end of a long series, perhaps hundreds, of exchanges.

Chapter 4

Workers Not Supported By Capital

BUT ONE DOUBT may linger. A farmer cannot eat a furrow; nor can a half-built loom weave clothes. John Stuart Mill asserted that people are maintained "not by the produce of present labor, but of past." Or, as another popular text put it, many months elapse between sowing the seed and baking the bread.*

An assumption is made in these passages that appears self-evident. Namely, that labor must subsist on capital produced by prior labor. This thought runs through the entire fabric of political economy. A related proposition is regarded as equally axiomatic. That is, that "population regulates itself by the funds which are to employ it, and, therefore, always increases or diminishes with the increase or diminution of capital."** This assumption, in turn, further influences economic reasoning.

On reflection, however, we see these propositions are not self-evident—they are absurd! They require the assumption that labor cannot be exerted until the products of labor are saved. This puts the product *before* the producer.

---

* Millicent Garrett Fawcett (1847-1929), *Political Economy for Beginners*, Chap. III, p. 25.
** David Ricardo (1772-1832), *Principles of Political Economy*, Chap. 11. The idea is common in many works.

To say a people eat breakfast before going to work is not to say that they cannot go to work unless an employer provides breakfast. People do not decide to eat or fast based on whether or not they propose to engage in productive labor. They eat because they are hungry.

The proposition that present labor must be maintained by past production is true only in the sense that lunch provides the fuel for the afternoon's work, or that before you eat a rabbit, it must be caught and cooked. Clearly this is not the sense in which the proposal is used in economic reasoning. That sense is that a stock to support workers must already exist before carrying out any effort that does not immediately yield wealth available for subsistence. Let us see if this is true.

Did Robinson Crusoe,* shipwrecked on an island, have to accumulate a stock of food before he began to build his canoe? Not at all. He needed only to spend part of his time getting food, and part of his time building the canoe.

Suppose a hundred people landed in a new country. Would they have to accumulate a season's worth of provisions before they could begin to cultivate the soil? Obviously not. What is required is that part of the group find enough fish, game, and berries to support them all. And that, through mutual self-interest or common desire, those gathering food in the present are willing to exchange it with those whose efforts are directed toward the harvest in the future.

What is true in these cases is true in all. Producing things that cannot be used immediately does not require

---

* Hero of the novel published in 1719 by Daniel Defoe (1660-1731), English writer.

the previous production of wealth for maintaining workers during production. All that is necessary is, within the circle of exchange, the contemporaneous production of sufficient subsistence—assuming a willingness to trade one for the other.

As a matter of fact, isn't it true that, under normal circumstances, consumption is supported by contemporaneous production? Imagine a wealthy idler who lives on an inheritance and does no productive work at all. Does he live on wealth accumulated in the past? On his table are fresh eggs, butter, and milk; meat from the butcher; vegetables from the garden. In short, hardly anything has not recently left the hand of productive labor, except perhaps some old bottles of wine.

What this man inherited—and what he lives on—is not actually wealth at all. It is only *the power to command wealth*, as others produce it. His sustenance is clearly taken from productive labor going on around him. (Remember we must include transporters and distributors, as well as those in the first stages of production.)

London contains more wealth than the same size space almost anywhere else. Yet if productive labor in London were to stop completely, within a few months hardly anyone would be left alive. It is the daily labor of the community that supplies its daily bread.

Workers engaged in long-term endeavors are supported by other workers producing sustenance. They engage in their respective work simultaneously. To build a modern public project taking years to complete, the government does not appropriate wealth already produced. It uses wealth yet to be produced—to be taken in taxes from producers as the work progresses.

There may be a thousand intermediate exchanges in the circle of exchange between two parties. A mechanic wants food, clothing, and shelter for her family. How does her work on an engine secure these items? Reduced to its most basic terms, the transaction really amounts to an exchange of labor between herself and the producers of those items.

What causes a mechanic to work on an engine? Someone with the power to give her what she wants is willing to exchange those things for an engine. In other words, there exists a demand for an engine from those producing bread, meat, and so on. Or, one step removed, there is a demand for an engine from others who are producing still other things that are wanted by those producing bread, meat, etc. Reversely, the demand of the mechanic for bread and meat directs an equivalent amount of labor toward the production of those things. Thus, her labor produces, implicitly, the things she spends her wage on. To put this in formal terms:

The demand for consumption determines the direction in which labor will be expended in production.

All the complexities of our subject disappear in light of this simple and obvious principle. We see the real objects and rewards of labor within the intricacies of modern production. We reach the same conclusions we did from observing the simpler forms of production and exchange in primitive society. We see that now, as then, each laborer is trying to obtain, by his or her work, the satisfaction of his or her own desires.

The minute division of labor assigns each worker only a small part—or perhaps nothing at all—of producing the particular things he desires. Even so, in helping to produce what others want, he is directing their labor to produce the things he wants. In effect, he is producing them himself.

Thus we see that, no matter what is taken or consumed by workers in return for their labor, there is no advance of capital.

If I have made knives and bought wheat, I have simply exchanged one for the other. I have added knives to the existing stock of wealth and taken wheat from it. It cannot even be said that I have lessened the stock of wheat. For by adding knives to the exchangeable stock of wealth and taking out wheat, I have directed other labor—at the end of a long series of exchanges—to produce more wheat. Just the same as the wheat grower, by putting in wheat and demanding knives, guided others to produce knives.

So farmers tend their fields, many months from harvest. Yet, by their exertion in plowing, they are producing the food they eat and the wages they receive. For though plowing is only part of producing a crop, it is as necessary a part as the harvesting. By the assurance it gives of a future crop, it releases other items from the general stock, which is constantly held. These then become the subsistence and wages of the plowman. This is not merely theoretically true. It is literally and practically true.

The series of exchanges that unite production and consumption may be likened to a curved pipe filled with water. If a quantity of water is poured in at one end, a like quantity is released at the other. It is not the identical water, but is its equivalent.

And so those who do the work of production put in what they take out. What they receive in subsistence and wages is but the product of their labor.

Chapter 5
The True Functions of Capital

WE HAVE SEEN that capital is not required to pay wages or support labor during production. What, then, are the true functions of capital?

Capital, as we discovered, is wealth used to procure more wealth. This we distinguish from wealth used to directly satisfy human desires. Therefore, capital may also be defined as wealth in the course of exchange.

Capital increases the power of labor to produce wealth in three ways:

(1) by applying labor in more effective ways (e. g., digging with a spade instead of by hand; or shipping by steamship instead rowing a boat). (2) by taking advantage of the reproductive forces of nature (e.g., growing more crops by sowing or more animals by breeding). (3) by permitting the division of labor. (This increases human efficiency by utilizing unique capabilities, acquiring special skills, and reducing waste. This allows people to produce each form of wealth where it is most favorable, by taking advantage of soil, climate, and location.)

The raw material that labor converts into wealth is not capital. Rather, it is material supplied by nature. Therefore, capital does not limit industry. The only thing that limits industry is access to natural materials.

It is clear, however, that capital may limit the *form* or

the *productiveness* of industry—by limiting the tools and the division of labor required for certain methods of production. Without the factory, there can be no factory worker; without the plow, no plowman. Without the exchange of great capital, the many special forms of industry concerned with exchanges would be impossible.

The tools available also limit productiveness. Does the farmer have enough capital for a plow, or must she use a spade? Must the mechanic use only a hammer, or the weaver a hand loom? Capital for the best tools can multiply production by tenfold.

Advanced civilization requires the minute subdivision of labor. The modern worker can exchange her labor with that of those around her, or even around the world. To do this, there must be stocks of goods in warehouses, stores, and ships. By analogy, for a city dweller to draw a glass of water, there must be millions of gallons stored in reservoirs and moving through miles of pipe.

But to say that capital may limit the form and productiveness of industry is a very different thing from saying that capital does limit industry.

We can, of course, imagine a community in which lack of capital would be the only obstacle to increased productiveness of labor. But the only examples that occur to me are the wholesale destruction of capital by war, fire, or natural disaster. Or possibly, the fresh settlement of civilized people in a new land. Yet it has long been known that capital is quickly replenished after war, and that a new community swiftly makes needed capital. Other than such rare and passing conditions, I am unable to think of any other cases where the productiveness of labor is really limited by lack of capital. There may be individuals in a community who cannot apply their labor as efficiently as they would like because they lack capital. Yet, so long as there is sufficient capital in the community at large, the real limitation is not capital, but its proper distribution.

Indeed, even the limitation of form or productiveness may be more theoretical than real. It is often said that poor countries need capital for development. But behind this "need", can't we perceive a greater want? One that includes—but is not the same as—lack of capital. Is it not the abuses of government, the insecurity of property, and the ignorance of the people that prevent the accumulation and use of capital? Bad government may steal capital belonging to workers. It may seize wealth that producers would use for improvements. The real limitation is misgovernment. The same with ignorance, custom, or other conditions that hamper the use of capital. The real limitations are these things, not the lack of capital—which would not be used even if placed there.

Giving a circular saw to a Terra del Fuegan or a locomotive to a Bedouin nomad would not add to their efficiency. The Apache and the Sioux are not kept from farming by want of capital. If provided with seeds and tools, they still would not use them productively—not until they chose to stop their wandering lifestyle and learned to cultivate the soil. They have certain items they are accustomed to using as their capital. Any wealth beyond these would be either consumed or left to waste. If all the capital in London were given to them in their present condition, it would simply cease to be capital. They would use only an infinitesimal part of it to assist them in the hunt.

Yet any capital they do desire, they manage to get,

sometimes despite great difficulties. These wild tribes hunt and fight with the best weapons that our factories produce, keeping up with all the latest improvements. It is only as they adopt our civilization that they seek other forms of capital. Otherwise, such things would not be of any use to them.

In the reign of George IV, missionaries brought a New Zealand chieftain, called Hongi, to England. His noble appearance and beautiful tattooing attracted much attention. When he was to return to his people, he was presented with a considerable stock of tools, implements, and seeds—thoughtful gifts from the monarch and some religious societies. The grateful chief did indeed use this capital to produce food—but in a manner his English benefactors could scarcely imagine. Returning through Australia, he exchanged his original capital for arms and ammunition. Once home, he waged war on another tribe with such success that, after the first battle, three hundred prisoners were cooked and eaten. Nowadays, Maoris have adopted European habits and stopped their warfare. Many of them have amassed considerable capital and put it to good use.

It would also be a mistake to attribute the simple economies found in new communities solely to the need for capital. These rude and inefficient modes of production and exchange require little capital. But when the conditions of such communities are considered, we find that they are, in reality, the most effective.

A modern printing press could produce thousands of pages, while a Franklin press might manage only a hundred. Yet to print a small edition of a country newspaper, the old-fashioned press is by far the more efficient machine. To occasionally carry two or three passengers, a canoe is a better means than a steamboat. And putting a great stock of goods into a backwoods store would be a waste of capital.

Generally, it will be found that these methods result not so much from lack of capital, as from inability to employ it profitably. No matter how much water you pour in a bucket, it can never hold more than a bucketful.

These observations lead us irresistibly to some practical conclusions, which justify the great pains we have taken to make sure of them. If wages come from labor, and not capital, then the current theories are invalid. We must disregard all remedies based on them, whether they are proposed by workers or professors of economics. Poverty cannot be alleviated by increasing capital or by restricting the number of workers. If each worker creates his or her own wages, then wages cannot be diminished by more workers. On the contrary, labor's efficiency clearly increases when there are more producers. Other things being equal, the more labor, the higher wages should be.

But the necessary proviso is "things being equal." This brings us to a question that must be disposed of before we can proceed: Do the productive powers of nature decrease as greater demands are made by a growing population?

Population and Subsistence

Chapter 6

The Theory of Population According to Malthus

IT IS SURPRISING that so many educated thinkers could have accepted a theory of wages that our analysis has shown to be utterly baseless. The explanation for this baffling fact can be found in the general acceptance of another theory. The theory of wages was never adequately examined because it seemed self-evident in the minds of economists when backed by the Malthusian theory.

This theory—published in 1798 by Rev. Thomas Malthus—postulates that population naturally tends to increase faster than nature can provide subsistence. The two doctrines, fitted together, frame the answer to the problem of poverty given by current economic thought.

Both theories derive additional support from a principle in Ricardo's theory of rent. Namely, that past a certain point, applying capital and labor to land yields a diminishing return. Together, these ideas provide a likely explanation for the phenomena of a highly organized, advanced society. This has prevented closer investigation.

Malthus based his theory on the growth of the North American colonies. This, he concluded, showed that population naturally tended to double every twenty-five years. Thus, population would increase at a geometrical ratio. Meanwhile, subsistence from land, under the most favorable circumstances, could not possibly increase faster than in an arithmetical ratio. That is, to increase the same amount every twenty-five years. In other words, population increases as 1, 2, 4, 8; while subsistence increases as 1, 2, 3, 4.

"The necessary effects of these two different rates of increase, when brought together," Mr. Malthus naively goes on to say, "will be very striking." He concludes that at the end of only the first century, two thirds of the population will be "totally unprovided for"; while in two thousand years, "the difference would be almost incalculable."

Such a result is, of course, prevented by the physical fact that no more people can exist than can find food. Hence, Malthus concludes that the tendency of population to indefinite increase may be held back by two means. Population may be limited by "moral restraint" [i.e., sexual abstinence]. Otherwise, various causes of increased mortality will do the job. He calls restraints on propagation the "preventive check." Increased mortality he names the "positive check."

This is the famous Malthusian doctrine, as promulgated by Malthus himself in his *Essay on Population*. The fallacious reasoning in assuming geometrical and arithmetical rates of increase, is hardly worth discussing. It merely provides a high-sounding formula that carries far more weight with many people than the clearest reasoning. But this assumption is not essential. It is expressly repudiated by some who otherwise accept the doctrine.

Regardless, the essence of Malthusian theory is that population tends to increase faster than the food supply. Malthus claims that population constantly tends towards increase. Unless restrained, it will ultimately press against the limits of subsistence, although such limits are elastic, not fixed. Nonetheless, it becomes increasingly difficult to produce subsistence. Thus, whenever growth, over time, is unchecked by conscious restraint, population will be kept in check by a corresponding degree of deprivation.

Malthus unashamedly makes vice and suffering the necessary result of natural instinct and affection. Despite being silly and offensive, as well as repugnant to our sense of a harmonious nature, it has withstood the refutations and denunciations, the sarcasm, ridicule, and sentiment directed against it. It demands recognition even from those who do not believe it. Today it stands as an accepted truth (though I will show it is false).

The reasons for its acceptance are not hard to find. It appears to be backed by an indisputable mathematical truth—that a continuously increasing population must eventually exceed the capacity of the earth to furnish food, or even standing room. It is supported by analogies in the animal and vegetable kingdoms, where life beats wastefully against the barriers holding different species in check.

Many obvious facts seem to corroborate it. For instance, the prevalence of poverty, vice, and misery amid dense populations. In addition, the general effect of material progress is to increase population without relieving poverty. It is pointed out that population grows rapidly in newly settled counties. It slows in more densely settled ones, apparently because of mortality among those condemned to poverty.

Malthusian theory furnishes a general principle to explain these facts. Moreover, it accounts for them in a way that harmonizes with the doctrine that wages are drawn from capital—and with all the principles deduced from it. Current wage theory says that wages fall as more workers compel a finer division of capital. Malthusian theory claims poverty arises as increased population forces further division of subsistence. It requires little to make the two propositions as identical formally as they already are substantially. Merely identify capital with subsistence, and the number of workers with population. This identification is already made in current economic writing, where the terms are often interchanged.

Ricardo furnished additional support a few years later, by correcting the mistake Adam Smith had made regarding the nature and cause of rent. Ricardo showed that rent increases as a growing population extends cultivation to less and less productive land.

This formed a triple combination of interlocking theories. The previous doctrine of wages and the subsequent doctrine of rent can be seen, in this view, as special examples of the general principle of the Malthusian theory of population. Wages fall and rents rise with increasing population. Both show the pressure of population against subsistence.

To a factory worker, the obvious cause of low wages and lack of work appears to be too much competition. And in the squalid ghettos, what seems clearer than that there are too many people? We may also note that, in our present state of society, most workers appear to depend upon a separate class of capitalists for employment. Under these conditions, we may pardon the masses—who rarely bother to separate the real from the apparent.

But the real reason for the triumph of the theory is that it does not threaten any vested right or antagonize any powerful interest. Malthus was eminently reassuring to the classes who wield the power of wealth and, thus, largely dominate thought. The French Revolution had aroused intense fear. At a time when old supports were falling away, his theory came to the rescue. It saved the special privileges by which only a few monopolize so much of this world.

It proclaimed a natural cause for want and misery. Malthus' purpose was to justify existing inequality by shifting the responsibility from human institutions to the laws of the Creator. For if those things were attributed to political institutions, they would condemn every government. Instead, he provided a philosophy to shield the rich from the unpleasant image of the poor; to shelter selfishness from question by interposing an inevitable necessity. Poverty, want, and starvation are not the result of greed or social maladjustment, it said. They are the inevitable result of universal laws, as certain as gravity. Even if the rich were to divide their wealth among the poor, nothing would be gained. Population would increase until it again pressed the limits of subsistence. Any equality that might result would be only common misery.

Thus, any reform that might interfere with the interests of any powerful class is discouraged as hopeless. Nothing can really be done, individually or socially, to reduce poverty. This theory, while exploiting the erroneous thoughts of the poor, justifies the greed of the rich and the selfishness of the powerful. Such a theory will spread quickly and strike deep roots. Recently, this theory has received new support from Darwin's theory on the origin of species. Malthusian theory seems but the application to human society of "survival of the fittest." Only "the struggle for existence," cruel and remorseless, has differentiated humans from monkeys, and made our century succeed the stone age.*

Thus seemingly proved, linked, and buttressed, Malthusian theory is now generally accepted as an unquestionable truth: Poverty is due to the pressure of population against subsistence. Or in its other form, the number of laborers will always increase until wages are reduced to the minimum of survival.

All social phenomena are now to be explained in this light—as for years the heavens were explained by supposing the earth was at the center of the universe. If authority were the only consideration, argument would be futile. This theory has received almost universal acceptance in the intellectual world, endorsed by economists and statesmen, historians and scientists, psychologists and clergy, conservatives and radicals. It is held, and habitually reasoned from, by many who have never even heard of Malthus, and haven't the slightest idea what his theory is.

Nevertheless, upon our investigation, the supporting arguments for wage theory evaporated. So too, I believe, will vanish the grounds for this doctrine, which is its twin.

---

*The debate between Darwin's theory and "Social Darwinism" has gone on into the 21st century.

Chapter 7
Malthus vs. Facts

DESPITE ITS ENDORSEMENT by respected authorities, I believe we will find Malthusian theory utterly without support when we apply the test of straightforward analysis. Facts marshaled in support do not prove it, and analogies do not uphold it. Further, there are facts that conclusively disprove it. There is no justification in experience or analogy for the assumption that there is any tendency for population to increase faster than the food supply.

The facts cited to support the Malthusian theory are taken from new countries where population is sparse, or among the poor classes in old countries where wealth is distributed unequally. In these cases, human life is occupied with the physical necessities of existence. Reproduction under such conditions is at a high rate, which, if it were to go unchecked, might eventually exceed subsistence. But it is not legitimate to infer that reproduction would continue at the same rate under conditions where population was sufficiently dense and wealth was distributed evenly. These conditions would lift the whole community above a mere struggle for existence. Nor can one assume that such a community is impossible because population growth would cause poverty. This is obviously circular reasoning, as it assumes the very point at issue. To prove that overpopulation causes poverty, one would need to show that there are no other causes that could account for it. With the present state of government, this is clearly impossible.

This is abundantly shown in Malthus' *Essay on Population* itself. This famous book is spoken of more often than read. The contrast between the merits of the book itself and the effect it produced is one of the most remarkable in the history of literature. His other works, though written after he became famous, had no influence. They are treated with contempt, even by those who consider his theory a great discovery.

Malthus begins with the assumption that population increases in a geometrical ratio, while subsistence can increase in an arithmetical ratio at best. That is no more valid than to assert than that, because a puppy doubled the length of its tail while adding so many pounds of weight, there is therefore a geometric progression of tail length and an arithmetical progression of weight. We can imagine Jonathan Swift, the great satirist, describing the logical inference from such an assumption. He might have the sages of a previously dogless island deducing from these two ratios the "very striking consequence" that by the time the dog grew to fifty pounds its tail would be over a mile long! This, of course, this would be extremely difficult to wag. Hence, they must recommend the "prudential check" of a bandage as the only alternative to the "positive check" of constant amputations.

After commencing with such an absurdity, the Rev. Malthus continues to show the most ridiculous incapacity for logical thought. The main body of the book is actually a refutation of the very theory it advances. His review of what he calls positive checks simply shows that the effects he attributes to overpopulation actually arise from other causes. He cites cases from around the world where vice and misery restrain population by limiting marriages or shortening life span. Not in a single case, however, can this be traced to an actual increase in the number of mouths over the power of the accompanying hands to feed them. In every case, vice and misery spring either from ignorance and greed, or from bad government, unjust laws, or war.

Nor has what Malthus failed to show been shown by anyone since. We may search the globe and sift through history in vain for any instance of a considerable country in which poverty and want can be fairly attributed to the pressure of an increasing population. Whatever dangers may be possible in human increase, they have never yet appeared. While this time may come, it never yet has afflicted mankind.

Historically, population has declined as often as increased. It has ebbed and flowed, while its centers have changed. Regions once holding great populations are now deserted, and their cultivated fields turned to jungle.

New nations have arisen and others declined. Sparse regions have become populous and dense ones receded. But as far back as we can go, without merely guessing, there is nothing to show continuous increase. We are apt to lose sight of this fact as we count our increasing millions. As yet, the principle of population has not been strong enough to fully settle the world. Whether the aggregate population of the earth in 1879 is greater than at any previous time, we can only guess. Compared with its capacities to support human life, the earth as a whole is still sparsely populated.

Another broad, general fact is obvious. Malthus asserts that the natural tendency of population to outrun subsistence is a universal law. If so, it should be as obvious as any other natural law, and as universally recognized.

Why, then, do we find no injunction to limit population among the codes of the Jews, Egyptians, Hindus, or Chinese? Nor among any people who have had dense populations? On the contrary, the wisdom of the ages and the religions of the world have always instilled the very opposite idea: "Be fruitful and multiply."

If the tendency to reproduce is as strong as Malthus supposes, then how is it that family lines so often become extinct? This occurs even in families where want is unknown. In an aristocracy such as England, hereditary titles and possession offer every advantage. Yet the House of Lords is kept up over the centuries only by the creation of new titles.

To find the single example of a family that has survived any great lapse of time, we must go to immutable China. There, descendants of Confucius still enjoy peculiar privileges and consideration. Taking the presumption that population tends to double every twenty-five years, his lineage after 2,150 years should include 859,559,193,106,709,670,198,710,528 souls. Yet, instead of any such unimaginable number, his descendants number about 22,000 total. This is quite a discrepancy!

Further, an increase of descendants does not mean an increase of population. This would only happen if all the breeding were in the same family. Mr. and Mrs. Smith have a son and a daughter, who each marry someone else's child. Each has two children. Thus, Mr. and Mrs. Smith have four grandchildren. Yet each generation is no larger than the other. While there are now four grandchildren, each child would have four grandparents.

Supposing this process were to go on and on. The line of descent might spread out to thousands, even millions. But in each generation, there would be no more individuals than in any previous generation. The web of generations is like lattice-work or the diagonal threads in cloth. Commencing at any point at the top, the eye follows lines that diverge widely at the bottom; but beginning at any point at the bottom, the lines diverge in the same way to the top. How many children a woman may have is variable. But that she had two parents is certain! And that these also had two parents each is also certain. Follow this geometrical progression through a few generations and see if it does not lead to quite as "striking consequences" as Mr. Malthus' peopling of the solar systems.

But let us now advance to specific cases. I assert that examples commonly cited as instances of overpopulation will not bear up under investigation. India, China, and Ireland furnish the strongest of these. In each, great numbers have died of starvation, while entire classes were reduced to abject misery or compelled to emigrate. But is this really due to overpopulation?

Comparing total population with total area, India and China are far from being the most densely populated countries of the world. The population densities [in 1873] of India and China were 132 and 119 per square mile, respectively. Compare this to England (442), Belgium (441), Italy (234), and Japan (233). The total population of the world was estimated to be just under 1.4 billion, for an average of 26.64 per square mile.

Both India and China have large areas not fully used,

or even unused. There is no doubt that they could support a much greater population—and in greater comfort. Labor is crude and inefficient. Meanwhile, great natural resources go untapped. This does not arise from any innate deficiency in their people. They devised the rudiments of many modern inventions while our ancestors were still wandering savages. The problem arises from the form which social organization has taken in both countries. This has shackled productive power and robbed industry of its reward.

In India, from time immemorial, working classes have been ground down by extortion and oppression into a condition of hopeless, and helpless, degradation. For ages, peasants considered themselves happy if they could keep enough to support life and save seed for the next crop. All the wealth that could be wrung from the people was in the possession of princes, who were little better than thieves. Some they gave to their favorites; the rest they wasted in useless luxury. Religion, reduced to an elaborate and terrible superstition, tyrannized their minds as physical force did their bodies.

Capital could not be accumulated safely nor used to assist production to any significant extent. Under these conditions, only arts that ministered to ostentation and luxury could advance. Elephants of the rajah blazed with gold of exquisite workmanship; umbrellas symbolizing his regal power glittered with gems. But the plow of the ryot (peasant) was only a sharpened stick. Tools were of the poorest and rudest description. Commerce could only be carried on by stealth.

It is clear that this tyranny and insecurity produced the want and starvation of India. Population did not produce want, and want tyranny. As a chaplain with the East India Company in 1796 noted:

"When we reflect upon the great fertility of Hindostan, it is amazing to consider the frequency of famine. It is evidently not owing to any sterility of soil or climate; the evil must be traced to some political cause, and it requires but little penetration to discover it in the avarice and extortion of the various governments. The great spur to industry, that of security, is taken away. Hence no man raises more grain than is barely sufficient for himself, and the first unfavorable season produces a famine."

The good Reverend then goes on to describe the misery of the peasant in gloomy detail. The continuous violence produced a state under which "neither commerce nor the arts could prosper, nor agriculture assume the appearance of a system." This merciless rapacity would have produced want and famine even if the population were but one to a square mile and the land a Garden of Eden.

British rule replaced this with a power even worse. "They had been accustomed to live under tyranny, but never tyranny like this," the British historian Macaulay* explained. "It resembled the government of evil genii, rather than the government of human tyrants."

An enormous sum was drained away to England every year in various guises. The effect of English law was to put a potent instrument of plunder in the hands of native money lenders. Its rigid rules were mysterious proceedings to the natives. According to Florence Nightingale,

---

* Lord Thomas Macaulay (1800-1859), English historian, in his essay on Lord Clive (1725-1774), the British general who led the conquest of India.

the famous humanitarian, terrible famines were caused by taxation, which took the very means of cultivation from farmers. They were reduced to actual slavery as "the consequences of our own [British] laws." Even in famine-stricken districts, food was exported to pay taxes.

In India now, as in times past, only the most superficial view can attribute starvation and want to the pressure of population on the ability of land to produce subsistence. Vast areas are still uncultivated, vast mineral resources untouched. If the farmers could keep some capital, industry could revive and take on more productive forms, which would undoubtedly support a much greater population. The limit of the soil to furnish subsistence certainly has not been reached.

It is clear that the true cause of poverty in India has been, and continues to be, the greed of man—not the deficiency of nature.

What is true of India is true of China. As densely populated as China is in many parts, the extreme poverty of the lower classes is not caused by overpopulation. Rather, it is caused by factors similar to those at work in India.

Insecurity prevails, production faces great disadvantages, and trade is restricted. Government is a series of extortions. Capital is safe only when someone has been paid off. Goods are transported mainly on men's shoulders. The Chinese junk must be constructed so it is unusable on the seas. And piracy is such a regular trade that robbers often march in regiments.

Under these conditions, poverty would prevail and any crop failure would result in famine, no matter how sparse the population. China is obviously capable of supporting a much greater population. All travelers testify to the great extent of uncultivated land, while immense mineral deposits exist untouched.

Neither in India nor China, therefore, can poverty and starvation be charged to the pressure of population against subsistence. Millions are not kept on the verge of starvation (and occasionally pushed beyond it) by dense population—but rather by causes that prevent the natural development of social organization and keep labor from getting its full return.

Let me be clearly understood. I do not mean only that India or China could maintain a greater population with a more highly developed civilization. Malthusian doctrine does not deny that increased production would permit a greater population to find subsistence.

But the essence of that theory is that whatever the capacity for production, the natural tendency of population is to press beyond it. This produces that degree of vice and misery necessary to prevent further increase. So as productive power increases, population will correspondingly increase. And in a little time, this will produce the same results as before.

I assert that nowhere is there an example that will support this theory. Nowhere can poverty properly be attributed to population pressing against the power to procure subsistence using the then-existing degree of human knowledge. In every case, the vice and misery generally attributed to overpopulation can be traced to warfare, tyranny, and oppression. These are the true causes that deny security, which is essential to production, and prevent knowledge from being properly utilized.

Later we will discover why population increase does not produce want. For now, we are only concerned with the fact that it has not yet done so anywhere.

This fact is obvious with regard to India and China. It also will be obvious wherever we track the true causes of results that, on superficial view, are often assumed to come from overpopulation.

Ireland, of all European countries, furnishes the great stock example of alleged overpopulation. It is constantly referred to as a demonstration of the Malthusian theory worked out under the eyes of the civilized world. Proponents cite the extreme poverty of the peasantry, the low wages, the Irish famine, and Irish emigration. I doubt if we could find a more striking example of how a pre-accepted theory has the power to blind people to the facts.

The truth is obvious. Ireland has never had a population it could not have maintained in ample comfort, given the natural state of the country and the current state of technological development. It is true, a large proportion has barely existed, clothed in rags, with only potatoes for food. When the potato blight came, they died by the thousands.

Did so many live in misery because of the inability of the soil to support them? Is this why they starved on the failure of a single crop?

On the contrary, it was the same remorseless greed that robbed the Indian ryot of the fruits of his labor and left him to starve where nature offered plenty. No merciless banditti plundered the land extorting taxes, as in Asia. But the laborer was stripped just as effectively by a merciless horde of landlords. The soil had been divided among them as their absolute possession, regardless of the rights of those who lived upon it. Most farmers dared not make improvements, even if the exorbitant rents left anything over. For to do so would only have led to a further increase in rent. So labor was inefficient and wasteful. It was applied aimlessly, whereas had there been any security for its fruits, it would have been applied continually.

Even under these conditions, it is a matter of fact that Ireland did support eight million plus. For when her population was at its highest, Ireland was still a food exporting country. Even during the famine, grain, meat, butter, and cheese destined for export were carted past trenches piled with the dead. So far as the people of Ireland were concerned, this food might as well have been burned or never even produced. It went not as an exchange, but as a tribute. The rent of absentee landlords was wrung from the producers by those who in no way contributed to production.

What if this food had been left to those who raised it? What if they were able to keep and use the capital produced by their labor? What if security had stimulated industry and more economical production? There would have been enough to support the largest population Ireland ever had, and in bounteous comfort. The potato blight might have come and gone without depriving even a single human being of a full meal.

It was not the imprudence of Irish peasants, as English economists coldly say, that made the potato the staple of their food. Irish emigrants do not live upon the potato when they can get other things. Certainly in the United States, the prudence of the Irish character to save something for a rainy day is remarkable. The Irish peasants lived on potatoes because rack rents stripped them of everything else. The truth is that the poverty and misery of Ireland have never been fairly attributable to overpopulation.

Writing this chapter, I have been looking over the literature of Irish misery. It is difficult to speak in civil terms about the complacency with which Irish want and suffering is attributed to overpopulation. I know of nothing to make the blood boil more than the grasping, grinding tyranny to which the Irish people have been subjected. It is this, not any inability of the land to support its population, that caused Irish poverty and famine.

No matter how sparse the population or what the natural resources, poverty and starvation are inevitable consequences when the producers of wealth are forced to work under conditions that deprive them of hope, self-respect, energy, and thrift. They are inevitable when absentee landlords drain away, without return, at least a fourth of the harvest. In addition, a starving industry must support resident landlords, with their horses and hounds, agents and jobbers, middlemen and bailiffs, as well as an army of policemen and soldiers to hunt down any opposition to the iniquitous system. Is it not blasphemy to blame this misery on natural law rather than on human greed?

What is true in these three cases will be found true in all cases—if we examine the facts. As far as our knowledge goes, we may safely say there has never been a case in which the pressure of population against subsistence has caused poverty—or even a decrease in the production of food per person.

Overpopulation is no more the cause of the famines of India, China, and Ireland than it is of the famines of sparsely populated Brazil. And the limitations of Nature are no more to blame for poverty than they are for the millions slain by Genghis Khan.

Chapter 8

Malthus vs. Analogies

ATTEMPTS TO SUPPORT the Malthusian theory with analogies are just as inconclusive as those which use facts.

The strength of the reproductive force in the animal and vegetable kingdoms is constantly cited, from Malthus to current textbooks. For instance, if protected from their natural enemies, a single pair of salmon might fill the entire ocean, or a pair of rabbits overrun a continent. Many plants scatter seeds by the hundreds, and some insects deposit eggs by the thousands. Each species constantly tends to press against the limits of subsistence, and when not limited by its enemies, apparently does so.

These examples attempt to prove that human population also tends to press against subsistence. Unless restrained by other means, this must necessarily result in low wages and poverty. And if that is not enough, then actual starvation will keep it within the limits of subsistence.

But is this analogy valid?

The human food supply is drawn from the animal and vegetable kingdoms. The reproductive force in the vegetable and animal kingdoms is greater than among humans. Hence, this analogy simply proves the power of subsistence to increase faster than population. All of the things that furnish human subsistence have the power to multiply many fold, sometimes a million fold. Meanwhile, humanity is merely doubling (even according to Malthus). Doesn't this show that even if human beings increase to the full extent of their reproductive power, population can never exceed subsistence?

There is one additional fact. The actual limit to each species lies in the existence of other species: its rivals, its enemies, or its food.

Humans, however, can extend the conditions that normally limit those species giving our sustenance. (In some cases, our mere appearance will accomplish this.) The reproductive forces of these species then begin to work in service of humans. This increase continues at a pace that our own powers of increase cannot rival. If we shoot hawks, birds will increase; if we trap foxes, rabbits will multiply.

This distinction between humans and all other forms of life destroys the analogy. Of all living things, only humans can manipulate reproductive forces stronger than their own to supply themselves with food. Bird, insect, beast, and fish take only what they find. They increase at the expense of their food. But the increase of humans will increase their food. The population of the United States, once small, is now forty-five million. Yet there is much more food per capita.

It is not the increase of food that has caused the increase of humans—rather, the increase of humans has brought about an increase of food. There is more food simply because there are more people. This is the difference: Both humans and hawks eat chickens—but the more hawks, the fewer chickens; while the more humans, the more chickens.

Moreover, human subsistence in any particular place is not bound by the physical limit of that place, but of the

globe. Fifty square miles, using present agricultural prac-
tices, will yield subsistence for only a few thousand people.
Yet over three million people reside in London—and their
subsistence increases as population increases. So far as the
limit of subsistence is concerned, London may grow to a
hundred million or five hundred million. For it draws upon
the whole globe for subsistence. Its limit is the limit of the
globe to furnish food for its inhabitants.

But another idea arises that gives Malthus great support: the diminishing productiveness of land. Beyond a
certain point, so the argument goes, land yields less and
less to additional labor and capital. Otherwise, a growing
population would not extend cultivation to additional land.
Acknowledging this appears to involve accepting the doctrine that a growing population increases the difficulty of
obtaining subsistence.

But if we analyze this proposition, we see that it depends on an implied qualification. It is true in a relative
context, but not when taken absolutely. Production and
consumption are only relative terms. Speaking absolutely,
people neither produce nor consume. They cannot ex-
haust or lessen the powers of nature. If the whole human
race were to work forever, they could not make the Earth
one atom heavier or lighter. Nor could they augment or
diminish the forces that produce all motion and sustain
all life.*

Water taken from the ocean must eventually return to
the ocean. So too, the food we take from nature is, from

---

* George was writing before Einstein showed that matter could be
converted into energy. Modern physics speaks of the conservation of
matter/energy, which still supports George's point.

the moment we take it, on its way back to those same reservoirs. What we draw from a limited extent of land may temporarily reduce the productiveness of that land. But the return will go to other land.

Life does not use up the forces that maintain life. We come into the material universe bringing nothing; we take nothing away when we depart. The human being, in physical terms, is just a transitory form of matter, a changing mode of motion.

From this, it follows that the limit to population can be only the limit of space—that the human race may not increase its numbers beyond the possibility of finding elbow room. Remote and shadowy as it is, this possibility is what makes Malthus' theory appear self-evident.

But there is still another difference: Humans are the only animals whose desires increase as they are fed—the only animal that is never satisfied. The wants of every other living thing are fixed. The ox of today aspires to no more than the ox that humans first yoked. The only use they can make of additional supplies, or additional opportunities, is to multiply.

But not so humans. No sooner are our animal wants satisfied than new wants arise. The beast never goes further, but humans have just set their foot on the first step of an infinite progression.

Once the demand for quantity is satisfied, we seek quality. As human power to gratify our wants increases, our aspirations grow. At the lower levels of desire, we seek merely to satisfy our senses. Moving to higher forms of desire, humans awaken to other things. We brave the desert and the polar sea, but not for food; we want to know how the earth was formed and how life arose. We toil to satisfy a hunger no animal has felt, a thirst no beast can know.

Given more food and better conditions, animals and vegetables can only multiply—but humans will develop. In the one case, the expansive force can only extend in greater numbers. In the other, it will tend to extend existence into higher forms and wider powers.

None of this supports Malthus' theory. Facts do not uphold it, and analogy does not support it. It is a pure figment of the imagination, like the preconceptions that kept people from recognizing that the earth was round and moved around the sun.

This theory of population is as unfounded as if we made an assumption about the growth of a baby from the rate of its early months. Say it weighed ten pounds at birth and twenty pounds at eight months. From this, we might calculate a result quite as striking as that of Mr. Malthus. By this logic it would be the size of an elephant at twelve, and at thirty would weigh over a billion tons.

The fact is, there is no more reason to worry about the pressure of population upon subsistence than there is to worry about the rapid growth of a baby. We are no more justified in assuming that overpopulation produces poverty than we are in assuming that gravity must hurl the moon to the earth and the earth into the sun.

Malthus asserted what he called positive and prudential checks. A third check comes into play with the development of intellect and increased standards of living. This is indicated by many well-known facts. The birth rate is lower among classes whose wealth has brought leisure, comfort, and a fuller life. It is higher among the poor who, though in the midst of wealth, are deprived of its advantages, and thus are reduced to an animal existence. It is also higher in new settlements.*

This shows the real law of population. The tendency to increase is not uniform. It is strong where a larger population would allow greater progress. It is also strong where dangerous conditions threaten the survival of the race. It weakens as higher development becomes possible, and survival is assured. In other words, the law of population conforms with, and is subordinate to, the law of intellectual development.

Any difficulty providing for an increasing population arises not from the laws of nature, but from social maladjustments. These are what condemn people to want in the midst of wealth.

In the last two chapters, we have supported a negative. That is, we have shown that Malthusian theory is not proved by the reasoning set forth to defend it. The next chapter will take the affirmative and show that it is actually disproved by the facts.

---

* This insight is referred to today as the "demographic shift," and is extensively documented. In addition to the correlation of improved living standards with lower fertility, modern researchers have found that better-educated women tend to have fewer children, even when their incomes do not actually increase.

Chapter 9
Malthusian Theory Disproved

FACTS are the supreme and final test. The wide acceptance of Malthusian theory is a remarkable example of how easily we can ignore facts when blinded by a preaccepted theory. The question is whether an increasing population necessarily tends to reduce wages and cause poverty. This is the same as asking whether it reduces the amount of wealth a given amount of labor can produce.

The accepted theory says that greater demands upon nature produce diminishing results. That is, less will be produced proportional to additional effort. Doubling labor will not double output. Thus, a growing population must reduce wages and deepen poverty. John Stuart Mill claimed a large population can never be provided for as well as a smaller one.

All this I deny. In fact, I assert that the very opposite is true.

I assert that a larger population can collectively produce more than a smaller one (in any given state of development).

I assert that poverty is not caused by overpopulation. It is caused by social injustice, not by any limitation of nature.

I assert that in the natural order of things, a growing population can produce more than is required to provide for the increased numbers.

I assert that, other things being equal, each individual would receive greater comfort in a larger population—under an equitable distribution of wealth.

I assert that in a state of equality, the natural increase of population would constantly tend to make every individual richer instead of poorer.

Thus taking issue with this theory, I submit the question to the test of facts.

But I must first warn the reader not to confuse the issue, as even writers of great reputation have done. For the question of fact into which this issue resolves itself is not, what size population produces the most subsistence? Rather it is, *what size population has the greatest power to produce wealth?*

Power to produce wealth in any form is the same as power to produce subsistence. Likewise, consumption of wealth in any form is equivalent to consumption of subsistence.

For instance, I may choose to buy food or cigars or jewelry. By spending on any particular item, I thereby direct labor to produce that item. We may say a set of diamonds has a value equal to so many barrels of flour. In other words, it takes (on average) the same amount of labor to produce those diamonds as it would to produce so much flour. So giving my wife diamonds is as much an exertion of subsistence-producing power as if I loaded her with so many barrels of flour as an extravagant display.

Similarly, a race horse requires care and labor enough for many work horses. A regiment of soldiers diverts labor that could otherwise produce subsistence for thousands of people.

Thus, the power of any population to produce the necessities of life is not to be measured only by the necessities actually produced. Rather, it is measured by the total expenditure of power in all forms of production. Therefore we must ask, does the relative power of producing wealth decrease with an increasing population?

There is no need for abstract reasoning; the question is one of simple fact. And the facts are so obvious that it is only necessary to call attention to them.

In modern times, we have seen many communities increase their population—and advance even more rapidly in wealth. Compare any communities having similar people in a similar stage of development. Isn't the most densely populated community also the richest? Aren't the more densely populated Eastern states richer in proportion to population than the more sparsely populated Western or Southern states? Isn't England, where population is even denser, also richer in proportion?

Where will you find wealth most lavishly devoted to nonproductive uses, such as extravagant buildings, fine furniture, gardens, and yachts? It is where population is dense rather than sparse. Where will you find the greatest proportion of those supported by the general production, without productive labor on their part? By this I mean the range of gentlemen of leisure, thieves, policemen, servants, lawyers, people of letters, and the like. It is where population is thick rather than thin. In which direction does capital for investment flow? It flows from densely populated countries to sparse ones.

Undeniably, wealth is greatest where population is densest. Therefore, the amount of wealth produced by a given amount of labor increases as population increases.

This is apparent wherever we look.

Let's examine a particular case: California. At first glance, this appears to be perhaps the best example supporting Malthus. While population has increased, wages have decreased. In addition, its natural productivity has obviously lessened.

The wave of immigration that poured into California with the discovery of gold found a country where nature was in the most generous mood. Primitive tools could easily extract gold from rivers where glittering deposits had been built up over thousands of years. The plains were alive with countless herds of horses and cattle, and soil was being tilled for the first time. Amid this abundance, wages and interest were higher than anywhere else in the world.

This virgin profusion has been steadily eroding under the demands of an increasing population. Mining now requires elaborate machinery and great skill. Cattle are brought in by rail. Some land now in use would barely yield a crop without irrigation. During this time, wages and interest have steadily declined. People will now work a week for what they once got per day.

But is this cause and effect? Are wages lower because the reduced productiveness of nature means labor yields less wealth? On the contrary!

The power of labor to produce wealth in California in 1879 is not less than in 1849—it is greater. During these years, the efficiency of labor has increased in many ways—by roads, harbors, steamboats, telegraphs, and machinery of all kinds; by a closer connection with the rest of the world; and by countless economies resulting from a larger population.

No one who considers this can doubt an increase in productiveness. The return that labor receives from nature is, on the whole, much greater now than it was in the days of unmined minerals and virgin soil. The increase in human power has more than compensated for the decline in natural factors.

In fact, consumption of wealth, compared to the number of laborers, is much greater now than it was then. Back then, population consisted almost exclusively of working men. Now there are many women and children who must also be supported. Others who do not produce wealth have also increased in greater proportion. Luxury has grown far more than wages have fallen. The best houses once were shanties; now there are mansions. The richest then would seem little better than paupers today.

In short, there is striking and conclusive evidence that the production and consumption of wealth has increased faster than population. If any class gets less, it is for one reason only—*because the distribution of wealth has become more unequal*.

The same thing is obvious wherever we look. The richest countries are not those where nature is most prolific, but those where labor is most efficient. Not Mexico, but Massachusetts. Not Brazil, but Britain. Other things being equal, countries with the densest population devote the largest proportion of production to luxury and the support of nonproducers. They are the countries where capital overflows. In emergency, such as war, they can stand the greatest drain. Though a much smaller proportion of the population is engaged in productive labor, a much larger surplus is available for purposes other than supplying physical needs.

On the other hand, in a new country the whole available workforce is involved in production. There are no paupers or beggars. Neither are there idle rich, nor whole classes whose labor is devoted to ministering to the convenience or caprice of the rich. There is no literary or scientific class, no criminal class, and no class maintained to guard against them.

Yet, even with the whole community devoted to production, there is no consumption of wealth as in the old country. The condition of the lower classes, however, is better. Everyone can earn a living. Yet no one gets much more. Few, if any, can live in anything that would be called luxury (or even comfort). In the older country, consumption of wealth in proportion to population is greater. At the same time, the proportion of labor devoted to the production of wealth is less. In other words, fewer laborers produce more wealth.

Let us consider one last argument. Could the greater wealth of older countries be due to the accumulation of wealth, not greater productive power?

The truth is, wealth can be accumulated only to a small degree. Wealth consists of the material universe transformed by labor into desirable forms. As such, it constantly tends to revert back to its original state. Some wealth will last only a few hours, others for days, months, or even a few years. But there are really very few forms of wealth that can be passed from one generation to another.

Take wealth in some of its most useful and seemingly permanent forms: ships, houses, machinery. Unless labor is constantly applied to preserve and repair them, they will quickly become useless. If labor were to stop in any community, wealth would vanish. When labor starts again, wealth will reappear almost immediately. It is like the jet of a fountain that vanishes when the flow of water is shut off.

This is clear where war or disaster has swept away

wealth—but left the population unimpaired. London has no less wealth today because of The Great Fire (1666). Nor Chicago because of its fire (1871). On those fire-swept acres, magnificent buildings, overflowing with goods, have arisen. A visitor, unaware of history, would never dream these stately avenues lay black and bare a few short years ago.

This same principle is obvious in every new city—namely, that wealth is constantly re-created. No one who has seen Melbourne or San Francisco can doubt that if the population of England were transported to New Zealand—leaving all accumulated wealth behind—it would soon be as rich as England is now. Conversely, if England were reduced to the sparseness of New Zealand, they would soon be as poor—despite their accumulated wealth. Wealth from generations past can no more account for present consumption than last year's dinners can give strength today.

In sum, a growing population means an increase—not a decrease—in the average production of wealth. The reason for this is obvious. It so vastly increases the power of the human factor that it more than compensates for any reduction in the natural factor. Twenty people working together, even where nature is scant, can produce more than twenty times the wealth one person can produce where nature is bountiful. The denser the population, the finer the division of labor, and the greater the economies of production and distribution.

Thus we see that the very reverse of Malthusian doctrine is true. In any given state of civilization, a greater number of people can produce a larger proportionate amount of wealth than can a smaller number.

Can anything be clearer? The weakness of natural forces is not the cause of poverty festering in the centers of civilization. Consider those countries where poverty is deepest. If their productive forces were fully employed, they could clearly provide enough for all. They could not merely provide comfort, but luxury. Industrial paralysis and depression obviously do not arise from lack of productive power. Whatever the trouble may be, it is clearly not a lack of ability to produce wealth.

Poverty appears where productive power is greatest and the production of wealth is largest. This is the enigma that perplexes the civilized world, the puzzle we are trying to unravel. It is obvious that Malthusian theory cannot explain it. That theory is utterly inconsistent with all the facts. It gratuitously attributes to the laws of God results that spring from the social maladjustments of humans. But we have yet to find exactly what does produce poverty amid advancing wealth.

Chapter 10
The Necessary Relation of the Laws of Distribution

OUR PRECEDING EXAMINATION has shown that the current explanation for the persistence of poverty despite increasing wealth is no explanation at all. But by demolishing it, we have made the facts appear even more inexplicable. We have, in short, proved that wages should be highest where they are actually lowest.

At least we have discovered where it is useless to look. The cause of poverty is not lack of capital. Nor is it the limitation of nature. In short, it is not found in laws governing the production of wealth. Therefore, we must examine the laws governing its distribution.

First, let's outline the distribution of wealth. Since land, labor, and capital join to produce wealth, the output must then be divided among these three. To discover the cause of poverty, we will have to find the law that determines what part is distributed to labor (wages). Then to make sure this law is correct, we must also find the laws fixing what part goes to capital (interest) and what part to landowners (rent).

Producing is not simply making things—it also includes increasing their value by transporting or exchanging them. Wealth is produced by the commercial community, just as it is by the agricultural or manufacturing community. In each case, some of it will go to the owners of capital, some to laborers, and some to the owners of land.

Additionally, since capital is constantly consumed and constantly replaced, a portion of the wealth produced goes toward the replacement of capital. It is not necessary to take this replacement of capital into account, however. It is eliminated by considering capital as continuous. We habitually do this, both in speaking and thinking of it.

The produce of the community is the general fund that supports all consumption. The term refers to wealth produced beyond what is required to replace any capital consumed in the process. Therefore, interest means what goes to capital after its replacement or maintenance.

Furthermore, some of the wealth produced is taken by government in taxes (except in the most primitive communities). Again, for our purposes in determining the laws of distribution, we may consider taxation either as not existing or as reducing output by that amount. Certain forms of monopoly exercise powers analogous to taxation, and may be treated likewise. (We will discuss these in Chapter 13.) After we have discovered the laws of distribution, we can then see what effect taxation has upon the process.

Economists do not understand these laws correctly, as we may see in any standard text. In all these works, we are told that the three factors of production are land, labor, and capital, and that the entire output is distributed to their corresponding parts. Therefore, three terms are needed. Each should clearly express one part to the exclusion of the others.

Rent is defined clearly enough as the part that goes to owners of land. The term wages is also defined clearly enough as the part that is the return to labor. The third term, then, should express the return for the use of capital.

But here, we find a problem. In standard economics books, there is a puzzling ambiguity and confusion. The term that comes closest to exclusively expressing the idea of return to capital is interest. Interest implies the return for the use of capital, exclusive of any labor in its use or management, and also exclusive of risk.

Note that the word profits simply means what is received in excess of what is expended. Such receipts may include rent and interest and wages, including compensation for risk.* Therefore, profits cannot be used to signify the share going to capital—as distinct from that going to labor and to landowners. The term has no place in discussing the distribution of wealth between the three factors of production, unless extreme violence is done to its meaning.

To speak of the distribution of wealth into "rent, wages, and profits" is like dividing mankind into "men, women, and human beings." Yet, to the utter bewilderment of the reader, this is what is done in all standard works. Undoubtedly, thousands have vainly puzzled over this confusion of terms, and abandoned their efforts in despair. Believing the fault could not be in such great thinkers, they assumed

---

* Today, some attribute risk-taking to a distinct factor, called "entrepreneurism". George defined labor as all human exertion in production, whether mental or physical.

it must be their own stupidity. Reading John Stuart Mill, you can see this confusion exemplified by the most logical of English economists—in a manner more striking than I care to characterize.

No text, to my knowledge, brings these laws together so the reader can recognize their relation to each other. Instead, each is enveloped in a mass of reflections and dissertations. The reason is not far to seek: Bringing together the three laws of distribution, as they are now taught, shows at a glance that they lack necessary relation.

The laws of distribution are obviously laws of proportion. They must relate to each other so that given any two, the third may be inferred. To say that one part of the whole is increased is to say that one or both of the other parts must be decreased (or vice versa).

Say Tom, Dick, and Harry are business partners. The agreement setting the share of one also sets the shares of the other two, either jointly or separately. If Tom gets thirty percent, that leaves seventy percent to be divided between Dick and Harry. If Tom gets thirty percent and Harry fifty percent, that fixes Dick's share at twenty percent.

But in standard economic texts, there is no such relation among the laws of distribution of wealth. If we fish these laws out and bring them together, we find them stated as follows:

Wages are determined by the ratio between capital available for labor and the number seeking employment.

Rent is determined by the margin of production. That is, rent equals the amount of produce in excess of what could be produced from the poorest land in use with the same amount of labor and capital.

Interest is determined by the demands of borrowers

and the supply of capital from lenders.

Or, if we take what is given as the law of profits, it is determined by wages, falling as wages rise and rising as wages fall. (What Mill calls "the cost of labor to the capitalist.")

Bringing these together, we immediately see a problem: They lack relation to each other, which the true laws of distribution must have. Since they do not correlate, at least two of the three must be wrong.

We must then seek the true laws of distribution that divide what is produced into wages, rent, and interest. The proof that we have found them will be in their correlation.

To recapitulate what we have discovered in our investigation:

Land, labor, and capital are the factors of production. Land includes all natural opportunities or forces. Labor includes all human exertion. Capital includes all wealth used to produce more wealth.

The output is distributed in returns to these three factors. Rent is that part that goes to owners of land as payment for the use of natural opportunities. Wages are that part that constitutes the reward for human exertion. Interest is that part that constitutes the return for the use of capital.

These terms mutually exclude each other. The income of any individual may be made up from any one, two, or all three of these sources. But to discover the laws of distribution we must keep them separate.

I think the error of political economy has now been abundantly revealed, and can be traced to an erroneous viewpoint.

We live in a society where capitalists generally rent land and hire labor. They thus seem to be the initiators or first movers in production. Living and making observations in this state, the great developers of economic science were led to look on capital as the prime factor in production. They saw land as its instrument, and labor as its agent or tool. This is apparent on every page. It is in the form and course of their reasoning, in the character of their illustrations, and even in their choice of terms. Everywhere capital is the starting point, and the capitalist the central figure.

This goes so far that both Smith and Ricardo use the term "natural wages" to express the minimum on which laborers can live.

On the contrary, unless injustice is natural, everything a laborer produces should be his natural wages. This habit of looking on capital as the employer of labor began when Adam Smith, in his first book, left the viewpoint that "the produce of labor constitutes the natural recompense or wages of labor." Instead, he adopted the view in which capital is considered as employing labor and paying wages.

But when we consider the origin and natural sequence of things, we see that this reverses the natural order of things. Capital does not come first, it comes last. Capital is not the employer of labor—it is, in reality, employed by labor.

The matter that labor converts into wealth comes only from land. There must be land before labor can be exerted. And labor must be exerted before capital can be produced. Capital is a result of labor, a form of labor, a subdivision of the general term. It is only stored-up labor, used by labor to assist it in further production. Labor is the active and initial force. Therefore, labor is the employer of capital, not vice versa—and it is even possible for labor to produce wealth without being aided by capital.

So the natural order is this: land, labor, capital.

Instead of using capital as our initial point, we should start from land.

Chapter 11

The Law Of Rent

RENT, IN THE ECONOMIC SENSE, is the part of the produce that accrues to the owners of land (or other natural capabilities) by virtue of ownership.

This differs from the everyday meaning in several respects. Common speech mixes payments for use of improvements with payments for use of bare land. When we speak of renting a house (or farm or factory), we combine the price for using land with the price for using buildings, machinery, fixtures, etc. But in the economic sense, rent means only what is paid for using land. We must exclude payments for the use of any product of human exertion. Anything paid for buildings or other improvements is compensation for the use of capital. This is properly called interest.

But the economic meaning is broader in a different sense. In common speech, we speak of rent only when the owner and the user are two different people. Yet in the economic sense, there is rent even when the same person is both. In this case, rent is what she might get if she rented the land to someone else. Or, to look at it another way, the return for her labor and capital (i.e., her wages and interest) is the part of her income equal to what she would make if she had to rent the land, instead of owning it.

Rent is also expressed in the selling price of land. This

price is payment for the right to perpetual use. In other words, it is rent capitalized. If I buy land and hold it until I can sell it for more, I will become rich—not from wages for my labor nor interest for my capital—but merely by rising rents.

Rent, in short, is the share of wealth given to landowners because they have an exclusive right to the use of those natural capabilities.

Wherever land has an exchange value, there is rent in the economic meaning of the term. If in use, there is actual rent. If land is not in use but still has a value, there is potential rent. It is this capacity of yielding rent that gives land its value.

Until ownership confers some advantage, land has no value. Therefore, land value does not arise from its productiveness or usefulness. No matter what its capabilities, land has no value until some one is willing to pay for the privilege of using it.

Rent does not, in any way, represent any aid or advantage to production. Rent is simply the power to take part of the results of production.

Furthermore, the amount anyone will pay for land does not depend on its capacity. Rather, it depends on its capacity *compared* to land that is available for free. Even very good land has no value as long as other land, just as good, is available without cost. But as soon as this other land is appropriated—and the best land now available for nothing is inferior (either in fertility, location, or some other quality)—then my land will have value and will begin to yield rent. Now, suppose my land becomes less productive. The rent I can get might still increase! Rent will increase if the productiveness of land available without charge decreases even more.

Rent, in short, is the price of monopoly. It arises from individual ownership of the natural elements—which human exertion can neither produce nor increase.

If one person owned all the land in a community, he or she could demand any price desired for its use. As long as that ownership was acknowledged, the others would have no alternative (except death or emigration). This, indeed, has been the case many times in the past.

In modern society, land is usually owned by too many different people for the price to be fixed by whim. While owners try to get all they can, there is a limit to what they can obtain. This market price (or market rent) varies with different lands and at different times.

The law of rent, then, will be the law or relation that determines what rent or price an owner can get under free competition. (To discover the principles of political economy, we must always assume free competition among all parties.)

Fortunately, economists agree on this point. It is an accepted dictum of political economy, with the self-evident character of a geometric axiom. Of course, in all the nonsense printed as economics in its present disjointed condition, it would be hard to find anything that has not been disputed. Yet all economic writers regarded as authorities endorse this law.

Often called Ricardo's law of rent,* it has been exhaustively explained by all leading economists after him. It applies not only to farmland, but to land used for other

---

* David Ricardo (1772-1823) English economist. Although not the first to state the law of rent, he brought it into prominence.

purposes, and to all natural agencies, such as mines, fisheries, etc. It says:

The rent of land is determined by the excess of its production over that which the same application can secure from the least productive land in use.

The effect of competition is to take the lowest reward for which labor and capital will engage in production and make that the highest they can claim. In other words, owners of more productive land are able to seize, in rent, everything above what labor and capital can obtain from the least productive land in use.

We can say the same thing in a slightly different form: Landowners can claim everything above what the same application of labor and capital could secure in the least productive occupation in which they can freely engage. Since any occupation requires the use of land, this amounts to precisely the same thing. Furthermore, all things considered, lands will be used until the poorest return equals the lowest compensation in other pursuits.

For instance, if farming paid more, clearly some labor and capital engaged in other pursuits would turn to agriculture. This will continue until the yield to labor and capital in both pursuits reaches the same level, all things considered. The process may be driven by extending cultivation to inferior land. Or the relative value of manufactured products may increase as production slows. In fact, both processes may be at work. Regardless, the final point at which manufacturing is still carried on will also be the point to which cultivation is extended.

The law of rent is, in fact, a deduction from the law of competition. In the final analysis, it rests on a principle as fundamental to political economy as the law of gravity is to physics. Namely, that people seek to gratify their desires with the least exertion.

Ever since Ricardo, the basic law itself has been clearly understood and recognized— but its corollaries have not. Yet these are as plain as the simplest geometry. Wealth is divided among rent, wages, and interest. Therefore, the law of rent is necessarily the law of wages and interest taken together.

In algebraic form:

Production = Rent + Wages + Interest.
Production – Rent = Wages + Interest.

Thus, wages and interest do not depend on what labor and capital produce—they depend on what is left after rent is taken out. No matter how much they might actually produce, they receive only what they could get on land available without rent—on the least productive land in use. Landowners take everything else. Hence, no matter how much productive power increases, neither wages nor interest can rise if the increase in rent keeps pace with it.

Recognizing this simple relationship immediately illuminates what had seemed inexplicable. Increasing rent is the key that explains why wages and interest fail to increase with greater productivity.

The wealth produced in every community is divided into two parts by what may be called the rent line—that is, by the return that labor and capital could obtain from natural opportunities available without rent. Wages and interest are paid from below this line. Everything above it goes to rent.

Thus, where land values are low, wages and interest are high—even if relatively little wealth is produced. We see this in new countries. In older countries, a larger amount of wealth may be produced. Yet where the value of land is high, wages and interest are low.

Productive power is increasing in all developing countries—but wages and interest do not follow. Rather, they are controlled by how rent is affected. Wages and interest can increase only when land values do not increase as quickly as productivity.

All of this is demonstrated in actual fact.

Chapter 12

The Cause of Interest

WE HAVE DETERMINED the law of rent and its necessary corollaries. Still, let's seek each law separately and independently—without deduction from the law of rent. If we discover them independently—and find they correlate—then our conclusions will be certain. To start, let's examine the general subject of interest.

I have already warned of confusing profits with interest. Additionally, the economic meaning differs from common usage. Interest properly includes all returns for the use of capital—not just payments from borrower to lender.

Further, the economic meaning excludes compensation for risk—which makes up a great part of what is commonly called interest. But compensation for risk is merely an equalization of return between different uses of capital. We want to discover what determines the general rate of interest proper.

Rates also vary considerably in different countries and at different times. Interest generally has been higher in the United States than in England. Indeed, it has long been well known that interest tends to sink as society progresses.

What can bind these variations together and reveal their cause? It is obvious that current explanations run counter to facts. It is easily proved that interest does not depend on productiveness, for interest is lowest where labor and capital are most productive. Nor does interest vary inversely with wages. The fact is, interest is high when and where wages are high. Likewise, low interest and low wages are found together.

So let us begin at the beginning. Even at the risk of digressing, we must establish the cause of interest before considering its law. In other words, why should borrowers pay back more than they received from lenders? Why should there be interest at all?

The standard texts all claim interest is a reward for abstinence. But abstinence is a passive quality, not an active one. Abstinence in itself produces nothing. So why should part of anything produced be given for it? If I bury my money for a year, I have exercised as much abstinence as if I had loaned it. Yet when loaned, I expect it to be returned with an additional sum as interest.

Some may say I provide a service to the borrower by lending my capital. But the borrower also does me a service by keeping it safely. Under some conditions, such a service may be very valuable. Many forms of capital must be constantly maintained, an onerous task if there is no immediate use for them. The secure preservation, the maintenance, or the restoration of capital is an offset to its use. So isn't the debt discharged when the capital is returned?

Accumulation is the purpose of abstinence. It can do no more. In fact, by itself, it can't even do this. Think how much wealth would disappear in just a few years if we simply abstained from using it!

Bastiat* and many others say the basis of interest is

---

* Frederic Bastiat (1801-1850), French economist, gave a well-known illustration of interest involving the loan of a carpenter's plane. George's analysis of the fallacies in this illustration is somewhat complex. It is not necessary for our discussion here.

"the power which exists in tools to increase the productiveness of labor." Clearly, however, this is not the basis in justice or in fact. A fallacy allows it to pass as conclusive to those who do not stop to analyze it. It is true that tools increase labor's productive power. The mistake lies in assuming that the loan transfers this power. This is really not involved.

The essential thing loaned is *not* the increased power that labor acquires. To suppose this, we would have to assume that such things were trade secrets or patent rights. In such case, the illustration would become one of monopoly, not capital. The essential thing loaned is this: the use of the concrete results of the effort expended in producing the tools—not the privilege of applying labor in a more effective way.

If interest were based on increased productiveness, the rate of interest would increase with technology. This is not so. Nor do I expect to pay more to borrow a fifty-dollar sewing machine than to borrow fifty dollars' worth of needles. Nor if I borrow a steam engine rather than a pile of bricks.

Capital, like wealth, is interchangeable. It is not one particular thing—it is anything within the circle of exchange. Moreover, tools and machinery do not add to the reproductive power of capital—they add to the productive power of labor.

Now, consider for a moment a world in which wealth consisted only of inert matter, and production was only working this inert matter into different shapes. Such things have no reproductive power of their own. If I put away hammers or barrels or money, they will not increase.

But suppose, instead, I put away wine. At the end

of a year, the wine will have improved in quality and its value will be greater. Or suppose I release a swarm of bees. At the end of a year, I will have more bees, as well as the honey they have made. Or suppose I put cattle out on the range. At the end of the year, I will, on average, also have an increase.

What provides the increase in these cases is something distinct and separate from labor. Though it generally requires labor to make use of it, we can readily distinguish it from labor. It is the active power of nature—the principle of growth, or reproduction, which characterizes all forms of what we call life.

It seems to me that this is the true cause of interest—that is, the increase of capital over and above that due to labor. Certain powers in nature—with a force independent of our own efforts—help us turn matter into forms we desire. In other words, they aid us in producing wealth.

Both types of things are included in the terms wealth and capital—things that have no innate power of increase, and things that yield over and above what can be attributed to labor. With inanimate things, labor alone is the efficient cause. When labor stops, all production stops. But in these other modes, time is an element. The seed grows whether the farmer sleeps or works.

Furthermore, there are also variations in the powers of nature and of people. Through exchange, these variations can be used to obtain an increase in net output. This somewhat resembles the increase produced by the vital forces of nature.

For instance, in one place a given amount of labor will secure either what we may call 200 units of vegetable food or 100 units of animal food. In another place, the conditions are reversed: The same amount of labor will produce 100 of vegetable or 200 of animal food. The relative value of animal to vegetable food will be two to one in one location, but one to two in the other. If equal amounts are required, the same amount of labor in either place will secure 150 units of both. But suppose in one place labor is used to procure vegetables, while in the other to procure animal food. Then an exchange is made in the quantity required. Thus, the people of each place—with the same amount of labor—will acquire 200 of both (less the losses and expenses of exchange). In each place, the product that is exchanged brings back an increase.

Since wealth is interchangeable, it necessarily involves an average between all types of wealth. So any special advantage that accrues from the possession of any one particular type must be averaged with all others. For no one would keep capital in one form when it could be changed into a more advantageous form.

So, in any circle of exchange, the power of increase that nature gives to some forms of capital must be averaged with all forms of capital. Thereby, those who lend money or bricks are not deprived of the power to obtain an increase. They will get the same as if they had lent (or used) an equivalent amount of capital in a form capable of increase.

This general averaging—or "pooling" of advantages—inevitably takes place wherever society carries on different modes of production simultaneously. Thus, all types of wealth maintain similar advantages. In the final analysis, the advantage given by time comes from the generative force of nature and from the varying powers of nature and of people. If the quality and capacity of matter everywhere were uniform, and if productive power existed only in humans, then there would be no interest.

If I have a thousand dollars, I can certainly loan it out at interest. But that does not arise because those without funds would gladly pay me for the use of it. Rather, it comes from the fact that capital, which my money represents, has the power to yield an increase. The price something will bring does not depend so much on what the buyer would be willing to give rather than go without it—it depends on what the seller can get otherwise. Interest is not a payment made for the use of capital—it is a return accruing from the increase of capital.

In short, then, when we analyze production, it falls into three modes:

ADAPTING—Changing natural products, in form or place, to fit them to satisfy human desire.

GROWING—Utilizing the vital forces of nature, as in raising vegetables or animals.

EXCHANGING— Increasing the general sum of wealth by exploiting local variations in the forces of nature, or variations among human forces due to situation, occupation, or character.

In adapting, capital gains its benefit in its use. In growing, the benefits arise not from use but from increase. In exchanging, capital is exchanged rather than used. The benefit is in the increase, or greater value, of things received in return. Essentially, benefits arising from use go to labor; those from increase go to capital.

But the division of labor and the interchangeability of wealth compel an averaging of benefits. For neither labor nor capital will pursue any method of production while another is available offering a greater return.

We can say this another way. In adapting, labor will not get the whole return—but less enough to give capital the increase it could have gotten in the other modes. Likewise, capital in the second and third modes will not get the whole increase—but less enough to give labor the reward it could have gotten from the first mode.

Thus, interest springs from the power of increase given to capital by the reproductive forces of nature, or by the analogous capacity of exchange. This is not arbitrary, it is natural. It is not the result of a particular social organization, but of laws of the universe.

Chapter 13
False Interest

THE BELIEF that interest is a form of robbery is, I am persuaded, largely due to a failure to discriminate between what is really capital and what is not. True interest is often confused with revenue from sources other than use of capital. In common speech, we call anyone a "capitalist" who makes money independent of labor. Further, anything received from any kind of investment is labeled interest. Before we decide whather labor and capital really are in conflict we should clear up some misconceptions that might cloud our judgment.

An enormous part of what is commonly called capital is actually land value—it is not capital at all. Rent is not the earnings of capital, and must be carefully separated from interest.

Additionally, what are properly termed "wages of superintendence" are often confused with the earnings of capital. This includes income derived from such personal qualities as skill, tact, and organizational ability.

Stocks and bonds constitute another large part of what is commonly called capital. These are not capital either— they are simply evidence of indebtedness. Always remember that nothing can be capital that is not wealth. It must consist of actual, tangible things that satisfy human desires. They can not be the spontaneous offerings of nature.

And they must fulfill our desires by themselves, directly or indirectly, but not by proxy.

Thus, a government bond is not capital—nor does it even *represent* capital. Any capital once received for it has been shot from cannons or used to keep men marching and drilling. The bond cannot represent capital that has been destroyed. It is simply a declaration that, some time in the future, the government will take, by taxation, so much wealth from the general stock then existing among the people. This it will turn over to the bondholders when the bond matures. Meanwhile, from time to time, it will take, by taxation, a certain amount to give as interest. The amount will be enough to make up whatever increase the bondholders would have received if they had kept the original capital. Immense sums are taken from the production of every modern country to pay interest on public debt. These are not the earnings or increase of capital. They are not even interest, in the strict sense of the term. They are taxes levied on labor and capital—leaving less for wages and less for true interest.

But suppose the bonds were issued for deepening a river bed or erecting a lighthouse? Or, to modify the illustration, suppose they were issued by a railroad company? These may be considered evidence of ownership of capital. But only so far as they represent real capital—existing and applied to productive uses—and not bonds issued in excess of actual capital used.

All too often, certificates are issued for two, three, or even ten times the amount of actual capital used. The excess (over what is due as interest on the real capital invested) is regularly paid out as "interest" or dividends on this fictitious amount. Large sums are also absorbed by management and never accounted for. All this is taken from the aggregate production of the community—but not for services rendered by capital.

There is another element contributing to the profits we are speaking of here. That element is monopoly.

When the king granted his minion the exclusive privilege to make gold thread, the handsome income enjoyed as a result did not arise from interest on capital invested in manufacturing. Nor did it come from the talent and skill of those who actually did the work. It came from an exclusive privilege. It was, in reality, the power to levy a tax (for private enjoyment) on all users of such thread.

Much of the profits commonly confused with earnings of capital come from a similar source. Receipts from patents granted to encourage invention are clearly attributable to this source. So are returns from monopolies created by protective tariffs under the pretense of encouraging home industry.

But there is another form of monopoly, far more general and far more insidious. The accumulation of large amounts of capital under consolidated control creates a new kind of power—essentially different from the power of increase. Increase is constructive in its nature. Power from accumulation is destructive. It is often exercised with reckless disregard, not only to industry but to the personal rights of individuals.

A railroad approaches a small town as a robber approaches his victim.* "Agree to our terms or we will bypass your town" is as effective a threat as "your money or your

---

* Nowadays, this could describe the way that "big-box" retail stores approach communities.

life." As robbers unite to plunder and divide the spoils, the trunk lines of railroads unite to raise rates and pool their earnings. The public is then forced to pay the cost of the whole maneuver, as the vanquished are forced to pay the cost of their own enslavement by a conquering army.

Profits properly due to the elements of risk are also frequently mislabeled interest. Some people acquire wealth by taking chances in ventures where most suffer losses. There are many such forms of speculation, especially that method of gambling known as the stock market. Nerve, judgment, and possession of capital give an advantage. Also, those skills known as the arts of the confidence man. But, just as at a gaming table, whatever one person gains someone else must lose.

Everyone knows the tyranny and greed with which capital, when concentrated in large amounts, is frequently wielded to corrupt, rob, and destroy. What I wish to call the reader's attention to here is this:

These profits should not be confused with the legitimate returns of capital as an agent of production. Any analysis will show that much of what is commonly confused with interest is really the result of the power of concentrated capital. For the most part, this should be attributed to bad legislation, blind adherence to ancient customs, and superstitious reverence for legal technicalities.

Examine the great fortunes said to exemplify the accumulative power of capital: the Rothschilds, the Vanderbilts, the Astors. They have been built up, to a greater or lesser degree, by the means we have been reviewing — not by interest. When we find the general cause that tends to concentrate wealth, and thus power, in advancing communities, we will have the solution to our problem.

Chapter 14

The Law Of Interest

WE MAY NOW SEEK the law of interest, recalling two things: Capital does not employ labor; labor employs capital. Capital is not a fixed quantity; the amount can be increased or decreased.

Capital is simply wealth applied in a certain way—wealth being the larger category. Therefore, capital can be increased (1) by applying more labor to its production; or (2) by converting wealth into capital. Likewise, capital can be decreased (1) by applying less labor; or (2) by converting capital back into wealth.

Under free conditions, the maximum that can be given for the use of capital is the increase it will bring. Above this, borrowing capital would involve a loss. The minimum is the replacement of capital, or else capital could not be maintained. Interest will vary between these two points.

We must repeat: the maximum is not fixed—as some writers carelessly state—by the increased efficiency capital gives to labor. Rather, the maximum is set by the average power of increase that belongs to capital in general.

The power of applying itself in advantageous forms is a power of labor. Capital, as capital, cannot claim nor share in this. Indians using only sticks and stones might kill one buffalo a week. Yet with bows and arrows, they may kill one every day. But the tribe's weapon maker would not claim six out of seven buffaloes. Neither will capital invested in a woolen factory entitle the owner to the difference between the output of the factory and what could be made with a spinning wheel. The march of knowledge has made these advantages a common property and power of labor.

We established (in chapter 12) that the cause of interest is the vital forces of nature that give an advantage to the element of time. And this should set the maximum rate of interest. But the reproductive force of nature varies enormously. For instance, if I raise rabbits and you raise horses, my rabbits will multiply faster than your horses. But my capital will not increase faster! The effect of the varying rates will be to lower the value of rabbits compared to horses. Thus, differences are brought to a uniform level that determines the average increase of capital.

Whatever this point, it must be such that the reward to capital and the reward to labor will be equal. That is to say, the normal point of interest will give an equally attractive result for the exertion or sacrifice involved.

For labor and capital are merely different forms of the same thing—human exertion. Capital is produced by labor. It is labor impressed upon matter. This labor has been stored up to be released as needed—as the heat of the sun is stored in coal. Capital can be used only by being consumed. In order for it to be maintained, labor must produce it in proportion to its consumption in aiding labor. Therefore, capital used in production is simply a mode of labor.

Under free competition, a principle operates to maintain this equilibrium between wages and interest. This principle is: People seek to gratify their desires with the least exertion.

The natural relation between interest and wages is an equilibrium at which both will represent equal return for equal exertion. Although this may be stated in a form that suggests opposition, this is only in appearance. For each gets only what they add to the common fund. Increasing the portion of one does not decrease what the other receives.

We are, of course, speaking of the general rate of wages and the general rate of interest. In a particular case or a particular occupation, this equilibrium may be impeded. But it will act quickly between the general rate of wages and the general rate of interest. A particular situation may have a clean line between labor and those who furnish capital. Yet even in communities where this distinction is the sharpest, the two shade off into each other by imperceptible gradations, until they meet in the same persons. Here, the interaction that restores equilibrium goes on without obstruction.

Furthermore, remember that capital is only a portion of wealth. It is distinguished from wealth only by the purpose it is used for. Hence, the whole body of wealth has an equalizing effect. This operates like a flywheel: taking up capital when there is excess, and giving it out again when there is lack. A jeweler may wear her diamonds while she is overstocked, but returns them to the showcase when stock is low. If interest rises above the equilibrium with wages, it produces two results: It will direct labor to produce capital. It will also direct wealth to be used as capital. Meanwhile, if wages rise above the equilibrium, that will also produce two results: Labor will turn away from producing capital. And the proportion of wealth used as capital will be reduced, as some will now be diverted to nonproductive uses.

Thus, there is a certain relation between wages and interest, which changes slowly, if at all. Hence, interest must rise or fall *with* wages.

To illustrate: The price of flour is determined by the price of wheat and cost of milling. Even over long intervals, the cost of milling hardly varies. But the price of wheat varies greatly and frequently. Hence, we correctly say that the price of flour is governed by the price of wheat.

To put this in the same form as the preceding discussion: The cost of milling fixes a certain relation between the value of wheat and the value of flour. This ratio is constantly maintained by the interaction between the demand for flour and the supply of wheat. Hence, the price of flour must rise and fall with the price of wheat. We can leave the connecting link, the price of wheat, to inference. We would then say that the price of flour depends upon the character of the seasons, wars, etc.

In the same way, we can put the law of interest in a form that connects it directly with the law of rent. The general rate of interest, then, will be determined by the return to capital on the poorest land freely available. That is to say, the return from the best land open to it without the payment of rent. The law of interest, therefore, is shown to be a corollary of the law of rent.

We can prove this conclusion another way. If we were to eliminate wages, we could plainly see that interest must decrease as rent increases. Of course, to do this we must imagine a place where production occurs without labor. Houses grow from seeds, and a jackknife thrown on the ground bears a crop of assorted cutlery.*

---

* A modern reader might imagine a land of robots in the near future.

Capitalists here would keep *all* the wealth produced from their capital—but only as long as none of it was demanded in rent. When rent arose, it would come from their interest. As rent increased, the return to the owners of capital must necessarily decrease. If this place were an island, interest would fall to just above its minimum (mere replacement) as soon as capital reached the limit of the island to support it. Landowners would receive almost the entire output—for the only alternative would be for capitalists to throw their capital into the sea.

This, in sum, is the law of interest:

> *The relation between wages and interest is determined by the average power of increase that attaches to capital from its use in reproductive modes. As rent arises, interest will fall as wages fall, or will be determined by the margin of production.*

In truth, the principal distribution of wealth is into two—not three—parts. Capital is simply a form of labor. Its distinction is a subdivision, like dividing labor into skilled and unskilled. That is to say, wealth is divided between the possessors of two factors: (1) natural substances and forces, and (2) human exertion. For all wealth is produced by the union of these two factors.

Chapter 15

The Law Of Wages

THERE IS no common rate of wages in the same sense as the common rate of interest, which is relatively specific at any given time and place. Wages vary with individual abilities. As society becomes more complex, there are also large variations among occupations. Nevertheless, there is a certain general relation between all wages. This concept—that wages are higher or lower at one time or place than another—is quite clear. So wages must rise and fall according to some law.

There is a law as basic to political economy as the law of gravity is to physics. The fundamental principle of human action is this:

People seek to gratify their desires with the least exertion.

Clearly, this principle will tend, through competition, to balance rewards for equal exertion under similar circumstances. When people work for themselves, this operates largely through price fluctuations. The same tendency governs relationships between those who work for themselves and those who work for others. Given free conditions, no one would work for someone else if they could make the same amount working for themselves.

But output does not depend only on the intensity or quality of labor. Wealth is the product of two factors—land and labor. A given amount of labor yields various results, depending on the powers of the natural opportunities to which it is applied. This is easily seen in fundamental occupations, which still form the base of production—even in the most highly developed societies.

People will not work at a lower point while a higher one is available. So, the highest point of natural productiveness available will be same as the lowest point at which production continues. This is called the margin of production.

Wages will be set by the output at the most productive point open to labor. They will rise or fall as this point rises or falls.

To illustrate, consider a simple society in which each person is self-employed. Let's say some hunt, some fish, some farm. At first, all land being used yields a similar return for similar effort. Allowing for differences of ease, risk, and so on, wages will be approximately equal in each. That is, equal exertions will yield equal results for hunting, fishing, or farming. Wages will be the total production of labor. (Remember, even though there are no employers yet, there are still wages—that is, the return for labor. But no one would work for someone else, at this stage, unless they received the full, average results of labor.)

Time passes. Cultivation now occurs on land of different quality. Wages will no longer be as before—the full, average production of labor. Instead, wages will be the average at the margin of production—the point of lowest return. Since people seek to satisfy their desires with the least exertion, this point will yield a return to labor equivalent to the average return in hunting and fishing.

This equalization in return will be brought about by prices. Labor no longer yields equal returns for equal exertion. Those working superior land get greater results, for the same exertion, than those on inferior land. Wages, however, are still equal. The excess received from superior land is, in reality, properly called rent. If land has been subjected to individual ownership, this is what gives it value.

Circumstances have changed. To hire others, an employer need pay only what the labor yields at the lowest point of cultivation. If the margin of production sinks lower, wages will also drop. If it should rise, wages must also rise.

We have deduced the law of wages from an obvious and universal principle—that people will seek to satisfy their wants with the least exertion. Wages depend on the margin of production. They will be greater or less depending on what labor can get from the best natural opportunities available to it.

We deduced this from simple states. If we examine the complex phenomena of highly civilized societies, the same law applies. Wages differ widely in these societies, but they still bear a fairly definite and obvious relationship to each other.

Of course, this relation is not invariable. A well-known entertainer may earn many times the wages of the best mechanic, yet at some other time the same entertainer may barely command the pay of a footman. Some jobs pay high wages in big cities, while in a small town the pay is low. We need not dwell on what causes wages to vary among different jobs. This has been admirably explained by Adam Smith and the economists who followed him.* They have

---

* Adam Smith has summarized these circumstances. They include: the difficulty of the job itself; the difficulty and expense of training; the constancy of employment; the degree of responsibility; and the probability of success. The last is analogous to the element of risk in profits It accounts for the high wages of successful doctors, lawyers, actors, etc.

worked out the details quite well—even if they failed to comprehend the main law.

It is perfectly correct to say that wages of different occupations vary according to supply and demand. Demand means the request that the community makes for particular services. Supply is the relative amount of labor available to perform those particular services.

However, when we hear (as we often do) that the general rate of wages is determined by supply and demand, those words are meaningless. For supply and demand can only be relative terms. Demand for labor can only mean that some product of labor is offered in exchange for (other) labor. Likewise, the supply of labor can only mean labor offered in exchange for the products of labor.

Thus, supply is demand, and demand is supply. In the whole community, they must be coextensive with each other. Wages can never permanently exceed the production of labor.

The high wages of some occupations resemble lottery prizes, where the great gain of one is taken from the losses of many others. This accounts for the high wages of successful doctors, lawyers, actors, and the like. It is also largely true of wages of superintendence in mercantile pursuits, for over ninety percent of such firms ultimately fail.

Greater abilities or skill, whether natural or acquired, command (on average) greater wages. These qualities are essentially analogous to differences in strength or quickness in manual labor. Higher wages, paid to those who can do more, are based on the wages of those who can only do an average amount. So wages in occupations requiring superior abilities must depend on common wages paid for ordinary abilities. In these occupations, the demand is more uniform and there is the greatest freedom to engage in them.

These gradations of wages shade into each other by imperceptible degrees. In each occupation, there are those who combine it with others, or alternate between fields. All mechanics could work as laborers, and many laborers could easily become mechanics. Mechanics generally earn more than laborers. Still, there are always some mechanics who do not make as much as some laborers. The best paid lawyers receive much higher wages than the best paid clerks. Yet, the best paid clerks make more than some lawyers. In fact, the worst paid clerks make more than the worst paid lawyers. Meanwhile, young people coming into the ranks are drawn to the strongest incentive and least obstruction.

Thus, the differences between occupations are so finely balanced that the slightest change is enough to guide their labor in one direction or another. Experience shows that this equilibrium will be maintained even in the face of artificial barriers. They may interfere with this interaction, but they cannot prevent it. They operate only as dams, which pile up the water of a stream above its natural level, but cannot prevent its overflow.

Thus, it is evident that wages in all strata must ultimately depend upon wages in the lowest and widest stratum. The general rate of wages will rise or fall as the lowest wages rise or fall. The primary and fundamental occupations, on which all the others are built, are those that obtain wealth directly from nature. Hence the law of wages applying to those occupations must be the general law of wages. And wages in such occupations clearly depend upon what labor can produce at the lowest point of natural productiveness to which it is regularly applied. Therefore:

Wages depend upon the margin of production. That is, wages depend on the yield labor can obtain at the highest point of natural productiveness open to it without the payment of rent.

Our demonstration is complete. The law just obtained is identical to the one we deduced as a corollary of the law of rent. It also harmonizes completely with the law of interest. It conforms with universal facts, and explains phenomena that seem unrelated and contradictory without it.

Specifically, it explains these four conditions: Where land is free and labor works without capital, the entire output will go to labor as wages. Where land is free and labor is assisted by capital, wages will consist of the whole produce less what is necessary to induce the storing up of labor as capital. Where land is subject to ownership and rent arises, wages will be fixed by what labor could secure from the highest natural opportunities open to it without paying rent (i.e., the margin of production). Where all natural opportunities are monopolized, wages may be forced by competition among laborers to the minimum at which they will consent to reproduce. Clearly, the margin cannot fall below the point of survival.

To recap: The law of wages is a corollary of Ricardo's law of rent. Like it, the law of wages contains its own proof, and is self-evident as soon as it is stated. It is only the application of the central truth that is the foundation of economic reasoning—namely, that people seek to satisfy their desires with the least exertion. All things considered, the average person will not work for an employer for less than can be earned in self-employment. Neither will a person choose self-employment for less than could be earned working for an employer. Hence, the return labor can get from free natural opportunities must set the wages for labor in general. Said another way, the line of rent is the necessary measure of the line of wages.

In fact, recognizing the law of rent depends upon accepting (often unconsciously) the law of wages. What makes it clear that land of a particular quality will yield rent equal to its surplus over the least productive land in use? Because we know that owners of better land can get others to work for them by paying what workers can get on poorer land.

The law of wages is so obvious that it is often understood without being recognized. People who do not trouble themselves about political economy grasp it in its simpler forms, just as those unconcerned with the laws of gravitation know that a heavy body falls to the earth. It does not require a philosopher to see that the general rate of wages would rise if natural opportunities were available where workers could earn more than the lowest wages. Even the most ignorant placer miners of early California knew that as these mines gave out or were monopolized, wages would fall.

It requires no finespun theory to explain why wages are so high relative to production in new countries where land is not yet monopolized. The cause is on the surface. No one will work for another for less than can be earned through self-employment—such as going nearby and independently operating a farm. It is only as land becomes monopolized, and these natural opportunities are shut off, that laborers are forced to compete with each other for work. It then becomes possible for a farmer to hire hands to do the work—while the farmer lives on the difference between what their labor produces and their wages.

Adam Smith himself saw the cause of high wages where land was still open to settlement. Unfortunately, he failed to appreciate the importance and the connection of the fact. In the *Causes of the Prosperity of New Colonies*, he reports:

> *Every colonist gets more land than he can possibly culti-*
> *vate. He has no rent and scarce any taxes to pay. He is*
> *eager, therefore, to collect laborers from every quarter and*
> *to pay them the most liberal wages. But these liberal wages,*
> *joined to the plenty and cheapness of land, soon make these*
> *laborers leave him in order to become landlords them-*
> *selves, and to reward with equal liberality other laborers*
> *who soon leave them for the same reason they left their*
> *first masters.* *

It is impossible to read the works of Adam Smith and other economists without seeing how, over and over again, they stumble over the law of wages without recognizing it. If it were a dog, it would bite them! Indeed, it is difficult to resist the notion that some of them actually saw it, but were afraid of its logical conclusions. To an age that has rejected it, a great truth is not a word of peace, but a sword!

Before closing this chapter, let me remind the reader that I am not using the word wages in the sense of a quantity, but in that of a proportion. When I say that wages fall as rent rises, I do not mean that the quantity of wealth laborers receive as wages is necessarily less. I mean that the proportion it bears to the entire output is less. The

---

* Chap. VII, Book IV, *Wealth of Nations*.

proportion may diminish while the quantity remains the same, or even increases.

For example, suppose the margin of production declines. (We will say from 25 to 20.) As rents increase by this difference, the proportion given in wages must decrease to the same extent. In the meantime, the productive power of labor has increased. Technology may have advanced, or increasing population may make possible greater economies of scale. The same effort at point 20 now produces as much wealth as point 25 used to. The *quantity* of wages remains the same, though the *proportion* has decreased.

This relative fall of wages will not be noticed in the comforts of the laborers. It will be seen only in the increased value of land—and in the greater income and extravagance of the rent-receiving class.

Chapter 16
Correlating The Laws of Distribution

THE CONCLUSIONS we have reached on the laws governing the distribution of wealth recast a large and important part of the science of political economy, as presently taught. They overthrow some of its most elaborate theories, and shed new light on some of its most important problems. Yet in doing this, we have not advanced a single fundamental principle that is not already recognized.

True, we have substituted a new law of wages and a new law of interest for those now taught. But these laws are necessary deductions from the most fundamental law: that people seek to gratify their desires with the least exertion. When viewed in relation to one of the factors of production, this becomes the law of rent.

Ricardo's statement of the law of rent has been accepted by every reputable economist since his day. Like an axiom of geometry, it only needs to be understood to be accepted. The laws of interest and of wages, as I have stated them, are necessary deductions from the law of rent. In recognizing the law of rent, they too must be recognized. For discerning the law of rent clearly rests on recognizing this fact: Competition prevents the return to labor and capital from being greater than what could be produced on the poorest land in use. Once we see this, we see what the owner of land will be able to claim as rent—everything that exceeds what an equal amount of labor and capital could produce on the poorest land in use.

The laws of distribution, as we now understand, clearly correlate with each other. This is in striking contrast to the lack of harmony of those given by current political economy. Let us state them side by side:

The Current Statement:

RENT depends on the margin of production, rising as it falls and falling as it rises.

WAGES depend upon the ratio between the number of laborers and the amount of capital devoted to their employment.

INTEREST depends upon the equation between the supply of and demand for capital. (Or, as is stated of profits, interest depends upon "the cost of labor", rising as wages fall and falling as wages rise.)

The True Statement:

RENT depends on the margin of production—rising as it falls, and falling as it rises.

WAGES depend on the margin of production—falling as it falls, and rising as it rises.

INTEREST depends on the margin of production—falling as it falls, and rising as it rises. (Its ratio with wages being fixed by the net power of increase that attaches to capital.)

In their current form, the laws of distribution have no mutual relation and no common center. They are not correlating divisions of a whole. Rather, they are measures of different qualities.

In the statement we have given, all the laws spring from a single point. They support and supplement each other. Together they form correlating divisions of a complete whole.

Chapter 17

The Problem Explained

WE HAVE NOW obtained a clear, simple, and consistent theory of the distribution of wealth. It accords with both basic principles and existing facts. Once understood, it is self-evident.

The old theory of wages had the support of the highest authorities, and was firmly rooted in common prejudices. Until it was proven groundless, it prevented any other theory from even being considered. Similarly, the theory that the earth was the center of the universe prevented any consideration that the earth circled the sun.

There is, in fact, a striking resemblance between the science of political economy, as currently taught, and astronomy prior to Copernicus. As they attempt to explain social phenomena, economists employ devices that may well be compared to the elaborate system of cycles and epicycles constructed by the learned people of the past. They tried to make celestial phenomena fit the dogmas of authority and the primitive perceptions of the uneducated. But as these elaborate theories could not explain observed phenomena, a simpler theory finally supplanted them.

At this point the parallel ceases. The thought that our solid earth is whirling through space is, at first, jarring to our sensibilities. But the truth I wish to make clear is seen naturally. It has been recognized early on by every society.

It is obscured only by the complexities of civilization, the distortions of selfish interests, and the false turns taken by intellectual speculation. It is a theory that will give political economy the simplicity and harmony that Copernican theory gave astronomy.

To recognize it, we need only return to first principles and simple perceptions. Nothing can be clearer than that wages fail to increase with increasing productive power, and that this is due to rising rent.

Three things unite in production: land, labor, and capital. Three parties divide the output: landowner, laborer, and capitalist. If the laborer and capitalist get no more as production increases, it is a necessary inference that the landowner takes the gain.

The facts agree with this inference. Neither wages nor interest keep step with material progress. Yet rising rents and land values invariably accompany advancement. Indeed, they are the mark of progress! Increasing rent explains why wages and interest do not increase. The same cause that gives more to the land owner also denies it to the laborer and capitalist.

Wages and interest are higher in new countries than in old. The difference is not due to nature, but to the fact that land is cheaper. Consequently, a smaller proportion is taken by rent. Wages and interest are not determined by total production, but by net production—after rent has been taken out. Wages and interest are not set by the productiveness of labor, but by the value of land. Wherever the value of land is relatively low, wages and interest are relatively high. Where land is relatively high, wages and interest are relatively low.

When society is in its earliest stages, all labor is applied directly to the land. All wages are paid from its production. It is obvious that if the landowner takes a larger share, the worker gets a smaller one. But in modern production, labor is applied after materials have been separated from the land, and exchange plays a far greater role.

These complexities may disguise the facts, but they do not alter them. All production is still the union of land and labor. Rent cannot increase except at the expense of wages and interest. The rent on land in a manufacturing or commercial city lessens the amount available to divide as wages and interest among those engaged in the production and exchange of wealth in that place. To see human beings in their most hopeless condition, do not go to the unfenced prairies or the log cabins of the backwoods where land is worth nothing. Go, instead, to the great cities, where owning a little patch of ground is worth a fortune.

It is a universal fact—seen everywhere—that the contrast between wealth and want grows as the value of land increases. The greatest luxury and the most pathetic destitution exist side by side where land values are highest.

In short, the value of land depends entirely on the power that ownership gives to appropriate the wealth created by labor. Land value always increases at the expense of labor. The reason greater productive power does not increase wages is because it increases the value of land. Rent swallows up the whole gain.

That is why poverty accompanies progress.

The Effect of Material Progress on the Distribution of Wealth

Chapter 18

Dynamic Forces Not Yet Explored

WE HAVE REACHED a conclusion of great significance. We have shown that rent—not labor—receives the increased production of material progress. Further, we have seen that labor and capital do not have opposing interests, as is popularly believed. In reality, the struggle is between labor and capital, on one side, and landownership on the other.

But we have not fully solved the problem. We know wages remain low because rent advances. Still, that is like saying a steamboat moves because its wheels turn. The further question is, what *causes* rent to advance? What is the force or necessity that distributes an increasing proportion of production as rent?

Ricardo and others focused only on population growth, which forces cultivation of poorer lands. But this principle does not fully account for the increase of rent as material progress goes on. Nor are all the conclusions drawn from it valid. There are other causes that conspire to raise rent. If we trace the effect of progress on the distribution of wealth, we will see what these are and how they operate.

Three changes contribute to material progress: (1) increased population; (2) improvements in production and exchange; and (3) improvements in knowledge, education, government, police, and ethics (to the extent they increase the power to produce wealth).

The latter two have essentially the same economic effect, so we can consider them together. But first, we will consider the effects of increasing population by itself.

Chapter 19

Population Growth and the Distribution of Wealth

HOW DOES A GROWING POPULATION increase rent? Current thought says a higher demand for subsistence forces production to inferior land. For example, if the margin of production is the place where the average laborer can produce 30, then on all lands where more than 30 is produced, there will be rent. A growing population requires additional supplies, which cannot be obtained without extending cultivation. This causes lands that were formerly free to bear rent. Say the margin is extended to 20. All land between 20 and 30 will acquire value and yield rent. All land over 30 will increase in value and bear higher rent. As explained by Ricardo (and later economists), this inability to procure more food except at a greater cost accounts for the increase in rent.

I will show, later, that rent would increase even if population remained steady. But first, we must clear up the misconception that using poorer land produces less aggregate production, proportional to labor expended. For increased population—of itself, and without any technological advances—makes possible an increase in the productive power of labor.

All things being equal, the labor of a hundred people will produce much more than one hundred times the labor of one person. And the labor of a thousand, much more than ten times the labor of a hundred. With every additional person, there is a more-than-proportionate addition to the productive power of labor. As population increases, naturally less productive land may be used—but without any reduction in the average production of wealth per worker. There will be no decrease even at the lowest point. If population doubles, land of only 20 (as per our earlier example) may yield as much as land of 30 could before, given the same amount of labor.

For it must not be forgotten (although it often is) that the productiveness of either land or labor is not measured by any one thing—but by all things we desire. A settler may raise as much corn a hundred miles from the nearest house as on land near a city. But in the city, one could make as good a living, with the same effort, on much poorer land (or on equal land after paying high rent). This is because labor becomes more effective in the midst of a large population. Not, perhaps, in the production of corn, but in the production of wealth. That is, in the ability to obtain the goods and services that are the real object of labor.

A growing population increases the effectiveness of labor by permitting greater economies. More wealth can be produced with the same effort. It increases productivity not only on the newer land, but on all the better land already in use.

If productivity rose faster than the need for less productive land, the average production of wealth would increase. Thus, the minimum return to labor would increase, although rent would still rise. In other words, wages would rise as a quantity—but fall as a proportion.

If productivity just compensated for the diminishing

productiveness of additional land, average production would still increase. Rent would increase (as the margin fell), without reducing wages as a quantity.

Finally, as growth forced even poorer quality land into use, the difference might be so great that even the increased power of labor could not compensate for it. The minimum return to labor would be reduced. Rents would rise, while wages would fall, both as a proportion *and* a quantity.

But even here, average production will still increase (unless the quality of land falls far more precipitously than has ever happened). Remember, the increase of population, which compels the use of inferior land, increases the effectiveness of labor at the same time. This increase affects all labor. Therefore, the gains on superior land will more than compensate for diminished production on the lowest quality.

In short, the aggregate production of wealth, compared with the aggregate expenditure of labor, will be greater— but its distribution will be more unequal. Rent will increase. Wages may or may not fall as a quantity. But wages—as a proportion—will fall. Increasing population seldom can—and probably never does—reduce the aggregate production of wealth compared to the aggregate expenditure of labor. On the contrary, a greater population increases wealth—and frequently increases it greatly.

But it is a mistake to think that lowering the margin is the only process that increases rent. Greater density raises rent without reference to the natural qualities of land. The enhanced powers of cooperation and exchange that come with a larger population are equivalent to a greater capacity to produce wealth. Indeed, I think we can say without metaphor that they actually increase the capacity of land.

Improved tools or methods give greater results to the same amount of labor. This is, in effect, equivalent to an increase in the natural powers of land. But I do not mean to say the power that comes with larger population is merely like this. Rather, it brings out a greater power in labor—and this power is localized on certain land. It does not belong to labor in general, but only to labor exerted on particular land. It resides in land as much as physical qualities such as soil, climate, mineral deposits, or natural situation. Like these, this power passes with possession of the land.

Consider an improvement in cultivation (or tools or machinery) that allows two crops a year instead of one. Clearly, the effect is the same as if the fertility of that land were doubled. But such improvements can be applied to any land, while increased fertility affects only that land. In large part, the increased productivity arising from population can be utilized only on certain land.

The Unbounded Savannah *

Imagine a vast, unbounded savanna, stretching off in endless sameness till the traveler tires of the monotony. The first family of settlers approaches and cannot tell where to settle—every acre seems as good as any other. There is no difference in location, fertility, or water. Perplexed by this embarrassment of riches, they stop somewhere, anywhere, and make themselves a home.

The soil is virgin and rich, the game abundant, the streams flash with trout. What they have would make them

---

*This famous narrative of a society's development has often been excerpted. A savannah is a grassy plain.

rich—if only they were among others. Instead, they are very poor. To say nothing of their mental cravings, which would lead them to welcome the sorriest of strangers, they labor under all the disadvantages of solitude. For any work requiring a union of strength, they are limited to their own family. Though they have cattle, they cannot often have fresh meat—to get a steak, they must kill a whole steer. They are their own blacksmith, carpenter, and cobbler; jacks of all trades and masters of none.

Their children can have no schooling, unless they pay the full salary of a teacher. Anything they cannot produce, they must buy in quantity to keep on hand—or go without. For they cannot constantly leave work and make a long journey to civilization. When forced to do so, getting medicine or replacing a broken tool may cost their labor and the use of their horses for several days.

Under such circumstances, though nature is prolific, the family is poor. It is an easy matter to get enough to eat. But beyond that, their labor can satisfy only the simplest wants in the rudest way.

Soon, though, other immigrants arrive. Though every acre is still as good as every other, there is no doubt where to settle. The land may be the same, but one place is clearly better than any other. And that is where there is already a settler, and they may have a neighbor.

Conditions improve immediately for the earlier pioneers. Many things that were once impossible are now practical—for two families can help each other do things one could never do. As others arrive, they are guided by the same attraction, until there are a score of neighbors around our first.

Labor now has an effectiveness that it could never approach in the solitary state. If heavy work is to be done, the community—working together—accomplish in a day what would have required years alone. There is fresh meat all the time. When one butchers a steer, the others share in it, returning the favor in their turn. Together they hire a schoolmaster. All their children are taught for a fraction of what it would have cost the first settler. And it becomes easy to send to the nearest town, for someone is always going. But there is less need for such journeys.

A blacksmith and a wheelwright soon set up shop. Now our settlers can have their tools repaired for a small part of the labor it formerly cost. A store opens, and they can get what they want, when they want it. A post office soon gives regular communication with the rest of the world.

Occasionally, a passing lecturer opens up a glimpse of the world of science, art, or literature. And finally comes the circus, talked of for months before. Children, whose horizon had been only the prairie, now visit the realms of imagination: princes and princesses, lions and tigers, camels and elephants.

Go to our original settlers now and make this offer: "You have planted so many acres, built a well, a barn, a house. Your labor has added this much value to this farm. But after farming for a few years, your land itself is not quite as good. Still, I will give you the full value of all your improvements—if you will go with your family into the wilderness again."

They would laugh at you. The land yields no more wheat or potatoes than before—but it does yield far more of the necessities and comforts of life. Labor brings no more crops than before—yet it brings far more of all the other things for which people work. The presence of others—the growth of population—has raised the productiveness of labor in these other things. This added productivity confers superiority over land of equal natural quality where there are no settlers.

If, however, there is a continuous stretch of equal land over which population is now spreading, it will not be necessary to go into the wilderness. A newcomer could settle just beyond the others, and get the advantage of proximity to them. The value or rent of land will then depend on the advantage it has: the advantage of being at the center of population over being at the edge.

As population continues to grow, so do the economies its increase permits. In effect, these add to the productiveness of the land. Our first settler's land is now the center of population. The store, the blacksmith, the wheelwright have set up nearby. A village arises, becoming the center of exchange for the whole district.

This land has no greater agricultural productiveness than it had at first. Yet it now begins to develop productiveness of a higher kind. Labor expended in raising crops will yield no more of those than at first. But labor will yield much greater returns in specialized branches of production—where proximity to others is required. The farmer may go further on, and find land yielding as great a harvest. But what of the manufacturer, the storekeeper, the professional? Their labor here, at the center of exchange, gives a much greater return than labor expended even a short distance away from it.

All this difference in productiveness, the landowner can claim. Our pioneers can sell a few building lots at prices they would not bring for farming, even if the fertility were multiplied many times over. With the proceeds, they build fine houses and furnish them handsomely. Or to state the transaction in its lowest terms: those who wish to use this land will build and furnish the houses for them. They do this on the condition that the landowners will allow the workers to avail themselves of the superior productiveness of this land—productiveness given solely by the increase in population.

The town grows into a city: a St. Louis, a Chicago, a San Francisco. Its population gives greater and greater utility to the land—and more and more wealth to its owners. Production is performed on a grand scale, using the latest machinery. The division of labor becomes extremely minute, wonderfully multiplying efficiency. Exchanges are of such volume and rapidity that they entail a minimum of friction and loss. This land now offers enormous advantages for the application of labor. Instead of one person farming a few acres, thousands work in buildings with floors stacked upon each other.

All these advantages attach to the land. On this land—and no other—they can be utilized. For here is the center of population: the focus of exchange, the marketplace, the workshop of industry. Density of population has given this land productive power equivalent to multiplying its original fertility a thousandfold.

Rent—which measures the difference between this added productivity and that of the least productive land in use—has increased accordingly.

Our settlers—or whoever has the rights to the land—are now millionaires. Like Rip Van Winkle, they may have lain down and slept. But they are still rich—not from anything they have done, but from the increase of population.

Nothing has changed in the land itself. It is the same

land that once, when our first settler came upon it, had no value at all. The vast difference in productiveness, which causes rents to rise, is not due to using inferior land. Rather, it is more the result of the increased productiveness that population gives to land already in use. This is how population acts to increase rent—as those living in an advancing country can see if they will just look around. The process is going on before their eyes.

The most valuable lands on earth, those with the highest rent, are not those with the highest natural fertility. Rather, they are lands given a greater usefulness by population density.

We sail through space as if on a well-provisioned ship.* If food above deck seems to grow scarce, we simply open a hatch—and there is a new supply. And a very great command over others comes to those who, as the hatches are opened, are permitted to say: "This is mine!"

---

* This may be the earliest mention of "Spaceship Earth"!

Chapter 20

Technology and the Distribution of Wealth

I INTEND TO SHOW that improved methods of production and exchange will also increase rent, regardless of population. When this is established, we will have explained why material progress lowers wages and produces poverty. No theory of pressure against the means of subsistence is needed, and Malthus's theory—and all doctrines related to it—will be completely disproved.

Inventions and increased productivity save labor. The same results are produced with less labor—or greater results are produced with the same labor. If all material desires were satisfied, labor-saving improvements would simply reduce the amount of labor expended. But such a society cannot be found anywhere. A person is not an ox, lying down to chew its cud when it has had its fill. A person is more like a leech—constantly asking for more.

Demand does not increase only when population does. It grows—in each individual—with the power of obtaining the things desired, and with every opportunity for additional gratification. This being the case, the effect of labor-saving improvements will be to increase the production of wealth.

Now, to produce wealth, two things are required: labor and land. Therefore, the effect of labor-saving improvements will be to extend the demand for land.

So the primary effect of labor-saving improvements is to increase the power of labor. But the secondary effect is to extend the margin of production. And the end result is to increase rent.

This shows that effects attributed to population are really due to technological progress. It also explains the otherwise perplexing fact that laborsaving machinery fails to benefit workers.

Yet, to fully grasp this, it is necessary to keep one thing in mind—the interchangeability of wealth. I mention this again, because it is so persistently forgotten. The possession or production of any form of wealth is—in effect—the possession or production of any other form of wealth for which it can be exchanged. If you keep this clearly in mind, you will see that all improvements tend to increase rent. Not only improvements applied directly to land—but all improvements that in any way save labor.

It is only because of the division of labor that any individual applies effort exclusively to the production of only one form of wealth. An increase in the power of producing one thing adds to the power of obtaining others.

I cannot think of any form of wealth that would not show an increased demand because of labor saved in the production of other forms. Coffins are cited as examples where demand is not likely to increase. But this is true only in quantity. Increased power of supply leads to a demand for fancier coffins.

In economic reasoning it is frequently—but erroneously—assumed that the demand for food is limited. It is fixed only in having a definite minimum; less than a certain amount will not keep a human being alive. But beyond this, the food a human being can use may be increased almost infinitely.

Adam Smith and Ricardo have said the desire for food is limited by the capacity of the human stomach. Clearly, this is true only in the sense that when a person's belly is filled, hunger is satisfied. But demands for food have no such limit. The stomach of a king can digest no more than the stomach of a peasant. Yet a small plot of ground supports the peasant, while thousands of acres supply the demands of the king. Besides his own wasteful use of the finest quality food, he requires immense supplies for his servants, horses, and dogs.

And so every improvement or invention that gives labor the power to produce more wealth, no matter what it may be, causes an increased demand for land and its products. Progress thus tends to force down the margin of production, the same as the demand of a larger population would. This being the case, every labor-saving invention has a tendency to increase rent. This is true whether it is a tractor, a telegraph, or a sewing machine. There will be a greater production of wealth—but landowners will get the whole benefit.

I do not mean to say that the change in the margin would always correspond exactly with the increase in production. Nor do I mean the process would have clearly defined steps. In any particular case, the margin may either lag behind or exceed the increase in productivity. Nor is it precisely true that all labor set free will seek employment. Some will pass from the ranks of the productive to the unproductive, and become idlers. Observation shows that this segment tends to increase with the progress of society.

All I wish to make clear is that even without any increase in population, the progress of invention constantly tends to give a greater proportion of the production to landowners. Therefore, a smaller and smaller share goes to labor and capital. Since we can assign no limits to the progress of invention, neither can we offer any limits to the increase of rent—short of the entire output. If wealth could be obtained without labor, there would be no use for either labor or capital. Nor would there be any possible way either could demand any share of the wealth produced. If anybody but landowners continued to exist, it would be at their whim or mercy—perhaps maintained for their amusement, or as paupers by their charity.

This scenario may seem very remote, if not impossible to attain. Yet it is a point towards which the march of invention is tending every day. In the great machine-worked wheat fields of Dakota, one may ride for miles and miles through waving grain without seeing a single dwelling. The tractor and reaping machine are creating, in the modern world, Roman latifundia*—the great estates of ancient Italy created by the influx of slaves from foreign wars. To many a poor person forced out of a home, it may seem as though these labor-saving inventions are a curse.

Of course, in the preceding, I have spoken about inventions and improvements when they are generally diffused. Sometimes an invention or improvement is used by so few that they derive a special advantage from it. It is hardly necessary to say that, to the extent it is a special advantage, it does not affect the general distribution of

---

* Latifundia were large estates created when the wealthy displaced smaller farmers. These once-independent farmers were then forced to join the poor masses in Rome, or sell their lives for food in the army.

wealth. The special profits arising from these situations are often mistaken for the profits of capital—but they are really the returns of monopoly.*

Improvements that directly expand productive power are not the only ones that increase rent. Advances in government, manners, and morals that indirectly increase productivity are also included. Considered as material forces, the effect of all these is to increase productive power. Like improvements in the productive arts, their benefit is ultimately monopolized by landowners.

A notable instance of this is England's abolition of laws protecting certain trades. The resulting free trade has enormously increased the wealth of Great Britain—but it has not reduced poverty. It has simply increased rent. And if the corrupt governments of our great American cities were made into models of purity and thrift, it would not raise wages or interest. It would simply increase the value of land.

---

* As explained in Chapter 13.

Chapter 21
Speculation

THERE IS ANOTHER CAUSE, not yet mentioned, that must be considered before we can fully explain the impact of progress on the distribution of wealth. It is the confident expectation that land values will increase in the future. The steady increase of rent in all growing countries leads to speculation—holding onto land for a higher price than it would otherwise bring at that time.

We have thus far allowed an assumption that is generally made in explaining the theory of rent. That is, that the actual margin of production always coincides with what may be termed the necessary margin of production. We have assumed that cultivation extends to less productive points only as it becomes necessary to do so—and that more productive points are fully utilized. This is probably the case in stable or slowly developing communities. But with rapid advancement, the swift and steady increase of rent gives confidence to calculations of further increase. It leads to land being withheld from use, as higher prices are expected. Thus, the margin of production is forced out farther than required by the necessities of production. As landowners confidently expect rents to increase further, they demand more rent than the land would provide under current conditions.

Settlers will take more land than they can use, if

possible, in the belief that it will soon become valuable. As they do, the margin is carried to even more remote points. It is also well known that private mineral land is often withheld from use, while poorer deposits are worked. In new states, it is common to find individuals who are called "land poor." They persist in holding land they cannot use themselves. They endure poverty, sometimes almost to deprivation, instead of selling their land. Or, they offer it at prices where no one else could use it profitably.

The same thing may be seen in every rapidly growing city. If superior land were always fully used before resorting to inferior land, no vacant lots would be left as a city extended. Nor would we find miserable shanties in the midst of costly buildings. Though some of these lots are extremely valuable, they are withheld from their fullest use, or any use at all. Instead, the owners prefer to wait for a higher price than they could currently get from those who are willing to improve them. They expect, of course, that land values will increase.

The result of land being withheld is that the margin of the city is pushed away so much farther from the center. The actual margin of building is at the limits of the city. This corresponds to the margin of production in agriculture. But we will not find land available at its value for agricultural purposes, as we would if rent were determined simply by present requirements. Instead, we find—for a long distance beyond the city—that land bears a speculative value. This is based upon the belief that it will be required for urban purposes in the future. To reach the point at which land can be purchased at a price not based upon urban rent, we must go very far beyond the actual margin of urban use.

We may conceive of speculation as extending the margin of production. Or, we can look at it as carrying the rent line past the margin of production. However we view it, the influence of speculation on increasing rent is an important fact. It cannot be ignored in any complete theory of the distribution of wealth in progressive countries. Speculation is the force, arising from material progress, that constantly tends to increase rent in a greater ratio than progress increases production. As material progress goes on and productive power increases, speculation thus constantly tends to reduce wages—not merely relatively, but absolutely.

We see this process operating full force in land speculation manias, which mark the growth of new communities. These are abnormal and sporadic manifestations, yet it is undeniable that the same cause operates steadily, with greater or less intensity, in all progressive societies.

With commodities, rising prices will draw forth additional supplies. This cannot limit the speculative advance in land values, however. Land is a fixed quantity, which human action can neither increase nor decrease.

There is, nevertheless, a limit to the price of land. It is set by the minimum that labor and capital require to engage in production. Hence, speculation cannot have the same scope to advance rent in countries where wages and interest are already near the minimum, as it does in countries where they are considerably above it.

Still, in all progressive countries, there is a constant tendency for the speculative advance of rent to exceed the limit at which production stops. This, I think, is shown by recurring seasons of industrial paralysis (i.e., recessions)—the matter to which we turn in the next chapter.

The Problem Solved

Chapter 22

The Root Cause of Recessions

WE HAVE COMPLETED our long inquiry, and now we can compile the results.

We will begin with depressions and recessions, which affect every modern society. We have shown how land speculation inflates land values, reduces wages and interest, and thereby checks production. There are other reasons as well, such as: the complexity and interdependence of production; problems with money and credit; the artificial barriers of protective tariffs. Nonetheless, it is clear that land speculation is the primary cause producing recessions. We can see this either by considering principles or by observing phenomena.

As population grows and technology advances, land values rise. This steady increase leads to speculation, as future increases are anticipated. Land values are carried beyond the point at which labor and capital would receive their customary returns. Production, therefore, begins to stop.

Production need not decrease absolutely—it may

simply fail to increase proportionately. In other words, new labor and capital cannot find employment at the usual rates.

Stopping production at some points must necessarily affect other points of the industrial network. Demand is interrupted, checking production elsewhere. Paralysis spreads through all the interlaced industry and commerce. The same events can seem to show either overproduction or overconsumption—depending on one's point of view.

The period of depression will continue until: (1) the speculative advance in rents is lost; or (2) the increased efficiency of labor (due to population growth and/or improved technology) allows the normal rent line to overtake the speculative rent line; or (3) labor and capital are willing to work for smaller returns. Most likely, all three will cooperate to produce a new equilibrium*. Production resumes in full. After rents begin to advance again, speculation returns; production is checked; and the same cycle repeats itself.

Modern civilization is characterized by an elaborate and complicated system of production. Moreover, there is no such thing as a distinct and independent industrial community. We should not expect to see cause followed by effect as clearly as we would in a simpler society. Nevertheless, the phenomena actually observed clearly correspond with what we have inferred. Deduction shows how the actual phenomena result from the basic principle.

---

*It is also possible for these forces to move in different directions at the same time. For example, in the 1990s, the speculative advance of rents continued apace, but was offset by increased productivity due to technological advancements.

If we reverse the process, it is just as easy to use induction to follow the phenomena and arrive at the principle. Depressions and recessions are always preceded by periods of activity and speculation. Some connection between the two is generally acknowledged. Depression is seen as a reaction to speculation, as this morning's hangover is a reaction to last night's debauch. There are two schools of thought as to how this occurs.

The school of overproduction says production has exceeded the demand for consumption. They point out unsold goods, factories working half time, money lying idle, and workers without jobs.

The school of overconsumption points to the very same things as evidence that demand has stopped. This, they say, is because people, made extravagant by fictitious prosperity, have lived beyond their means. The pinch was not felt at the time, much as spendthrifts do not notice the loss of their fortunes while squandering them. Now they must retrench and consume less.

Each of these theories expresses one side, but fails to comprehend the full truth. Each is equally preposterous as an explanation of observed phenomena.

People want more wealth than they can get. The basis of wealth is labor. How can there be overproduction as long as people are willing to give their labor in return for things? Likewise, when workers and machinery are forced to stand idle, how can one claim overconsumption? The desire to consume coexists with the willingness to produce. So industrial and commercial paralysis cannot be attributed to either overproduction or overconsumption.

Clearly, the trouble is that production and consumption cannot meet and satisfy each other. This, it is commonly agreed, arises from speculation. But speculation in the products of labor simply tends to equalize supply and demand. It steadies the interplay of production and consumption, much like a flywheel in a machine. This has been well shown, and spares me the need to illustrate it.

Therefore, the problem must be speculation in things that are not the product of labor. Yet it must be things needed for production. And finally, it must be things of fixed quantity.

The cause of recurring recessions must be speculation in land.

This process is obvious in the United States. During each period of industrial activity, land values rose steadily, culminating in speculation that drove them up in great jumps. This was invariably followed by a partial cessation of production, reducing effective demand as a correlative. A commercial crash generally accompanied this. A period of comparative stagnation followed, during which equilibrium was slowly reestablished. Then the same cycle began again.

In common parlance, we say "buyers have no money." But this ignores the fact that money is only a medium of exchange. All trade is really the exchange of commodities for other commodities. What would-be buyers really lack is not money—it is commodities they can turn into money. Sales may decline and manufacturing orders fall off, yet a widespread desire for these things remains. This simply shows that the supply of other things—which would be exchanged for them in the course of trade—has declined. Reduced consumer demand is just a result of decreased production.

This is seen quite clearly in mill towns when workers

are thrown out of work. Since workers have no means to purchase what they desire, storekeepers are left with excess stock. They must then discharge some of their clerks. The decreased demand leaves manufacturers with an overstock, and forces them to discharge their workers in the same way. Somewhere—and it may be at the other end of the world—a check in production has produced a check in demand.

Demand is lessened without want being satisfied. People want things as much as ever. But they do not have as much to give for them. The obstruction then spreads through the whole framework of industry and exchange.

Since the industrial pyramid clearly rests on land, some obstacle must be preventing labor from expending itself on land. That obstacle is the speculative advance in land values. It is, in fact, a lockout of labor and capital by landowners. Though habit has made us used to it, it is a strange and unnatural thing that people, who are willing to work to satisfy their wants, cannot find the opportunity to do so.

We speak of the supply of labor and the demand for labor. Obviously, these are relative terms. Labor is what produces wealth. So the demand for labor always exists—for people always want things that labor alone can provide.

We speak of a lack of jobs, but clearly it is not work that is short. The supply of labor cannot be too great, nor the demand for labor too small, when people still want those things that labor produces. Trace this inactivity from point to point, and you will find that unemployment in one trade is caused by unemployment in another. This cannot arise from too large a supply of labor or too small a demand for labor.

The real trouble must be that supply is somehow prevented from satisfying demand. Somewhere, there is an obstacle keeping labor from producing the things that laborers want.

Put a few of the vast army of unemployed on an island cut off from all the advantages of a civilized community, without the cooperation and machinery that multiply productivity. Using only their own hands, they can feed themselves—but where productive power is at its highest, they cannot. Is this not because they have access to nature in one case, but are denied it in the other? The only thing that can explain why people are forced to stand idle when they would willingly work to supply their wants is that labor is denied access to land.

When we speak of labor creating wealth, we speak metaphorically. People create nothing. If the whole human race worked forever, it could not create the tiniest speck of dust floating in a sunbeam. In producing wealth, labor merely manipulates preexisting matter into desired forms by using natural forces. Therefore, labor must have access to this matter and to those forces to produce wealth. That is to say, they must have access to land.

Land is the source of all wealth. It is the substance to which labor gives form. When labor cannot satisfy its wants, can there be any other cause than that labor is denied access to land?

The foundation of the industrial structure is land. Hat makers, opticians, and craftsmen are not the pioneers of new settlements. Miners did not go to California because shoemakers, tailors, and printers were there. Rather, those trades followed the miners. The storekeeper does not bring the farmer, rather the farmer brings the storekeeper. It is not the growth of the city that develops the country, but the development of the country that raises the city.

Therefore, when people of all trades cannot find opportunity to work, the difficulty must arise in the occupations that create demand for all other employment. It must be because labor is shut out from land.

In great cities like Philadelphia or London or New York, it may require a grasp of basic principles to see this. But elsewhere, industrial development has not become so elaborate—nor has the chain of exchange become so widely separated. There, one has only to look at the obvious facts.

San Francisco ranks among the great cities of the world, though barely thirty years old. Yet certain symptoms are already beginning to appear. In older countries, these are taken as evidence of overpopulation. But it is absurd to talk of excess population in a state* with greater natural resources than France, but less than a million people.

Still, unemployment has been growing for a number of years. When the harvest season opens, the workers go trooping out; when it is over, they come back again to the city. Clearly, there are unemployed in the city because they cannot find employment in the country.

It is not that all the land is in use. Within a few miles of San Francisco is enough unused land to employ everyone who wants work. I do not mean that everyone could— or should—become a farmer if given the chance. But enough would do so to give employment to the rest.

What prevents labor from using this land? Simply that land has been monopolized. It is held at speculative prices, based not on present value, but on value that will come

* California in 1879

with future population growth. This speculative advance is held with great tenacity in developing communities. Owners hold on as long as they can, believing prices must eventually rise.

Thus, the speculative advance in rent outran the normal advance. Production was checked, and demand decreased. Labor and capital were turned away from occupations directly concerned with land. So they glutted those where land is a less apparent element. This is how, for instance, the rapid expansion of railroads was related to the succeeding depression.

It may seem as if I have overlooked one thing in saying the primary cause of depressions is land speculation. Such a cause should operate progressively; it should resemble a pressure, not a blow. Yet industrial depressions seem to come on suddenly.

Let me offer an explanation for this. Exchange links all forms of industry into one interdependent organization. For exchanges to be made between producers far removed by space and time, large stocks must be kept in store and in transit. (This is the great function of capital, in addition to supplying tools and seed.) These exchanges are made largely on credit: the advance is made on one side before the return is received on the other.

As a rule, these advances are made from more developed industries to fundamental ones. Natives who trade coconuts for trinkets get their return immediately. Merchants, on the contrary, let out their goods a long while before getting a return. Farmers sell their crops for cash as soon as they are harvested. Manufacturers must keep large stocks, ship goods long distances, and generally sell on installments.

Thus, advances and credits are generally from what we may call secondary to primary industries. It follows that any check to production that proceeds from the primary will not immediately manifest itself in the secondary. The system is, as it were, an elastic connection: it will give considerably before breaking. But when it breaks, it breaks with a snap.

Let me illustrate what I mean another way. A pyramid is composed of layers, with the bottom layer supporting the rest. If we could somehow make this bottom layer gradually smaller, the upper part would retain its form for some time. Eventually, gravity would overcome the adhesiveness of the material. At this point, it would not diminish gradually, but would break off suddenly, in large pieces.

The industrial organization may be likened to such a pyramid. As each form of industry develops, through the division of labor, it rises out of the others. Ultimately, everything rests upon land. For without land, labor is as powerless as a person would be in the void of space.

We have now explained the main cause and general course of recurring paroxysms of industrial depression, which are a conspicuous feature of modern life. Political economy can only—and need only—deal with general tendencies. The exact character of the phenomena cannot be predicted, because the actions and reactions are too diverse. We know that if a tree is cut, it will fall. But the precise direction will be determined by the inclination of the trunk, the spread of the branches, the impact of the blows, the direction and force of the wind, and so on.

I have given a cause that clearly explains the main features of recessions. This is in striking contrast to the contradictory—and self-contradictory—attempts based on current theories. It is clear that a speculative advance in land values invariably precedes each recession. That these are cause and effect is obvious to anyone who considers the necessary relation between land and labor.

The recession runs its course and a new equilibrium is established as the normal rent line and the speculative rent line are being brought together by three factors: (1) The fall of speculative land values, as shown by reduced rents and shrinkage of real estate values in major cities. (2) The increased efficiency of labor arising from population growth and new technology. (3) The lowering of customary standards of wages and interest.

When equilibrium is reestablished, renewed activity will set in. This will again result in a speculative advance of land values. But wages and interest will not recover their lost ground. The net result of all these disturbances is the gradual forcing of wages and interest toward their minimum.

Chapter 23

The Persistence of Poverty Despite Increasing Wealth

THE GREAT PROBLEM IS SOLVED. We are able to explain social phenomena that have appalled philanthropists and perplexed statesmen all over the civilized world. We have found the reason why wages constantly tend to a minimum, giving but a bare living, despite increase in productive power:

As productive power increases, rent tends to increase even more—constantly forcing down wages.

Advancing civilization tends to increase the power of human labor to satisfy human desires. We should be able to eliminate poverty. But workers cannot reap these benefits because they are intercepted. Land is necessary to labor. When it has been reduced to private ownership, the increased productivity of labor only increases rent. Thus, all the advantages of progress go to those who own land. Wages do not increase—wages *cannot* increase. The more labor produces, the more it must pay for the opportunity to make anything at all.

Mere laborers, therefore, have no more interest in progress than Cuban slaves have in higher sugar prices. Higher prices may spur their masters to drive them harder. Likewise, a free laborer may be worse off with greater productivity. Steadily rising rents generate speculation. The effects of future improvements are discounted by even higher rents. This tends to drive wages down to the point of slavery, at which the worker can barely live. The worker is robbed of all the benefits of increased productive power.

These improvements also cause a further subdivision of labor. The efficiency of the whole body of laborers is increased, but at the expense of the independence of its constituents. Individual workers know only a tiny part of the various processes required to supply even the commonest wants.

A primitive tribe may not produce much wealth, but all members are capable of an independent life. Each shares all the knowledge possessed by the tribe. They know the habits of animals, birds, and fishes. They can make their own shelter, clothing, and weapons. In short, they are all capable of supplying their own wants. The independence of all of the members makes them free contracting parties in their relations with the community.

Compare this savage with workers in the lowest ranks of civilized society. Their lives are spent in producing just one thing or, more likely, the smallest part of one thing. They cannot even make what is required for their work; they use tools they can never hope to own. Compelled to oppressive and constant labor, they get no more than the savage: the bare necessaries of life. Yet they lose the independence the savage keeps.

Modern workers are mere links in an enormous chain of producers and consumers. The very power of exerting their labor to satisfy their needs passes from their control. The worse their position in society, the more dependent they are on society. Their power may be taken away by the actions of others. Or even by general causes, over which they have no more influence than they have over the motion of the stars.

Under such circumstances, people lose an essential quality: the power of modifying and controlling their condition. They become slaves, machines, commodities. In some respects, they are lower than animals.

I am no sentimental admirer of the savage state. I do not get my ideas of nature from Rousseau. I am aware of its material and mental lack, its low and narrow range. I believe that civilization is the natural destiny of humanity, the elevation and refinement of our powers.

Nevertheless, no one who faces the facts can avoid the conclusion that—in the heart of our civilization—there are large classes that even the sorriest savage would not want to trade places with. Given the choice of being born an Australian aborigine, an arctic Eskimo, or among the lowest classes in a highly civilized country such as Great Britain, one would make an infinitely better choice in selecting the lot of the savage.

Those condemned to want in the midst of wealth suffer all the hardships of savages, without the sense of personal freedom. If their horizon is wider, it is only to see the blessings they cannot enjoy. I challenge anyone to produce an authentic account of primitive life citing the degradation we find in official documents regarding the condition of the working poor in highly civilized countries.

I have outlined a simple theory that recognizes the most obvious relations. It explains the conjunction of poverty with wealth; of low wages with high productivity; of degradation amid enlightenment; of virtual slavery in political liberty. It flows from a general and unchanging law. It shows the sequence and relation between phenomena that are separate and contradictory without this theory.

It explains why interest and wages are higher in new communities, even though the production is less. It explains why improvements that increase the productive power of labor and capital do not increase the reward of either. It shows that what is commonly called a conflict between labor and capital is, in fact, a harmony of interests between them. It proves the fallacies of protectionism, while showing why free trade fails to benefit the working class.

It explains why want increases with abundance, and why wealth tends to greater and greater concentration. It explains periodic recessions and depressions—and why large numbers of potential producers stand idle, without the absurd assumption that there is too little work to do or too many hands to do it. It explains the negative impact of machinery, without denying the natural advantages it gives. It explains why vice and misery appear among dense populations, without attributing to the laws of God those defects arising only from the shortsighted and selfish decrees of humans.

This is an explanation in accordance with all the facts. Look at the world today. The same conditions exist in different countries—regardless of the type of government, industries, tariffs, or currency. But everywhere you find poverty in the midst of wealth, you will find that land is monopolized. Instead of being treated as the common property of all the people, land is treated as the private property of individuals. And before labor is allowed to use it, large sums are extorted from the earnings of labor.

Compare different countries. You will see that it is not the abundance of capital, nor the productiveness of labor, that makes wages high or low. Rather, wages vary with the extent to which those who monopolize land can levy tribute in the form of rent.

It is well-known, even among the most ignorant, that new countries are always better for workers than rich countries. In new countries, although the total amount of wealth is small, land is cheap. Whereas in rich countries, land is costly. Wherever rent is relatively low, you will find wages relatively high. Wherever rent is high, wages are low. As land values increase, poverty deepens and beggars appear. In the new settlements, where land is cheap, any inequalities in condition are very slight. In great cities, where land is so valuable it is measured by the foot, you will find the extremes of poverty and luxury.

The disparity between the two extremes of the social scale may always be measured by the price of land. Land is more valuable in New York than San Francisco; and in New York, the squalor and misery would make the San Franciscan stand aghast. Land is more valuable in London than in New York; and in London, the squalor and destitution is worse than in New York.

The same relation is obvious if you compare the same country in different times. The enormous increase in the efficiency of labor has only added to rent. The rent of agricultural land in England is many times greater than it was 500 years ago.* Yet wages, measured as a proportion

---

*Prof. James Rogers (1823-1900) estimated the increase in rent at fourteen times, if measured in wheat, or 120 times if measured in money.

of total production, have decreased everywhere.

The Black Death brought a great rise in wages in England in the fourteenth century. There can be no doubt that such an awful decline in population decreased the effective power of labor. However, less competition for land lowered rent to an even greater extent. This allowed wages to rise so much that land holders enacted penal laws to keep them down.

The reverse effect followed the monopolization of land during the reign of Henry VIII. The commons were enclosed, and church lands divided among parasites who were thus enabled to found noble families. The result was the same as from a speculative increase in land values. According to none other than Malthus, a worker in the reign of Henry VII would get half a bushel of wheat for about one day's common labor. By end of Elizabeth's reign, it would take three days of labor to purchase the same amount. The rapid monopolization of land carried the speculative rent line beyond the normal rent line, and produced tramps and paupers. We have lately seen similar effects from similar causes in the United States.

We may as well cite historical illustrations of the attraction of gravity; the principle is just as universal and just as obvious. Rent must reduce wages. This is as clear as an equation: the larger the subtractor, the smaller the remainder.

The truth is self-evident. Put this question to anyone capable of consecutive thought:

"Suppose some land should arise from the English Channel. This land will remain unappropriated—like the commons that once comprised a part of England. An unlimited number of workers can have free access to it.

Here, a common laborer could make ten shillings a day. What would be the effect upon wages in England?"

They would at once tell you that common wages throughout England must soon rise to ten shillings a day.

Ask, "What would be the effect on rents?"

After a moment's reflection, they would tell you, "Rents must fall."

If they thought out the next step, they would tell you that all this would happen without much labor being diverted to the new natural opportunities. Nor would the forms and direction of industry change much. The only loss would be the kind of production that now yields, to labor and landlord together, less than labor could secure on the new opportunities.

The great rise in wages would be at the expense of rent.

Next take some hardheaded business owners who have no theories, but know how to make money. Say to them: "Here is a little village. In ten years, it will be a great city. The railroad and the electric light are coming; it will soon abound with all the machinery and improvements that enormously multiply the effective power of labor."

Now ask: "Will interest be any higher?"

"No!"

"Will the wages of common labor be any higher?"

"No," they will tell you. "On the contrary, chances are they will be lower. It will not be easier for a mere laborer to make an independent living; chances are it will be harder."

"What, then, will be higher?" you ask.

"Rent, and the value of land!"

"Then what should I do?" you beg.

"Get yourself a piece of ground, and hold on to it."

If you take their advice under these circumstances, you need do nothing more. You may sit down and smoke your pipe; you may lie around like an idler; you may go up in a balloon, or down a hole in the ground. Yet without doing one stroke of work, without adding one iota to the wealth of the community—in ten years you will be rich!

In the new city you may have a luxurious mansion. But among its public buildings, will be an almshouse.

In all our long investigation, we have been advancing to this simple truth:

> *Land is required for the exertion of labor in the production of wealth. Therefore, to control the land is to command all the fruits of labor, except only enough to enable labor to continue to exist.*

We have been advancing as through enemy country, in which every step must be secured, every position fortified, and every bypath explored. This simple truth, and its application to social and political problems, is hidden from the masses—hidden partly by its very simplicity. And in greater part by widespread fallacies and erroneous habits of thought. These lead us to look in every direction but the right one for an explanation of the evils that oppress and threaten the civilized world.

In back of these elaborate fallacies and misleading theories is an active, energetic power. This is the power that writes laws and molds thought. It operates in every country, no matter what its political forms may be. It is the power of a vast and dominant financial interest.

But this truth is so simple and clear, that to fully see it once is to recognize it always. There are pictures that, though looked at again and again, present only a confused pattern of lines. Or, perhaps they seem to be only a landscape, trees, or something of the kind. Then, attention is called to the fact that these things make up a face or a figure. Once this relation is recognized, it is always clear. It is so in this case.

In the light of this truth, all social facts group themselves in an orderly relation. The most diverse phenomena are seen to spring from one great principle. It is not the relations of capital and labor, not the pressure of population against subsistence, that explains the unequal development of society.

The great cause of inequality in the distribution of wealth is inequality in the ownership of land.

Ownership of land is the great fundamental fact that ultimately determines the social, the political, and consequently the intellectual and moral condition of a people. And it must be so.

For land is the home of humans, the storehouse we must draw upon for all our needs. Land is the material to which we must apply our labor to supply all our desires. Even the products of the sea cannot be taken, or the light of the sun enjoyed, or any of the forces of nature utilized, without the use of land or its products.

On land we are born, from it we live, to it we return again. We are children of the soil as truly as a blade of grass or the flower of the field. Take away from people all that belongs to land, and they are but disembodied spirits. Material progress cannot rid us of our dependence on land; it can only add to our power to produce wealth from land.

Hence, when land is monopolized, progress might go on to infinity without increasing wages or improving the condition of those who have only their labor. It can only add to the value of land and the power its possession gives.

Everywhere, in all times, among all peoples, possession of land is the base of aristocracy, the foundation of great fortunes, the source of power. As the Brahmins said, ages ago:

"To whomsoever the soil at any time belongs, to him belong the fruits of it. White parasols and elephants mad with pride are the flowers of a grant of land."

The Remedy

Chapter 24

Ineffective Remedies

OUR CONCLUSIONS point to a solution. It is so radical that it will not be considered if we believe less drastic measures might work. Yet it is so simple that its effectiveness will be discounted until more elaborate measures are evaluated. Let us review current proposals to relieve social distress. For convenience, we may group them into six categories:

1. More efficient government
2. Better education and work habits
3. Unions or associations
4. Cooperation
5. Government regulation
6. Redistribution of land

1. More efficient government

Social distress is largely attributed to the immense burdens of government: huge debts, military establishments, and general extravagance (which is especially characteristic of large cities). We must also include the robbery of protective tariffs, which take a dollar or more out of the pockets of consumers for every quarter they put in the treasury.

The connection between these immense sums, taken from the people, and the privations of the lower classes seems obvious. From a superficial viewpoint, we might naturally suppose that reducing this enormous burden would make it easier for the poor to make a living. However, considering the economic principles we have identified, we can see that this would not be the effect.

Reducing taxes taken from production would be equivalent to increasing productivity. It would, in effect, add to the productive power of labor—just as increasing population and technological improvements do. As it does in those cases, any advantage would go to landlords in higher rents. The great advances of power and machinery have not alleviated poverty—they have only increased rent. And so would this.

I will not dispute that if these things could be done suddenly, without the destruction of a revolution, there might be a temporary improvement in the condition of the lowest classes. Unfortunately, such reform is clearly impossible. Yet even if it were possible, any temporary improvement would ultimately be swallowed up by increased land values. Ultimately, the condition of those who live by their labor would not be improved.

A dim consciousness of this is beginning to pervade the masses, and it constitutes a grave political difficulty closing in around the American republic. Those with nothing but their labor care little about the extravagance of government. Many—especially in the cities—are disposed to look upon it as a good thing, "furnishing employment" and "putting money in circulation."

"Boss Tweed"* robbed New York as a guerrilla chief might a captured town. He was one of the new banditti grasping control of government in all our cities. His thievery was notorious, his spoils blazoned in big diamonds and lavish personal expenditure. Yet he was undoubtedly popular with a majority of the voters.

Let me be clearly understood. I am not saying economy in government is not desirable. I am simply saying that reducing the cost of government will have no direct effect on eliminating poverty or increasing wages—*as long as land is monopolized.*

Nonetheless, every effort should be made to reduce useless expenditures. The more complex and extravagant government becomes, the more it becomes a power distinct from, and independent of, the people. We face momentous problems, yet the most important questions of government are barely considered. The average American voter has prejudices, party feelings, and general notions of a certain kind. But he or she gives as much thought to the fundamental questions of government as a streetcar horse gives to the profits of the line. Were this not the case, so many hoary abuses could not have survived, nor so many new ones been added.

Anything that tends to make government simple and inexpensive tends to put it under control of the people. But no reduction in the expenses of government can, of itself, cure or mitigate the evils arising from a constant tendency toward unequal distribution of wealth.

---

* William Marcy Tweed (1823-1878), political leader of the infamous Tammany Hall, an organization that stole millions from the citizens of New York City. Tweed held several public offices, and died in prison.

2. Better education and work habits

Many believe that poverty is due to lack of industry, frugality, and intelligence. This soothes any sense of responsibility and flatters by its suggestion of superiority. They attribute their better circumstances to superior industry and superior intelligence—to say nothing of a superior lack of conscience, which is often the determining quality of a millionaire.

Yet anyone who has grasped the laws determining the distribution of wealth, which we discovered in previous chapters, will see the mistake. It is true that any one of several competitors may win a race, but it is impossible that every one can.

This being the case, industry, skill, frugality, and intelligence can help the individual only in so far as they are superior to the general level. Just as in a race, speed benefits a runner only if it exceeds that of the competitors. If one person works harder or with superior skill or intelligence than ordinary people, that person will get ahead. But if the average is brought up to this higher point, the extra effort will bring only average wages. To get ahead, one must then work harder still.

For once land acquires value, wages do not depend upon the real earnings or product of labor—they depend on what is left after rent is taken out. When all land is monopolized, rent will drive wages down to the point at which the poorest class will consent to live and reproduce.

Life might be more comfortable for many poor families if they were taught to prepare cheap dishes. But if the working class generally came to live like that, wages would ultimately fall proportionally. If American workers came down to the Chinese standard of living, they would ultimately come down to the Chinese standard of wages. The potato was introduced into Ireland to improve the condition of the poor by lowering their cost of living. The actual result was to raise rents and lower wages. When the potato blight came, the population had already reduced its standard of comfort so low that the next step was starvation.

So if one individual works longer, that one may earn more. But the wages of all cannot be increased this way. It is well-known that occupations with longer hours do not have higher wages. In fact, the longer the working day, the more helpless the laborer generally becomes. Likewise, in industries where it has become common for a wife and children to supplement earnings, the wages of a whole family rarely exceed that of an individual in other occupations. Bohemian cigar makers of New York employ men, women, and children in their tenements. They have thus reduced wages to less than the Chinese were getting in San Francisco.

These general facts are well known, and are fully recognized in standard economics texts. However, they are explained away by the Malthusian theory of the supposed tendency of population to multiply to the limit of subsistence. The true explanation, as I have sufficiently shown, is in the tendency of rent to reduce wages.

As to the effects of education, it may be especially worthwhile to say a few words, for there is a prevailing tendency to attribute some magical influence to it. College graduates often think no better, and sometimes not as well, as those who have never been to college. Be this as it may, education can operate on wages only by increasing the effective power of labor. (At least until it enables the masses to discover and remove the true cause of unequal distribution of wealth.)

Education, therefore, has the same effect as increased skill or industry. It can raise the wages of an individual only in so far as it renders one superior to others. When reading and writing were rare accomplishments, a clerk commanded high wages. Now that they are nearly universal, they give no advantage. The Chinese are virtually all literate; yet wages in China are the lowest possible.

The diffusion of intelligence cannot raise wages generally, nor in any way improve the condition of the lowest class. One senator called them the "mudsills" of society: those who must rest on the soil, no matter how high the superstructure is built. The only hope of education is that it may make people discontented with a state that condemns producers to a life of toil while non-producers loll in luxury.

No increase in the power of labor can increase general wages—*so long as rent swallows up all the gain.* This is not merely a deduction from principles; it is a fact proven by experience. The growth of knowledge and the progress of invention have multiplied the effective power of labor over and over again without increasing wages.

It is true that greater prudence and higher intelligence are associated with better material conditions. But this is the effect, not the cause. Wherever conditions have improved, improvement in personal qualities has followed. Wherever conditions have worsened, these qualities have decayed. Yet, nowhere do we find that increased industry, skill, prudence, or intelligence have improved conditions among those condemned to toil for a bare living.

Qualities that raise people above animals are superimposed on those they share with animals. Only when we are relieved from the wants of our animal nature can our intellectual and moral nature grow. Condemn people to drudgery for the necessities of an animal existence, and they will do only what they are forced to do.

Improvements may not show immediately. Increased wages may first be taken out in idleness and dissipation. But ultimately they will bring industry, skill, intelligence, and thrift. If we compare different countries, or different classes in the same country, or different periods for the same people, we find an invariable result: personal qualities appear as material conditions are improved.

To make people industrious, prudent, skillful, and intelligent, they must be relieved from want. If you would have a slave show the virtues of a free person, you must first make the slave free.

3. Unions or associations

The laws of distribution show that combinations of workers actually can advance wages—and not at the expense of other workers, as is sometimes claimed; nor at the expense of capital, as is generally believed. Ultimately, it is at the expense of rent. The misconceptions arise from the erroneous idea that wages are drawn from capital.

Unions have secured higher wages in particular trades without lowering wages in other trades or reducing the rate of profits. Wages affect an employer in comparison to other employers. The first employer who succeeds in reducing wages gains an advantage; the first compelled to pay more is put at a disadvantage. But the differential ends when the competitors are also included in the change. Any gain or loss is purely relative, and disappears when the whole community is considered.

If the change in wages creates a change in relative

demand, then capital fixed in machinery, buildings, or other things may become more (or less) profitable. But a new equilibrium is soon reached. If there is too little capital in a certain form, the tendency to assume that form soon brings it up to the required amount. If there is too much, reduced production soon restores the level.

A change in wages in any particular occupation may cause a change in the relative demand for labor—but it cannot produce a change in total demand. Suppose a union raises wages in a particular industry in one country. Meanwhile, wages go down in the same industry in another country. If the change is great enough, part of the demand in the first country will now be supplied by imports from the second. Higher imports of one kind cause a corresponding decrease in imports of other kinds, or else a corresponding increase in exports. For one country can obtain the products of another country only by exchanging the products of its own labor and capital.

If all wages in any particular country were doubled, that country would continue to export and import the same things, and in the same proportions. Exchange is determined by the relative, not the absolute, cost of production. If wages in some industries doubled while others increased less, there would be a change in the proportion of the various things imported. Still, there would be no change in the proportion between exports and imports.

Therefore, most of the objections to trade unions are groundless. Their success cannot reduce other wages, nor decrease the profits of capital, nor injure national prosperity. Nevertheless, the difficulties confronting effective combinations of workers are so great that the good they can accomplish is limited. In addition, there are inherent disadvantages in the process. All any union has done is to raise wages in a particular occupation. This is a task that grows in difficulty. As wages of any particular kind rise above the normal level of other wages, there is a strong tendency to bring them back.

For instance, say a union can raise wages for typesetters by ten percent. Immediately, relative supply and demand are affected. On the one hand, there will be less demand for typesetting. On the other, higher wages will tend to increase the number of typesetters. This occurs in ways even the strongest combination cannot prevent. If the increase were twenty percent, these tendencies would be stronger still.

As a practical matter, unions can do relatively little to raise wages, even when supporting each other. They do not affect the lower strata of unorganized laborers, who need help the most. And those wages ultimately determine all above them. The effective approach would be by a general combination including workers of all kinds. Unfortunately, such a combination is practically impossible. The difficulties of combination are hard enough in the smallest and most highly paid trades. They become greater as we go down the industrial scale.

The only method unions have, the strike, is a struggle of endurance. And do not forget who is really pitted against whom. It is not labor against capital; it is labor on one side, and landowners on the other. For wages cannot increase unless rent decreases. But landowners can sit and wait. While landowners are inconvenienced, capital is destroyed, and laborers starve.

Land is absolutely necessary for production. It is certain to increase in value in all growing countries. These facts alone produce among landowners—without any for-mal alliance—the same effect that the most rigorous fed-eration of workers or capitalists would. The struggle of endurance involved in a strike is really what it has often been compared to: war. Like all war, it reduces wealth. Like war, the organization for a strike must be tyrannical. Those who would fight for freedom give up their personal free-dom on entering the army. They become a mere cog in a great machine. So it must be with workers who organize for a strike. Unions are, therefore, necessarily destructive of the very things that workers seek to gain through them: wealth and freedom.

4. Cooperation

It has become the fashion to preach cooperation as a remedy for the grievances of the working class. Since these evils do not arise from any conflict between labor and capi-tal, cooperation cannot raise wages nor relieve poverty.

Two kinds of proposals have been made: cooperation in supply and cooperation in production. Cooperation in supply is simply a device to save labor and eliminate risk. No matter how many middlemen it eliminates, it only re-duces the cost of exchange. Its effect upon distribution is the same as improvements and inventions. These have wonderfully facilitated trade in modern times—yet the effect is only to increase rent.

Cooperation in production is simply the substitution of proportional wages for fixed wages. There are occasional instances of this in almost all occupations. Sometimes management is left to the workers, and the capitalist only takes a fixed proportion of net production. All that is claimed for cooperation in production is that it makes the worker more active and industrious. In other words, it increases the efficiency of labor. Its effect, therefore, is in the same direction as other forms of material progress. It can produce only the same result—higher rent.

It is striking proof of how basic principles are ignored that cooperation is proposed as a means of raising wages and relieving poverty. It can have no such general tendency. Imagine that cooperation of supply and cooperation of production replaced present methods. Cooperative stores connect producer and consumer with a minimum of expense. Cooperative factories, farms, and mines abolish capitalist employers who pay fixed wages.

All this greatly increases the efficiency of labor. What of it? It becomes possible to produce the same amount of wealth with less labor. Consequently, owners of land—the source of all wealth—could command a greater amount for the use of their land. This is not just theory; it is proven by facts. Experience has shown that improvements in the methods and machinery of production and exchange have no tendency to improve the condition of the lowest class. Wages are lower and poverty is deeper where trade goes on at the least cost, and where production has the best technology. The advantage only adds to rent.

But what if there were cooperation between producers and landowners? That would simply amount to the payment of rent in kind. Call it cooperation, if you choose, but the terms would still be fixed by the laws that determine rent. Wherever land is monopolized, any increase in productive power simply gives landowners the power to demand a larger share.

Nonetheless, in many instances where it has been tried, it seems that cooperation has noticeably improved the condition of those immediately engaged in it. This is due to the fact that these cases are isolated. Industry or skill may improve the condition of those who possess them in superior degree. When these improvements become widespread, however, they cease to have the same effect. Likewise, one may benefit from a special advantage in procuring supplies or a special efficiency given to some labor. But these benefits would be lost as soon as the improvements became so prevalent as to affect the general relationships of distribution.

Increased productive power does not add to the reward of labor. This is not because of competition, but because competition is one-sided. There can be no production without land—and land is monopolized. Producers must compete for its use, and this forces wages to a minimum. It gives all the advantage of increasing productive power to landowners—in higher rents and increased land values. Destroy this monopoly, and competition would accomplish what cooperation attempts: giving everyone what they fairly earn. Destroy this monopoly, and industry must become the cooperation of equals.

5. Government Regulation

Space will not permit a detailed examination of proposals to alleviate poverty by government regulation of industry and accumulation. In their most comprehensive forms, we generally call these methods socialism. Nor is analysis necessary, for the same defects apply to all of them. They substitute governmental control for the freedom of individual action. They attempt to secure by restraint what can better be secured by freedom. We should not resort to them if we can achieve the same ends any other way.

For instance, a graduated income tax aims to mitigate the immense concentration of wealth. The end is good;

but look at the means required. It employs a large number of officials with inquisitorial powers. There are temptations to bribery, perjury, and all other means of evasion, which beget a demoralization of opinion. It puts a premium upon unscrupulousness and a tax upon conscience. Finally, in proportion to accomplishing its effect, it weakens the incentive to accumulate wealth, one of the driving forces of industrial progress.

If these elaborate schemes for regulating everything and finding a place for everybody could be carried out, we would have a state of society resembling that of ancient Peru. Modern society cannot successfully attempt socialism in anything approaching such a form. The only force that has ever proved effective for it, a strong religious faith, grows fainter every day. We have passed out of the socialism of the tribal state. We cannot enter it again, except by retrogression that would involve anarchy and perhaps barbarism.

The ideal of socialism is grand and noble. I am convinced it is possible to achieve. But such a state of society cannot be manufactured—it must grow. Society is an organism, not a machine. It can live only by the individual life of its parts. In the free and natural development of all its parts, the harmony of the whole will be secured. All that is necessary is "Land and Liberty."*

6. *Redistribution of Land*

Many suspect that possession of land is somehow connected with our social problems. Most propositions look toward a more general division of land. Some seek to restrict the size of individual holdings. Grants to assist in the settlement of public lands have even been sug-

---

* Motto of Russian revolutionaries, called Nihilists, in 1878.

gested. Such measures would merely allow ownership of land to more quickly assume the form to which it tends.

Ownership in Great Britain and the United States has been steadily concentrating. While statistical tables are sometimes quoted to show a decrease in the average size of holdings, ownership of land may still be concentrating.

As land passes to more intense use, the size of holdings tends to diminish. A stock range becomes a large farm, a small farm becomes a vegetable garden, a patch of land too small for even this makes a large property in the city. Thus, growing population naturally reduces the size of holdings by putting lands to higher or more intense uses. This process is very conspicuous in new countries. Average holdings of one acre in a city may show a much greater concentration of ownership than average holdings of 640 acres in a new township.

I refer to this to show the fallacy of assertions that land monopoly is an evil that will cure itself. On the contrary, it is obvious that the proportion of landowners to the whole population is constantly decreasing.

We clearly see a strong tendency toward concentration in agriculture. Small farms are being combined into larger ones. Only a few years ago, 320 acres would have made a large farm anywhere. In California there are now farms up to sixty thousand acres, while Dakota farms embrace a hundred thousand acres.

The reason is obvious. The use of machinery causes a general tendency towards large-scale production. Agriculture is beginning to exhibit the same trend that replaced independent hand weavers with factories. Therefore, any measure that merely allows a greater subdivision of land would be ineffective. Further, any measure to force it would reduce productivity. If land can be cultivated more cheaply in large parcels, restricting ownership to small ones will reduce the aggregate production of wealth.

Therefore, any effort to achieve a fairer division of wealth by such restrictions is subject to the drawback that it lessens the amount to be divided. It would be like the story of the monkey dividing cheese between cats, who equalized matters by taking a bite off the biggest piece. A further and fatal objection is that restriction will not secure the only end worth aiming at: a fair division. It will not reduce rent. Therefore it cannot increase wages. It may make the comfortable classes larger, but it will not improve the condition of the lowest class. Thus, subdivision of land does nothing to cure the evils of land monopoly. It may even discourage adoption of more sweeping measures. It strengthens the existing system by interesting a larger number of people in its maintenance.

Let us abandon all attempts to eliminate land monopoly by restricting ownership. An equal distribution of land is impossible. Yet anything short of that would be only a relief, not a cure. Indeed, it would be a relief that would prevent the adoption of a cure.

Nor is any remedy worth considering that does not flow with the natural direction of social development. There can be no mistaking that concentration is the order of development. The concentration of people in large cities, of handicrafts in large factories, of transportation by railroad and steamship lines, and of agricultural operations in large fields, all affirm this. To successfully resist this trend we would have to banish steam and electricity from human service.

Chapter 25

The True Remedy

WE HAVE TRACED the unequal distribution of wealth, the curse and menace of modern civilization, to the institution of private property in land. As long as this institution exists, no increase in production will permanently benefit the masses. On the contrary, any improvements must depress their condition further. We have examined the remedies currently proposed to relieve poverty and improve the distribution of wealth, and found them all ineffective or impractical. Poverty deepens as wealth increases; wages fall while productivity grows. All because land, the source of all wealth and the field of all labor, is monopolized.

Deduction and induction have brought us to the same truth: Unequal ownership of land causes unequal distribution of wealth. And because unequal ownership of land is inseperable from the recognition of individual property in land, it necessarily follows that there is only one remedy for the unjust distribution of wealth:

We must make land common property.

But this is a truth that will arouse the most bitter antagonism, given the present state of society. It must fight its way, inch by inch. It will be necessary to meet the objections of those who, even when forced to admit this truth, will contend that it cannot be practically applied. In doing this we shall bring our previous reasoning to a new and crucial test. Just as we test addition by subtraction and multiplication by division, so we can we test our conclusions by the adequacy of our remedy. If it is practical, it proves our conclusions are correct.

The laws of the universe are harmonious. If the remedy to which we have been led is the true one, it must be consistent with justice; it must be practical in application; it must accord with the tendencies of social development; and it must harmonize with other reforms.

All this I propose to show.

The laws of the universe do not deny the natural aspirations of the human heart. The progress of society can be toward equality, not inequality. Economic law will prove the perceptions of Marcus Aurelius: "We are made for cooperation—like feet, like hands, like eyelids, like the rows of the upper and lower teeth."

Editor's note: In the chapters that follow the bold and controversial statement, "We must make land common property," George shows how his method of doing so would secure to labor and capital the private possession of land and ownership of the improvements thereon.

Justice of the Remedy

Chapter 26

The Injustice of Private Property In Land

JUSTICE IS FUNDAMENTAL to the human mind, though often warped by superstition, habit, and selfishness. When I propose to abolish private property in land, the first question to be asked is that of justice. Only what is just can be wise; only what is right will endure. I bow to this demand and accept this test. If private property in land is just, then what I propose is false. If private property in land is unjust, then my remedy is true.

What constitutes the rightful basis of property? What allows someone to justly say, "This is mine!"? Is it not, primarily, the right of a person to one's own self? To the use of one's own powers? To enjoy the fruits of one's own labor? Each person is a definite, coherent, independent whole. Each particular pair of hands obeys a particular brain and is related to a particular body. And this alone justifies individual ownership.

As each person belongs to himself or herself, so labor belongs to the individual when put in concrete form. For this reason, what someone makes or produces belongs to that person—even against the claim of the whole world. It is that person's property, to use or enjoy, give or exchange, or even destroy. No one else can rightfully claim it. And this right to the exclusive possession and enjoyment wrongs no one else. Thus, there is a clear and indisputable title to everything produced by human exertion. It descends from the original producer, in whom it is vested by natural law.

The pen that I write with is justly mine. No other human being can rightfully lay claim to it, for in me is the title of the producers who made it. It has become mine because it was transferred to me by the stationer, to whom it was transferred by the importer, who obtained the exclusive right to it by transfer from the manufacturer. By the same process of purchase, the manufacturer acquired the vested rights of those who dug the material from the ground and shaped it into a pen.

Thus, my exclusive right of ownership in the pen springs from the natural right of individuals to the use of their own faculties—the source from which all ideas of exclusive ownership arise. It is not only the original source, it is the only source.

Nature acknowledges no ownership or control existing in humans, except the results of labor. Is there any other way to affect material things except by exerting the power of one's own faculties? All people exist in nature on equal footing and have equal rights. Nature recognizes no claim but labor—and without respect to who claims it. When a pirate ship spreads its sails, wind fills them; as it would those of a missionary. Fish will bite whether the line leads to a good child who goes to Sunday school or a bad one playing truant. The sun shines and the rain falls on the just and unjust alike.

The laws of nature are the decrees of the Creator. They recognize no right but labor. As nature gives only to labor, the exertion of labor in production is the only title to exclusive possession.

This right of ownership springing from labor excludes the possibility of any other right of ownership. A person is rightfully entitled to the product of his or her labor (or the labor of someone else from whom the right has been received).

It is *production* that gives the producer the right to exclusive possession and enjoyment. If so, there can be no right to exclusive possession of anything that is *not* the product of labor. Therefore, private property in land is wrong.

The right to the product of labor cannot be enjoyed without the right to free use of the opportunities offered by nature. To admit a right to property in nature is to deny the right of property as the product of labor. When non-producers can claim a portion of the wealth created by producers—as rent—then the right of producers to the fruits of their labor is denied to that extent.

There is no escape from this position. To affirm that someone can rightfully claim exclusive ownership of his or her own labor—when embodied in material things—is to deny that any one can rightfully claim exclusive ownership in land. Property in land is a claim having no justification in nature—it is a claim founded in the way societies are organized.

What keeps us from recognizing the injustice of private property in land? By habit, we include all things made subject to ownership in one category—which we call "property." The only distinctions are drawn by lawyers, who distinguish only personal property from real estate—

things movable from things immovable. The real and natural distinction, however, is between the product of labor and the free offerings of nature. In the terms of political economy, between wealth and land. To class them together is to confuse all thought regarding justice or injustice, right or wrong.

A house and the lot on which it stands are classed together by lawyers as real estate. Yet in nature and relations they differ widely. One is produced by human labor (wealth). The other is a part of nature (land).

The essential characteristic of wealth is that it embodies labor. It is brought into being by human exertion. Its existence or nonexistence, its increase or decrease, depends on humans. The essential characteristic of land is that it does not embody labor. It exists irrespective of human exertion, and irrespective of people. It is the field, or environment, in which people find themselves; the storehouse from which their needs must be supplied; the raw material on which—and the forces with which—they can act.

The moment this distinction is recognized, we see that the sanction natural justice gives to one kind of property is denied to the other. The rightfulness of property that is the product of labor implies the wrongfulness of the individual ownership of land. The recognition of the former places all people upon equal terms, and gives them the due reward of their labor. Whereas the recognition of the latter is to deny the equal rights of people. It allows those who do not work to take the natural reward of those who do. Whatever may be said for the institution of private property in land, it clearly cannot be defended on the grounds of justice.

The equal right of all people to the use of land is as clear as their equal right to breathe the air—a right proclaimed by the very fact of their existence. We cannot suppose that some people have a right to be in this world and others do not. If we are all here by permission of the Creator, we are all here with an equal title to the bounty of nature.

This is a right that is natural and inalienable. It is a right that vests in every human being who enters the world. During each person's stay in the world it can be limited only by the equal rights of others. If all people living were to unite to grant away their equal rights, they could not grant away the rights of those who follow them. Have we made the earth, that we should determine the rights of those who come after us? No matter how long the claim, nor how many pieces of paper are issued, there is no right that natural justice recognizes to give one person possession of land that is not equally the right of all other people. The smallest infant born in the most squalid room of the most miserable tenement acquires, at the moment of birth, a right to land equal to millionaires. And that child is robbed if that right is denied.

Our previous conclusions were irresistible in and of themselves. They now stand confirmed by the highest and final test. Translated from economics into ethics, they show that the source of increasing misery amid progress is a great fundamental wrong: the appropriation of land as the exclusive property of some. For it is land on which—and from which—all people must live. From this fundamental injustice flow all the injustices that endanger modern development. They condemn the producer of wealth to poverty, while pampering the non-producer in luxury.

There is nothing strange or inexplicable in the phenomena now perplexing the world. It is not that material progress is not in itself a good thing. It is not that nature has produced children it has failed to provide for. It is not that the Creator has left injustice in natural laws, such that material progress should bring such bitter fruits. It is not due to any lack of nature—but to human injustice.

Vice and misery, poverty and pauperism, are not the legitimate results of growing population and industrial development. They follow them only because land is treated as private property. They are the direct and necessary result of violating the supreme law of justice—giving to the exclusive possession of a few, what nature has provided for all.

Since labor cannot produce wealth without using land, denying equal right to use land is, necessarily, denying the right of labor to its own product. If one person controls the land on which others must labor, that person can appropriate the product of their labor as the price of permission to labor. This violates the fundamental law of nature: that a person's enjoyment of the fruits of nature requires that person's exertion.

The unjust distribution of wealth stemming from this fundamental wrong is separating modern society into the very rich and the very poor. The continuous increase of rent is the price labor is forced to pay for the use of land. It strips the many of wealth they justly earn, and heaps it in the hands of a few who do nothing to earn it. The few receive without producing, while others produce without receiving. One is unjustly enriched—the others are robbed.

Why should those who suffer from this injustice hesitate for one moment to sweep it away? Why should landholders be permitted to reap what they have not sown?

Consider for a moment the utter absurdity by which we gravely pass down titles giving the right to exclusive possession of the earth, and thus absolute dominion over others. In California, land titles go back to the government of Mexico, which took them from the Spanish King, who took them from the Pope. The Pope, by a stroke of the pen, divided lands—yet to be discovered!—between Spain and Portugal.

In a word, ownership of land rests upon conquest. Everywhere, there is not a right that binds, but a force that compels. And when a title rests only on force, no complaint can be made when force annuls it. Whenever the people, having the power, choose to annul those titles, no objection can be made in the name of justice. People have had the power to take or hold exclusive possession of portions of the earth's surface. But when and where did there ever exist the human being who had such a right?

The right to exclusive ownership of anything of human production is clear. No matter how many hands it has passed through, at the beginning there was human labor. Someone produced or procured it by exertion, thus gaining clear title to it against all the rest of mankind. That person could justly pass it from one to another by sale or gift.

But at the end of what string of transfers or grants can we find, or even suppose, a similar title to any part of the material universe? To improvements, such an original title can be shown. But this is a title only to the improvements, and not to the land itself. If I clear a forest, drain a swamp, or fill a bog, all I can justly claim is the value given by these exertions. It gives me no right to the land itself. I have no claim other than my equal share with every other member of the community toward the value added by the growth of the community.

But it will be said: There are improvements that, in time, become indistinguishable from the land itself. Very well, then the title to the improvements becomes blended with the title to the land. The individual right is lost in the common right. It is the greater that swallows up the less; not the less that swallows up the greater. Nature does not proceed from humans, but humans from nature. And it is into the bosom of nature that we and all our works must return again.

Still, it will be said: Everyone has a right to the use and enjoyment of nature. In order to gain the full benefit of labor applied to land, a person must have the exclusive right to its use. There is no difficulty, however, in determining where the individual right ends and the common right begins. A delicate and exact test is supplied by value. With its aid, there is no difficulty in determining and securing the exact rights of each, and the equal rights of all. This can be determined, no matter how dense population becomes.

The value of land, as we have seen, is the price of monopoly. It is the relative, not the absolute, capability of land that determines its value. No matter what its intrinsic qualities may be, land that is no better than other land that can be had for free can have no value. The value of land always measures the difference between it and the best land that may be had for free.

Thus, the value of land expresses, in exact and tangible form, the right the community has in land held by an individual. And rent, therefore, expresses the exact amount an individual should pay the community to satisfy the equal rights of all other members.

We now have a method to reconcile the stability of tenure, required for improvement, with a full and complete recognition of the equal rights of all to the use of land. We can concede the undisturbed use of land to priority of possession—if we collect rent for the benefit of the community.

What of the deduction of a complete and exclusive individual right to land from priority of occupation? That is, if possible, the most absurd ground on which land ownership can be defended. How can order of occupation give exclusive and perpetual title to the surface of a globe on which countless generations succeed each other! Did the last generation have any better right to the use of this world than we? Or those of a hundred years ago? Or of a thousand years ago?

Does the first person to arrive at a banquet acquire the right to turn back all the chairs and claim that no other guests can eat the food unless they agree to the first person's terms? Does the first person with a ticket at the theater have the right to shut the doors and have the performance go on for him or her alone? Does the first passenger who enters a railroad car obtain the right to scatter baggage over all the seats and force all subsequent passengers to stand?

These cases are perfectly analogous. We arrive and we depart. We are guests at a banquet continually spread, spectators and participants in an entertainment where there is room for all who come. We are passengers on an orb whirling through space. Our rights to take and possess cannot be exclusive. They must be bounded, everywhere, by the equal rights of others.

A passenger in a railroad car may spread baggage around only until other passengers come in. So may settlers take and use as much land as they choose, until it is needed by others. This fact is shown by land acquiring a value when the initial right must be curtailed by the equal rights of the others. But no priority of appropriation can give a right that will bar the equal rights of others. If this were not the case, then—by priority of appropriation— one person could acquire the exclusive right to a whole township, a whole state, a whole continent. If one could concentrate the individual rights to the whole surface of the globe, that person alone of all the teeming billions would have the right to live, and could expel all the rest of the inhabitants.

In point of fact, this absurd supposition actually does occur, though on a smaller scale. I will refer to Britain only because land ownership is more concentrated there, and it affords a striking illustration of what private property in land necessarily involves. But it is true everywhere, including the United States. The territorial lords of Great Britain have, over and over again, expelled the native population from large areas. People, whose ancestors had lived on the land from time immemorial, have been forced to emigrate, become paupers, or starve. The vast body of the British people and their subjects are forced to pay enormous sums to a few—for the privilege of being permitted to live on the land they so fondly call their own.

Chapter 27
The Enslavement of Labor

AS CHATTEL SLAVERY, the owning of people, is unjust—so private ownership of land is unjust. Ownership of land always gives ownership of people. To what degree, is measured by the need for land. When starvation is the only alternative, the ownership of people involved in the ownership of land becomes absolute. This is simply the law of rent in different form.

Place one hundred people on an island from which there is no escape. Make one of them the absolute owner of the others—or the absolute owner of the soil. It will make no difference—either to owner or to the others—which one you choose. Either way, one individual will be the absolute master of the other ninety-nine. Denying permission to them to live on the island would force them into the sea.

The same cause must operate, in the same way and to the same end, even on a larger scale and through more complex relations. When people are compelled to live on—and from—land treated as the exclusive property of others, the ultimate result is the enslavement of workers. Though less direct and less obvious, relations will tend to the same state as on our hypothetical island. As population increases and productivity improves, we move toward the same absolute mastery of landlords and the same abject helplessness of labor. Rent will advance; wages will fall. Landowners continually increase their share of the total production, while labor's share constantly declines.

To the extent that moving to cheaper land becomes difficult or impossible, workers will be reduced to a bare living—no matter what they produce. Where land is monopolized, they will live as virtual slaves. Despite enormous increase in productive power, wages in the lower and wider layers of industry tend—everywhere—to the wages of slavery (i.e., just enough to maintain them in working condition).

There is nothing strange in this fact. Owning the land on which—and from which—people must live is virtually the same as owning the people themselves. In accepting the right of some individuals to the exclusive use and enjoyment of the earth, we condemn others to slavery. We do this as fully and as completely as though we had formally made them chattel slaves.

In simple societies, production is largely the direct application of labor to the soil. There, slavery is the obvious result of a few having an exclusive right to the soil from which all must live. This is plainly seen in various forms of serfdom. Chattel slavery originated in the capture of prisoners in war. Though it has existed to some extent in every part of the globe, its effects have been trivial compared to the slavery that originates in the appropriation of land.

Wherever society has reached a certain point of development, we see the general subjection of the many by the few—the result of the appropriation of land as individual property. Ownership of land gives absolute power over people who cannot live except by using it. Those who possess the land are masters of the people who dwell upon it.

The idea of individual ownership naturally and justly attaches to things of human production. But when it is extended to land, the rest is just a matter of time. The strong and cunning easily acquire a superior share in this species of property. For it is to be had, not by production, but by appropriation. In becoming lords of the land, they necessarily become lords of other people.

Ownership of land is the basis of aristocracy. It was not nobility that gave land, but the possession of land that gave nobility. All the enormous privileges of the nobility of medieval Europe flowed from their position as the owners of the soil. This simple principle of ownership produced the lord on one side, and the vassal on the other. One having all the rights, the other none.

The same cause has enslaved the masses of workers in every age. It is still acting in the civilized world today. We may say that personal liberty—freedom to move about— is universally acknowledged. In the United States and most civilized countries, political and legal inequality have been abolished. Yet the greatest cause of inequality remains— revealing itself in the unequal distribution of wealth.

The essence of slavery is that everything workers produce is taken from them, except enough to support a bare existence. Under existing conditions, the lowest wages of free labor invariably tend toward this same state. No matter how much productivity increases, rent steadily swallows up the whole gain (or even more). Thus, the condition of the masses in every civilized country is tending toward virtual slavery—under the forms of freedom.

Of all kinds of slavery, this is probably the most cruel

and relentless. Laborers are robbed of their production and forced to toil for mere subsistence. But their taskmasters assume the form of inescapable demands. It does not seem to be one human being who drives another, but "the inevitable laws of supply and demand." And for this, no one in particular is responsible. Even the selfish interest that prompted the master to look after the well-being of his slaves is lost.

Labor has become a commodity, and the worker a machine. There are no masters and slaves, no owners and owned—only buyers and sellers.

When Southern slaveholders saw the condition of the free poor in civilized countries, it is no wonder they easily persuaded themselves to accept slavery. There can be no doubt that Southern field hands were (as a class) better fed, better lodged, and better clothed than agricultural laborers in England. In the South during slavery, it would have been scandalous for masters to force their slaves to live and work under conditions that large classes of free white men and women did in Northern cities. If public opinion had not restrained them, their own selfish interest in maintaining the health and strength of their slaves would have.

Is it any wonder that demands to abolish slavery seemed hypocritical to slaveholders? And now that slavery has been abolished, the planters find they have sustained no loss. Ownership of the land—on which the freed slaves must live—gives them almost as much control of labor as before. Yet they are relieved of some very expensive responsibilities.

As population increases and land becomes more valuable, the planters will get a greater share (proportionately) of the earnings of their laborers than they did under slavery. Of course, labor will get a smaller share. At least slaves got enough to keep them in good physical health. But in countries such as England, there are large classes of laborers who do not get even that.

These modifying influences are lost in the complicated processes of modern production, where serfdom assumes a less obvious form. Those whose labor is appropriated and those who appropriate it are widely separated through many intermediate gradations. This makes relations between members of the two classes indirect and general, while before they were direct and particular.

That such conditions are not more common here is due to the great extent of fertile land available on this continent. This has not only provided an escape valve for the older sections of the Union, it has greatly relieved the pressure in Europe. But this avenue of relief cannot last forever. It is already closing up fast. As it closes, the pressure must become greater.

The working class is being driven into this helpless, hopeless poverty by a force like a resistless and unpitying machine. It drives people to acts barbarians would refuse. The Boston collar manufacturer who pays his workers two cents an hour may sympathize with their condition. But, like them, he is governed by the law of competition. His business cannot survive if he pays more. And so it goes, through all the intermediate gradations. It seems to be the inexorable laws of supply and demand that forces the lower classes into the slavery of poverty. And an individual can no more dispute this power than the winds and tides.

But in reality, it is the same cause that always has, and always must, result in slavery:

The monopolization by some of what nature meant for all.

As long as we recognize private property in land, our boasted freedom will inevitably involve slavery. Until it is abolished, Declarations of Independence and Acts of Emancipation are in vain. So long as one person can claim exclusive ownership of land—from which other people must live—slavery will exist. Indeed, as material progress grows, it must grow and deepen.

Chapter 28
Are Landowners Entitled to Compensation?

THERE CAN BE NO ESCAPE from this truth: There can be no honest title to exclusive possession of the earth. Private property in land is a bold, bare, enormous wrong—like chattel slavery. The majority of people do not recognize this, simply because the majority of people do not think. To them, whatever is, is right. It continues to appear so until its injustice has been pointed out repeatedly. In general, they are ready to crucify whoever first attempts this.

Yet it is impossible to think at all about the production and distribution of wealth, without seeing that property in land is a fundamentally different thing from property in objects of human production. Furthermore, our examination has also shown that private property in land cannot be justified on the grounds of utility. On the contrary, it is the great cause of poverty and misery. Expediency, therefore, joins justice in demanding that we abolish it.

This institution has no stronger ground than a mere municipal regulation. So what reason can there be for hesitation?

One worry—even among those who clearly see that land, by right, is common property—is this: Restoring common rights to land appears to be an injustice to those who have purchased it with their rightful wealth. Land being treated as private property for so long, they have based their calculations upon its permanence. So, it is said, justice requires that we compensate the owners if we abolish it.

The essential defect in this lies in the impossibility of bridging the radical difference between right and wrong. For the interests of landholders to be conserved, the interests and rights of others must be disregarded. If landholders lose nothing of their special privileges, the people at large can gain nothing.

Buying individual property rights would only give landholders a claim of the same kind and amount that their possession of land now gives them, only in another form. Through taxation, it would give them the same proportion of the earnings of labor and capital that they now appropriate in rent. The unjust advantage of landowners would be preserved, while the unjust disadvantage of others would be continued.

Yet even this discussion is a hopeful sign. Cries for justice are timid and humble when first protesting a time-honored wrong. We have been educated to look upon the "vested rights" of landowners with all the superstitious reverence that ancient Egyptians looked upon the crocodile.

But ideas grow when times are ripe, even though their first appearances are insignificant. The antislavery movement in the United States began with talk of compensating owners. But when four million slaves were emancipated, the owners got no compensation. Nor did they clamor for any. One day, the people of England or the United States will be sufficiently aroused to the injustice and disadvantages of individual ownership of land to reclaim it. And they will not trouble themselves about compensating land-owners.

Nor should there be any concern. How absurd! If the land of any country belongs to the people of that country, what right—in morality or justice—do landowners have to compensation? If the land belongs to the people, why should they pay its value *for their own land?*

Herbert Spencer once wrote,* "Had we to deal with the parties who originally robbed the human race of its heritage, we might make short work of the matter." Why not make short work of it anyhow?

For this robbery is not like the robbery of a horse or some money. That theft ceases with the act. This is a con-tinuous robbery that goes on every hour of every day. It is a toll levied upon labor constantly and continuously. It is not merely a robbery in the past—it is a robbery in the present. And a robbery that deprives the newborn of their birthright. Why should we hesitate to make short work of such a system?

Just because I was robbed yesterday and the day be-fore and the day before that, must I allow myself to be robbed today and tomorrow as well? Is there any reason to conclude that the robber has acquired a vested right to rob me? If land belongs to the people, why continue to permit landowners to take rent? And why compensate them in

---

* Herbert Spencer (1820-1903), English philosopher, *Social Statics*, page 142. This reference is from the edition published—with his con-sent—from 1864 to 1892. Thereafter, he repudiated it, and issued a new edition that eliminated all references declaring property in land to be unjust. Henry George addressed Spencer's reversal in a later book, *A Perplexed Philosopher.*

any manner for their "loss" of rent?

Consider what rent really is. It represents a value created by the whole community. It does not arise spontaneously from the land. Nor is it due to anything that landowners have done.

Let landowners have, if you please, everything land would give them—in the absence of the rest of the community. But rent is the creation of the whole community. So it necessarily belongs to the whole community.

Suppose we were to try the case using common law—which has been built by and for landowners. What does the law allow someone who innocently buys land later judged to belong to another? Nothing at all.

That fact that one purchased in good faith gives no right or claim whatsoever. The law simply says: "The land belongs to A, let the sheriff put him in possession!" It gives no claim to the innocent purchaser of a wrongful title, and allows no compensation.

Not only this, but it takes all improvements made in good faith. The buyers may have paid a high price, making every effort to see that the title is good. They may have held undisturbed possession for years, without hint of an adverse claimant. They may have even erected buildings more valuable than the land itself.

Yet clever lawyers may find a technical flaw in the papers. Or they may hunt up some forgotten heir who never dreamed of such rights. Then, not only the land, but all the improvements may be taken away.

And there is even more! According to common law, after surrendering the land and giving up the improvements, the buyers may be called upon to account for all the profits derived from use of the land during the time of possession.

These dictates of justice have been formulated into law by landowners themselves. They are applied every day in American and English courts. If we were to apply them to the case of "The People vs. The Landowners," we would not think of giving landholders any compensation. Indeed, we would take all the improvements and whatever else they may have as well.

But I do not propose to go that far. It is sufficient if the people resume ownership of the land. Let the landowners retain their improvements and personal property in secure possession.

By this measure of justice, there would be no oppression and no injury to any class. The great cause of the unequal distribution of wealth would be swept away. And with it, the suffering, degradation, and waste that it entails. All would share in the general prosperity. The gain of small landholders would be enormous; that of large landholders would still be real.

For in welcoming justice, peace and plenty will follow—bringing good not just to some, but to all. For justice itself is the highest and truest expediency. How true this is, we shall shortly see.

Chapter 29

History of Land as Private Property

ANY CUSTOM that has existed for a long time seems natural and necessary to us. This is merely habit. Nonetheless, this, more than anything else, keeps us from realizing the basic injustice of private property in land—and prevents us from considering any proposal to abolish it. We are so used to treating land as individual property that the vast majority of people never think of questioning it. It is thoroughly recognized in our laws, manners, and customs.

Most people even think it is required for the use of land. They are unable to conceive of society as possible without reducing land to private possession. The first step in improving land is to find an owner. A person's land is looked on as property to sell, lease, give, or bequeath—the same as houses, cattle, goods, or furniture. The "sacredness of property" has been preached so constantly—especially by the "conservators of ancient barbarism," as Voltaire called lawyers—that most people view private ownership of land as the very foundation of civilization. They fancy returning land to common ownership as some wild fantasy—or an attempt to return society to barbarism.

Even if it were true—which it is not—that land had always been treated as private property, this would not prove the justice or necessity of continuing to treat it as such. The universal existence of slavery was once affirmed.

Yet that did not prove it just or necessary. Not long ago, monarchy seemed all but universal. Not only kings, but the majority of their subjects, really believed that no country could survive without a king. Yet France, to say nothing of America, gets along quite well without a king. And the Queen of England has as much power to govern the realm as the wooden figurehead of a ship has to determine its course.

But the assumption that land had always been treated as private property is not true. On the contrary, the common right to land has always been recognized as the primary right. Private ownership has appeared only as the result of usurpation—that is, being seized by force.

The primary and persistent perception of mankind is that everyone has an equal right to land. The opinion that private property in land is necessary to society is a comparatively modern idea, as artificial and as baseless as the divine right of kings. It is only the result of an ignorance that cannot look beyond its immediate surroundings. History, research, and the observations of travelers prove that wherever human society has formed, the common right of people to use the earth has been recognized. Unrestricted individual ownership has never been freely adopted. It has always been born in war and conquest—and in the selfish use the cunning have made of law and superstition.

Wherever we can trace the early history of society— in Europe, Asia, Africa, America, and Polynesia—land was once considered common property. All members of the community had equal rights to the use and enjoyment of the land of the community.

This recognition of the common right to land did not prevent the full recognition of the exclusive right to the products of labor. Nor was it abandoned when the development of agriculture imposed the necessity of recognizing exclusive possession of land—to secure the results of labor expended in cultivating it.

How, then, has private ownership of land become so widespread? Why was the original idea of equal rights supplanted by the idea of exclusive and unequal rights? The causes are the same ones that led to the establishment of privileged classes. We can summarize them briefly: (1) The concentration of power in the hands of chieftains and the military. (2) Conquest that reduces the conquered to slavery and divides their lands, with a disproportionate share going to the chiefs. (3) The differentiation and influence of a priestly class. (4) The differentiation and influence of a class of professional lawyers.

The interests of priests and lawyers were served by the substitution of exclusive property in place of common land. In Europe lawyers have been especially effective in destroying all vestiges of the ancient tenure by substituting Roman law—exclusive ownership.

Unfortunately, inequality, once produced, always tends toward greater inequality. This struggle—between equal rights to the soil and the tendency to monopolize it in individual possession—caused the internal conflicts of ancient Greece and Rome. But the final triumph of the tendency toward ownership eventually destroyed both.

By the power with which the great attracts the less, small family estates became part of the great estates—the latifundia—of enormously rich patricians. The former owners were forced into slave gangs, or became virtual serfs. Others fled to the cities, swelling the ranks of the proletariat, who had nothing to sell but their votes. As a result, population declined, art sank, the intellect weakened, and once splendid civilizations became empty shells.

The hardy virtues born of personal independence died out, while exhaustive agriculture impoverished the soil. At length the barbarians broke through; a civilization once proud was left in ruins. During Rome's grandeur, such a fate would have seemed as impossible as it seems to us now that the Comanches could conquer the United States or Laplanders desolate Europe.

The fundamental cause was tenure of land. On the one hand, denial of the common right to land resulted in decay; on the other, equality gave strength. Every family in the German villages was entitled to an equal share of common land. This impressed a remarkable character on the individual, which explains how small bands of barbarians overran a great empire. Rome perished from "the failure of the crop of men."

After the Roman Empire fell, the idea of common rights was blended with the idea of exclusive property. The feudal system was the result.

But side by side and underneath the feudal system, a more primitive organization revived. Based on the common rights of cultivators, it has left traces all over Europe, and still survives in many places.

Feudalism clearly recognized—in theory at least—that land belongs to society at large, not to the individual. A fief (a feudal estate) was essentially a trust to which certain obligations attached. The sovereign was, theoretically, the representative of the collective power and rights of the whole people. Though land was granted to individual possession, specific duties were required. Through these, some equivalent to the benefits received from the common right was rendered back to the commonwealth.

Under the feudal scheme, crown lands supported public expenditures. Church lands defrayed the cost of public worship and instruction, as well as care for the sick and destitute. The military tenant was under obligation to raise a certain force when needed.

These duties were a rude and inefficient recognition— but unquestionably still a recognition—of a fact obvious to the natural perceptions of all men: Land is not individual property, but common property.

Amid the feudal system there were communities who tilled the soil as common property, though subject to feudal dues. Of course the lords, if they had the power, claimed pretty much all they thought worth claiming. Yet the idea of common right was strong enough to attach itself, by custom, to a considerable part of the land.

The commons must have been a very large proportion of most European countries in those times. After centuries of appropriation by the aristocracy, France still retains almost ten million acres of communal land. In England, while over eight million acres have been enclosed since 1710, some two million acres still remain as commons, though mostly worthless soil.

But these are not the only things that prove the universality and persistence of a common right to the soil. There are also the very institutions under which modern civilization has developed. Certain things persist in our legal systems that point to this common right, though they have lost their original meaning. For instance, the doctrine of eminent domain arises from nothing but the recognition of the sovereign or government as representing the collective rights of the people. Legal terminology also distinguishes between real and personal property. This very difference is the survival of a primitive distinction between what was originally looked on as common property and what, from its nature, was always considered the exclusive property of the individual.

The general course of development of modern civilization since the feudal period has subverted the natural and primary ideas of collective ownership of the soil. Paradoxical as it may appear, the emergence of liberty from feudal bonds has been accompanied by a tendency toward a form of land ownership that enslaves the working class. This is being felt all over the civilized world. Political economists mistake it for the pressure of natural laws, while workers mistake it for the oppression of capital.

It is clear that in Great Britain today, the right of the people as a whole to the soil of their native country is much less fully acknowledged than it was in feudal times. The commons, once so extensive, largely contributed to the independence and support of the lower classes. Today, all but a small remnant of worthless land has been appropriated for individual ownership and enclosed. Most crown lands have passed into private possession. Now the British workingman must pay to support the royal family and all the petty princelings who marry into it.

A smaller proportion of the people now own the land. And their ownership is much more absolute. Thirty thousand people have legal power to expel the whole population from five-sixths of the British Islands. The vast majority of the British people have no right whatsoever to their native land, except to walk the streets.

The reason, I take it, that the idea of private property in land has grown alongside the idea of personal freedom is this:

In the progress of civilization, the grosser forms of supremacy connected with land ownership were dropped, or abolished, or became less obvious. Parliamentary government gradually stripped the great lords of individual importance and repressed their most striking abuses. As this happened, attention was diverted from the more insidious—but really more potent—forms of domination.

Meanwhile, there was a steady progression of legal ideas drawn from Roman law, the great storehouse of modern jurisprudence. This tended to level the natural distinction between property in land and property in other things. Landowners were then able to put property in land on the same basis as other property.

Moreover, the political power of land barons was not broken by the revolt of those classes who could clearly feel the injustice of land ownership. What broke their power was the growth of the artisan and trading classes. But the relation between their wages and rent is not as obvious.

These classes developed under a system of guilds and corporations. As I explained previously, trade unions and monopolies enabled them to somewhat fence themselves off from the general law of wages. But those were more easily maintained then than now, when population is steadily becoming more mobile due to improved transportation, education, and access to current news.

These classes did not see—and still do not see—that land tenure is the fundamental fact that ultimately determines the conditions of industrial, social, and political life. And so the tendency has been to assimilate the idea of property in land with that of property in things of human production.

The original landholders of England got their land on terms that required them to provide military defense and meet other conditions, which amounted to a considerable part of their rent. Had the form of feudal dues simply been changed into ones better adapted to the changed times, English wars need never have incurred a single pound of debt. English labor and capital need not have been taxed a single farthing. All this would have come from rent. But since that time, landholders have appropriated it to themselves.

What if landholders had been kept to this contract? What if any land enclosed required similar terms? There would be no need for customs duties, excise, license, or income taxes. The income accruing to the nation from these landowners would meet all present expenditures and, in addition, leave a large surplus. This could be used for any purpose aiding the comfort or well-being of the people as a whole.

Looking back, wherever there is light to guide us, we see that people recognized the common ownership in land in their earliest perceptions. Private property in land is a usurpation, a creation of force and fraud.

Chapter 30

History of Property in Land in the United States

IN EARLIER STAGES of civilization, land was always regarded as common property. Turning from the dim past to our own times, we see that people still instinctively recognize equal rights to the bounty of nature—if placed under circumstances where the influence of education and habit are weakened.

The discovery of gold in California brought diverse people together in a new country. Probably not one in a thousand had ever dreamed of any distinction between land and wealth. They had long been used to thinking of land as individual property. Things might have been different had the land been agricultural or grazing or forest land; or had its value come from its location for commercial purposes. Then, they would have applied the land system they had been used to, and reduced it to private ownership in large tracts.

But here was land where gold could be had simply by washing it out. This novelty broke through their habitual ideas, and they were thrown back upon first principles. By common consent, it was declared that gold-bearing land should remain common property. No one could take more than could reasonably be mined, nor hold it for longer than it was being used. Title to the land remained with the government. No individual could acquire more than a possessory claim.

Miners in each district established the size of an individual claim, plus the amount of work required to constitute use. If this work were not done, any one could relocate on the ground. The essential idea was to prevent monopoly. No one was allowed to play "dog in the manger," and hinder, forestall, or lock up natural resources. Labor was acknowledged as the creator of wealth, and its reward was secured.

As placer mining declined, the familiar idea of private property finally prevailed. A law was passed to permit the ownership of mineral lands. The only effect was to lock up opportunities. It gave owners the power to say that no one else may use what they do not use themselves. In many cases mining land was withheld from use for speculative purposes—just as valuable building lots and agricultural land are.

If the first English settlers in North America had found circumstances that called their attention anew to the question of land ownership, they no doubt would have reverted to first principles. For they reverted to first principles in matters of government. Just as aristocracy and monarchy were rejected, so too, individual ownership of land would have been rejected. But in the country from which they came, this system had not yet fully developed itself. Nor had its effects been fully felt.

In the new country, an immense continent invited settlement. The question of the justice in private property in land did not arise. At first, no harm seemed done by treating land as property. In a new country, equality seemed sufficiently assured if no one took land to the exclusion of the rest. And there was plenty of land left for others. The problems stemming from individual ownership of land had not yet appeared.

In the South, where settlement had an aristocratic character, land was carved into large estates. The natural complement of this was the introduction of slavery. But in New England, the first settlers divided the land as their ancestors had divided Britain twelve centuries before. The head of each family was given his town lot and his seed lot. Beyond these lay the free commons. English kings attempted to create great proprietors by huge land grants. Settlers saw the injustice of this attempted monopoly, and no one got much from these grants. However, because land was so abundant, attention was not called to the injustice in individual ownership of land. But even when tracts are small, this must involve monopoly when land becomes scarce.

So it came to pass that the great republic of the modern world adopted an institution that destroyed the republics of antiquity. They proclaimed the inalienable right of all people to life, liberty, and the pursuit of happiness. Yet they accepted without question a principle that ultimately denies the equal right to life and liberty—by denying equal and inalienable right to the soil. At the cost of a bloody war, they abolished chattel slavery. Yet they allowed a more widespread and dangerous form of slavery to take root.

The continent seemed so wide, so vast. The unsettled land prevented the full effect of private appropriation from being felt, even in older sections. Besides, why shouldn't some take more land than they could use—even if this forced those who needed it later to pay them for the privilege of using it? Why should it seem un-just, when others in their turn might do the same thing by going farther on?

But worse, the fortunes resulting from appropria-tion of land were heralded as prizes of labor—when, in reality, they have been drawn from levies upon the wages of labor. Our landed aristocracy is in its first generation in the newer states, and to a considerable degree, even in the older states. Those who profit by the increase in land values have been largely people who began life without a cent. Their great fortunes seem, to them and to many others, the best proof that existing social con-ditions reward prudence, foresight, industry, and thrift.

Whereas the truth is, these fortunes are only the gains of monopoly. They are necessarily made at the expense of labor. The fact that those thus enriched started as laborers hides this. Every ticket-holder in a lottery delights in the imagination at the magnitude of the prizes. This same feeling has prevented even the poor from quarreling with a system that has made many poor people rich.

In short, the American people have failed to see the essential injustice of private property in land, because they have not yet felt its full effects. We are insulated by the vast extent of land not yet reduced to private possession, the enormous common to which the ener-getic always turned.

This great public domain is the key fact that has formed our national character and colored our thought. It is not that we have rejected a titled aristocracy; nor that we elect our officials; nor that our laws are in the name of the people instead of a prince; nor that our judges do not wear wigs. None of these are why we have avoided the ills of the effete despotism of the Old World.

Whence comes our general intelligence, our comfort, our active invention, and our power of adaptation and assimilation? And further, our free, independent spirit, the energy and hopefulness that have marked our people? They are not causes—*they are results*. They have sprung from unfenced land.

Our vast public domain has been the force that transforms unambitious European peasants into self-reliant Western farmers. Even those dwelling in crowded cities gain a consciousness of freedom from it. It is a wellspring of hope even to those who never take refuge in it. As children grow to adulthood in Europe, they find all the best seats at the banquet of life marked "taken." They must struggle with each other for the crumbs that fall, without one chance in a thousand of finding a seat. In America, whatever their condition, there has always been the consciousness that the public domain lay before them.

The knowledge of this fact has penetrated our whole national life, both in acting and reacting. It gives us generosity and independence, elasticity and ambition. All that we are proud of in the American character, all that makes our conditions and institutions better than those of older countries, may be traced to this fact:

Land has always been cheap in the United States, because new soil has been open to the settler.

But now our advance has reached the Pacific. The public domain is almost gone. Its influence is already rapidly failing; its influence will soon end. The republic has entered upon a new era—in which the monopoly of land will show itself with accelerating effect.

I do not mean to say that there will be no public domain. For a long time to come, there will be millions of acres of public lands carried on the books. But what remains are the great mountain ranges, sterile deserts, and high plains fit only for grazing. California appears, on paper, to have the most land available. Yet much of this is covered by railroad grants. Some is held, but not yet reported by survey. Much is monopolized by locations that control the water. As a matter of fact, it is difficult to point to any part of the state where settlers can take up a farm. Weary of the quest, they end up buying land or renting it on shares. There is no scarcity of land in California—but appropriation has gotten ahead of the settlers, and manages to keep ahead.

There is no question the United States can support a population of hundreds of millions. But in view of such an increase, what becomes of the public domain? In a very short time, all useful land will have an owner.

We are making the land of a whole people the exclusive property of some. The evil effects of this process will not wait until the final appropriation of the public domain to show themselves. It is not necessary to contemplate them in the future; we may see them in the present. They have grown with our growth, and are still increasing.

We plow new fields and build new cities. We cross the land with railroads and lace the air with telegraph wires. We build schools and colleges, and add invention after invention.

Yet it becomes no easier for the masses to make a

living—on the contrary, it is becoming harder. The wealthy become wealthier; the poor become more dependent. The gulf between boss and worker grows wider. Social contrasts become sharper and beggars are common.

We call ourselves the most progressive people on earth. But what is the goal of our progress, if these are its fruits?

These are the results of private property in land. They are the effects of a principle that must act with ever increasing force. It is not that laborers have increased faster than capital. It is not that population is pressing against subsistence. It is not that machinery has made work scarce. Nor is there is any real antagonism between labor and capital.

It is simply that land is becoming more valuable. And the terms on which labor can obtain access to natural opportunities—which alone enable it to produce—are becoming harder and harder.

The public domain is receding and narrowing, while property in land is concentrating. The proportion of people with no legal right to the land on which they live grows steadily larger. The scale of cultivation recalls the latifundia that destroyed Rome. In California, a large proportion of farmland is rented—at rates from one-fourth to even one-half the crop.

Lower wages, hard times, increasing poverty are simply the results of the natural laws we have traced—laws as universal and as irresistible as gravitation.

We did not establish a republic when we set forth inalienable human rights. We shall never establish a republic until we carry out that declaration—by giving the poorest child born among us an equal right to the soil!

We did not abolish slavery with the Fourteenth Amendment. To abolish slavery we must abolish exclusive ownership of land!

Unless we come back to first principles, unless we recognize our natural perceptions of justice, unless we acknowledge the equal right of all to land—our free institutions will be in vain. And all our discoveries and inventions will only add to the force that presses the masses down.

Application of the Remedy

Chapter 31

Private Property in Land is Inconsistent with the Best Use of Land

WHEN WE CONFUSE the accidental with the essential, the result is a delusion. It is a delusion that land *must* be private property to be used effectively. It is a further delusion that making land common property—as it once was in the past—would destroy civilization and reduce us to barbarism. Lawmakers have done their best to expand this delusion, while economists have generally consented to it.

A story* tells how the Chinese accidentally discovered roast pork, after a hut caught fire. For a long time, the story goes, they thought you must burn down a house to cook a pig. Finally, a sage arose to show the people this was not necessary.

But it does not take a sage to see that absolute ownership of land is not required to make improvements—only security for those improvements.

This is obvious to anyone who looks. Private property

---

* By Charles Lamb (1775-1834), English author.

in land is as crude, wasteful, and uncertain a device for securing improvement, as burning down a house is for roasting a pig. But we do not have the excuse Lamb's characters had, for they had never heard of a pig being roasted except when a house burned.

To us, however, it is quite common for land to be improved by those who do not own it. Most of London is built on leased ground. Tenant farmers cultivate the bulk of land in Great Britain. In the United States, the same system is prevalent.

If rent were collected by the government, wouldn't land be used to the same extent as now—when rent goes to private individuals? Wouldn't land be improved as well and as securely as now? Of course! Treating land as common property in no way interferes with its proper use.

What is necessary is not private ownership, but security of improvements. It is only necessary to tell someone "whatever your labor or capital produces on this land is yours"—not "this land is yours." People sow only to reap; they build to live in houses. These are the natural rewards of their labor. Owning land has nothing to do with it.

It was for security that landholders surrendered ownership to feudal lords. When a landlord pledged not to claim rent for twenty years, Irish peasants turned a barren mountain into lush gardens. On the mere promise of a fixed ground rent for a term of years, the most costly buildings in London and New York are erected on leased ground.* If those who make such improvements are guaranteed security, we may safely abolish private property in land.

---

* For instance, Rockefeller Center, The Empire State Building, and The World Trade Center were built on leased land.

The complete recognition of common rights to land need not interfere, in any way, with the complete recognition of individual rights to improvements or production. Two people may own a ship without sawing it in half. A railway may have thousands of shareholders, yet run as well as under a single owner.

Everything could go on exactly as it does now—and still recognize the common right to land—simply by appropriating rent for the common benefit.

In the center of San Francisco there is a lot in which the common rights of the people are still legally recognized. It is not cut up into tiny pieces; nor is it unused. It is covered with fine buildings, which are the property of private individuals. They stand there in perfect security. The only difference between this lot and those around it is this: Its rent goes to the common school fund—while the other rent goes into private pockets. What is to prevent the land of the whole country being held by the people in the same manner?

Consider those conditions commonly thought to demand private ownership. It would be difficult to find a place where these exist in higher degree than certain islands in the Aleutian Archipelago of Alaska, which are the breeding grounds of the fur seal. To prevent their utter destruction, the harvest of furs must be carefully managed. For without this resource, the islands are of no use.

If such a fishery were open to anyone, it would be in the interest of each party to kill as many as they could at once, without reference to the future. In a few seasons it would be utterly destroyed, as fisheries in other oceans have been.

But despite this danger, it is not necessary to make

these islands private property. Instead, the islands have been leased out and have already added over two million dollars to the national treasury—without diminishing their value. Under the careful management of the Alaska Fur Company, the seals have increased, not decreased.

These islands are still the common property of the people of the United States. Yet for far less convincing reasons, the great public domain of the American people has been made into private property as fast as anybody could take it.

Far from private property being necessary for the proper use of land, the contrary is true. Treating land as private property, in actual fact, *stands in the way of its proper use.*

If land were treated as public property, it would be used and improved as soon as there was need. But as private property, an individual owner is allowed to prevent others from using what the owner cannot—or will not—use. Large tracts are kept idle at the caprice of the owner, held out of use waiting for higher prices. Meanwhile, others are forced to use places where their labor will be far less productive. In every city, valuable lots may be seen vacant for this reason. This means of using land is as wasteful, unnecessary, and uncertain as burning down houses to roast pigs.

If the best use of land is the test, then private property in land is condemned—as it is condemned by every other consideration.

Chapter 32
Securing Equal Rights To Land

WE HAVE WEIGHED every objection and found nothing—in either justice or efficiency—to deter us from making land common property by confiscating rent. But the question of method remains: How shall we do it?

We could simply abolish private titles and declare all land public property. Then, lease lots to the highest bidders, under conditions guaranteeing the right to improvements. This would give a complex society the same equality of rights achieved in simpler communities through equal shares of land. And by leasing land to whoever could obtain the most from it, we would secure the greatest production.

But such a plan, though perfectly feasible, is not the best option. Rather, I propose to accomplish the same results in a simpler, easier, and quieter way.

To formally confiscate all land would involve a needless shock, and would require a needless extension of government. Both can be avoided. Great changes are best brought about under old forms. When nature makes a higher form, it takes a lower one and develops it. This, too, is the law of social growth. Let us work with it.

I do not propose to purchase or confiscate private property in land. Let those who now hold land retain possession, if they want. They may buy and sell or bequeath it.

Let them even continue to call it "their" land. We may safely leave them the shell, if we take the kernel.

It is not necessary to confiscate land—only to confiscate rent.

Taking rent for public use does not require that the state lease land; that would risk favoritism, collusion, and corruption. No new government agency need be created; the machinery already exists. Instead of extending it, all we have to do is to simplify and reduce it.

Government already takes some rent in taxation. With a few changes in our tax laws, we could take almost all. Letting owners keep a small percentage would cost much less than renting through a state agency. Using the existing machinery of government, we may assert the common right to land without any shock.

Therefore, I propose that we appropriate land rent for public use, through taxation.

This simple yet effective solution will raise wages, increase the earnings of capital, eliminate poverty, reduce crime, and provide full employment. It will unleash human power and elevate society. In its form, ownership of land would remain just as it is now. No owner need be dispossessed. No restriction need be placed upon the amount of land any one could hold.

If rent were taken by the state in taxes, then land would really be common property—no matter in whose name or in what parcels it was held. Every member of the community would participate in the advantages of its ownership.

Land values increase as population grows and progress advances. In any civilized country, this is enough to bear all government expenses. In better developed countries, it is much more than enough. In fact, when rent exceeds current government revenues, it will be necessary to actually increase the land tax to absorb excess rent. Taxation of rent would increase as we abolish other taxes. So, we may put our proposition into practical form by proposing:

To abolish all taxes—except on land values.

This is the first step in the practical struggle. Experience has taught me that wherever this idea is considered, it makes headway. But few who would benefit most from it see its full significance and power. It is difficult for workingmen to give up the notion that there is some basic antagonism between capital and labor. It is difficult for small farmers and homesteaders to get over the idea that this plan would unduly tax them. It is difficult for both classes to let go of the idea that exempting capital from taxation would benefit only the rich.

A great wrong always dies hard. These erroneous ideas spring from confused thought. But behind ignorance and prejudice, there is a powerful interest—one that has dominated literature, education, and public opinion. The great wrong that condemns millions to poverty will not die without a bitter struggle.

Chapter 33

The Canons of Taxation

THE BEST MEANS of raising public revenues will be one that meets these conditions:

1. It should bear as lightly as possible on production— least impeding the growth of the general fund, from which taxes must be paid and the community maintained.

2. It should be easily and cheaply collected, and it should fall as directly as possible on the ultimate payers— taking as little as possible from the people beyond what it yields the government.

3. It should be certain—offering the least opportunity for abuse and corruption, and the least temptation for evasion.

4. It should bear equally—giving no one an advantage, nor putting another at a disadvantage.

Let us consider what form of taxation best fits these conditions.

1. The Effect of Taxes on Production

It is obvious that all taxes come from the product of land and labor. There is no source of wealth other than the union of human exertion with the materials and forces of nature. But equal taxes may have very different effects on production, depending on how they are imposed.

Taxes that reduce the rewards of producers lessen the incentive to produce. Taxes based on the use of any of the three factors of production—land, labor, or capital—inevitably discourage production. Such taxes introduce artificial obstacles to the creation of wealth.

The method of taxation is, in fact, just as important as the amount. A small burden poorly placed may hinder a horse that could easily carry a much larger load properly adjusted. Similarly, taxes may impoverish people and destroy their power to produce wealth. Yet the same amount of taxes, if levied another way, could be borne with ease. A tax on date trees caused Egyptian farmers to cut down their trees; but twice the tax, imposed on land, had no such result.

Now, taxes on labor as it is exerted, on wealth as it is used as capital, or on land as it is developed will clearly discourage production—much more than taxes levied on laborers whether they work or play, on wealth whether used productively or fruitlessly, or on land whether cultivated or left idle.

To a greater or lesser degree, impediments to production are characteristic of most taxes modern governments use to raise revenue. Many kinds of production and exchange are seriously crippled by taxes that divert industry from more productive to less productive forms. These include all taxes on manufacturing, all taxes on commerce, all taxes on capital, and all taxes on improvements. All such taxes tend to reduce the production of wealth. Their tendency is the same as the Egyptian tax on date trees, though their effect may not be seen as clearly. They should never be used when it is possible to use means that do not check production.

The great class of taxes that do not interfere with production are taxes on monopolies. The profit of monopoly is in itself a tax on production. Taxing it would simply divert into public coffers what producers must pay anyway.

There are various sorts of monopolies. Some businesses are, in their nature, monopolies. These are generally the proper function of government. Delivering the mail, for example. For the same reason, railroads should belong to the public, as roads do.

Patent and copyright laws create temporary monopolies. Though the two are often confused, they are not alike.* Indeed, they are essentially different. Copyright does not prevent others from using facts, ideas, knowledge, laws, or combinations for similar productions. It only prohibits using the identical form. That is, it protects the actual labor expended in producing the work. It does not interfere with the similar right of anyone else to do likewise. It rests, therefore, upon our natural, moral right to enjoy the products of our own exertion—and it would be unjust and unwise to tax them.

The patent, on the other hand, prohibits anyone from doing a similar thing. Therefore, it is an interference with the equal liberty on which the right of ownership rests. Everyone has a moral right to think what I think, or to perceive what I perceive, or to do what I do. It does not matter whether someone gets the hint from me or independently of me.

Discovery can give no right of ownership. Whatever

---

* George said that he fell into this error himself in the first edition of this book. He subsequently acknowledged and corrected it.

is discovered must have already been there to be discovered. If someone makes a wheelbarrow, a book or a picture, the inventor has a moral right to that particular product, but no right to prevent others from making similar things. Though such a prohibition is intended to stimulate discovery and invention, in the long run it actually discourages them.

Finally, there are also onerous monopolies resulting from the aggregation of capital in certain businesses. (See Chapter 20.) It would be much better to abolish such monopolies than to try to tax the returns of their monopoly.

But all these other monopolies are trivial compared with the monopoly of land. The value of land expresses a monopoly, pure and simple. The value of a railroad or a telegraph line, or the price of gas or a patent medicine may partly express the cost of monopoly. But it also expresses the effort of labor and capital. On the other hand, the value of land does not include labor or capital at all. It expresses nothing but the advantage of appropriation. It is, in every respect, tailored for taxation.

A tax on land (unless it exceeds actual rent) cannot check production in the slightest degree—unlike taxes on commodities, or exchange, or capital, or any of the tools or processes of production. The value of land does not express the reward of production. It is not like the value of cattle, crops, buildings, or any of the things called personal property and improvements.

Land value expresses the exchange value of monopoly. It is not in any way the creation of the individual who owns the land. It is created by the growth of the community.

Hence, the community can take it all without reducing

the incentive to improvement, and without decreasing the production of wealth. Taking the entire rent in taxes will not reduce the wages of labor or the reward of capital one iota. Nor will it increase the price of a single commodity. It will not make production more difficult in any way.

But there is more than this. Taxes on land actually tend to increase production—by destroying speculative rent, which impedes production when valuable land is withheld from use. Industrial depressions originate in speculative land values. They then propagate themselves over the whole civilized world, paralyzing industry.

Taking rent for public use through taxation would prevent all this. If land were taxed near its rental value, no one could afford to hold unused land. This land would be made available to those who would use it. Consequently, labor and capital could produce much more with the same exertion.

With regard to production, a tax on land value is the best tax that can be imposed. Tax manufacturing, and you inhibit manufacturing. Tax improvements, and you lessen improvement. Tax commerce, and you prevent exchange. Tax capital, and you drive it away. But take the whole value of land in taxation, and the only effect will be to stimulate industry, open new opportunities, and increase the production of wealth.

2. Ease and Cost of Collection

Of all taxes, a tax on land is the easiest and cheapest to collect. Land cannot be hidden or carried off. Its value can be easily determined. Once the assessment is made, nothing but a receiver is required for collection.

The machinery for that purpose already exists. Part of

public revenue currently comes from taxes on land. We could just as easily collect all the rent as a part of it. Substituting this single tax for all other taxes would save the entire cost of collecting them. What an enormous saving this might be can be inferred by observing the horde of officials now engaged in this endeavor. This saving would greatly reduce the difference between what taxation now costs the people and the revenue it yields to the government.

But a land tax would reduce this difference in an even more important way. A tax on land is paid directly by those on whom it falls. It does not add to prices. In contrast, taxes on things of variable quantity are shifted from seller to buyer in the course of exchange, and they increase as they go.

A tax on money loaned has often been attempted. In this case, the lender will simply charge the tax to the borrower. The borrower must pay the increase or not get the loan. If the borrower uses it in business, the tax must be regained from customers. Otherwise the business becomes unprofitable.

If we tax buildings, the tenants must finally pay it. Construction will stop until rents rise enough to pay the regular profit and the tax besides.

If we tax goods, manufacturers or importers will charge higher prices to wholesalers, wholesalers to retailers, and retailers to consumers. The tax ultimately falls on consumers, who pay not only the tax itself—but a profit on it at each step of the process.

Each dealer requires profit on capital advanced to pay taxes, as much as profit on capital advanced to pay for goods.

For instance, an importer in San Francisco sells Manila cigars to wholesalers for $70 a thousand. The cigars cost $14, while the customs duty adds $56. Dealers must make a profit not just on $14 (the real cost of the cigars), but on the $70 they must shell out (cost plus duty). In this way all taxes that add to prices are shifted from hand to hand. They increase as they go, until they ultimately rest on the consumer—who ends up paying much more than what is received by the government.

Taxes raise prices by increasing the cost of production. This, in turn, reduces supply. But land is not something made by human production. Taxes on rent, therefore, cannot check supply.

Though taxing land makes landowners pay more, it gives them no power to obtain more. For there is no way this can reduce the supply of land. On the contrary, it forces those who hold land on speculation to sell or rent for what they can get. A land tax increases competition among owners. This lowers the price of land.

Thus, in all respects, a tax on land values is the cheapest way by which a large revenue can be raised. It gives government the largest net revenue in proportion to the amount taken from the people.

3. Certainty of Collection

Certainty is an important element in taxation. Collection provides opportunities for corruption on one side, and evasion or fraud on the other. The bulk of our revenues are collected by methods to be condemned on this ground, if on no other.

In earlier days, coasts were lined with one army of people trying to prevent smuggling, and another engaged in evading them. Clearly, the maintenance of both groups had to come from the production of labor and capital. The expenses and profits of smugglers, as well as the pay and bribes of custom officers, constituted a tax upon the industry of the nation. And this was in addition to what was received by the government!

We can also include all inducements to assessors, and moneys expended electing pliable officials to procure favorable acts or decisions. And do not forget all the expenses of legal proceedings and punishments, not only to the government but to those prosecuted. These evasions take so much from the general fund of wealth, without adding to revenue.

Yet this is the least part of the cost. Taxes that lack the element of certainty have the most terrible effect upon public morals. Our revenue laws might as well be entitled, "Acts to promote the corruption of public officials, to suppress honesty and encourage fraud, to promote perjury, and to divorce law from justice." This is their true character, and they succeed admirably.

But we need not resort to arbitrary assessments. A tax on land values is the least arbitrary of taxes, and possesses the highest degree of certainty. It may be assessed and collected with precision because of the immovable and unconcealable nature of land itself.

Taxes on land may be collected to the last cent. Though assessment of land is now often unequal, assessment of personal property is far more uneven. Inequalities arise mostly from taxing improvements along with land. If all taxes were placed on land values, regardless of improvements, the design of taxation would be simple and clear. It would be open to public observation. Assessment could be made with the certainty of a real estate agent determining the price a seller can get for a lot.

4. Equality

The common idea that our system of taxing everything vainly attempts to carry out is this: Citizens should pay taxes in proportion to their means, or in proportion to their incomes. But even ignoring all the insurmountable practical difficulties of taxation according to means, it is clear that justice cannot be attained through this.

Let us turn to Nature and read the mandates of justice in its laws. Nature gives to labor, and to labor alone. Even in a Garden of Eden, people would starve without exertion. Now, take two people of equal incomes. One gets income from labor; the other, from the rent of land. Is it just that they should contribute equally to the expenses of the state? Certainly not.

The worker's income represents wealth created and added to the general wealth of the state. The landowner's income represents only wealth taken from the general stock, with nothing given in return. The worker's right to income comes from the justification of Nature, which returns wealth to labor. The landowner's claim is a mere fictitious right, created by municipal regulation. It is unknown and unrecognized by Nature. It is a monopoly of natural opportunities—gifts that Nature offers impartially to all, and in which all have an equal birthright.

Value created and maintained by the community can justly be called upon to meet community expenses. What kinds of value are these? Only the value of land. This value does not arise until a community is formed; it grows as the community grows. It exists only as the community exists. Scatter the largest community, and land, once so valuable, would have no value at all. With every increase of population, the value of land rises; with every decrease, it falls.

A tax upon land values is, therefore, the most just and equal of all taxes. It falls only on those who receive a unique and valuable benefit from society. And it falls on them in proportion to the benefit they receive. It is taking by the community, for the use of the community, from the value that is the creation of the community. It is the application of the common property to common uses.

When all rent is taken by taxation for the needs of the community, equality will be attained. No citizen will have an advantage over any other, except through personal industry, skill, and intelligence. People will gain what they fairly earn. Only then, and not until then, will labor get its full reward, and capital its natural return.

Chapter 34
Endorsements And Objections

EVER SINCE the nature of rent and law of rent were first determined, every credible economist has acknowledged, expressly or tacitly, the grounds by which we have concluded that a tax on land values is the best method of raising public revenues.*

David Ricardo says a tax on rent would fall wholly on landlords, and could not be shifted to consumers. Rent would not be altered by such a tax, and it would not discourage the cultivation of land at the margin.

John McCulloch objects to a land tax. However, he bases this solely on the assumption that we cannot distinguish the value of land from improvements. But supposing we could? He agrees we could then tax the entire amount paid to landlords for permission to use the natural powers of the soil. He also agrees they could not pass this on to anyone else, and that it would not affect prices.

John Stuart Mill not only admits all this, but expressly declares the expediency and justice of a tax on rent. He asks what right landlords have to accept riches that come

---

* We have paraphrased quotations found in the original text. These writers, all British, include: David Ricardo (1772-1823). John Ramsey McCulloch (1789-1864). John Stuart Mill (1806-1873). Millicent Garrett Fawcett (1847-1929).

to them from the general progress of society—without any work, risk, or thrift on their part? He proposes to take all future increase, since they belong to society by natural right.

Millicent Fawcett says that land tax is in the nature of a rent paid by the landowner to the state. The "economic perfection" of this system is obvious, she notes.

In fact, the accepted doctrine of rent involves the idea that rent should be the particular subject of taxation, both on grounds of practicality and justice. It may be found, in embryonic form, in the works of all economists who have accepted Ricardo's law of rent.

Why didn't they take these principles to their inevitable conclusion, as we have done? Apparently, there was an unwillingness to offend the enormous interests involved in private ownership of land. In addition, false theories about the causes of poverty have dominated economic thought.

But there has been one school of economists who perceived what is clear to man's natural perception when not influenced by habit. Revenues from common property—land—should be appropriated for common purposes. The French *Economistes* or Physiocrats* of the eighteenth century proposed what I have—to abolish all taxes except those on the value of land. Regrettably, the French Revolution overwhelmed their ideas just as they were gaining strength among the thinking classes.

Without knowing anything of their doctrines, I have reached the same conclusion, on grounds that cannot be questioned. The only objection found in standard econom-

---

* The Physiocrats were led by Francois Quesnay (1694-1774), and his student, Robert Jacques Turgot (1727-1781).

ics texts actually concedes its advantages. That is, the difficulty of separating land from improvements might cause us to tax something else besides rent.

Macaulay* once remarked that if the law of gravity were unfavorable to any substantial financial interest, there would soon be no lack of arguments against it. Here is an illustration of this truth!

Assume that it is impossible to perfectly separate the value of land from improvements. Is the fear of accidentally taxing *some* improvements any reason to continue taxing *all* improvements? To tax values that labor and capital have intimately combined with land might discourage production. How much greater discouragement must come from taxing not only these, but *all* values that labor and capital create?

But, as a matter of fact, the value of land can always be readily distinguished from the value of improvements. In countries like the United States much valuable land has never been improved. In many states, assessors regularly estimate the value of land and the value of improvements separately. Only afterward are they reunited under the term "real estate."

Where land has been occupied from time immemorial, there is still no difficulty determining the value of bare land. Frequently, land is owned by one person and buildings by another. When a fire destroys improvements, a clear and definite value remains in the land. In the oldest country in the world, no difficulty whatever can attend the separation. We need only separate the value of clearly distinguishable improvements, made within a reasonable

---

* Thomas Macaulay (1800-1859), English historian.

period of time, from the value of the land, should the improvements be destroyed. This, manifestly, is all that justice or policy requires.

Absolute accuracy is impossible under any system. Attempting to separate everything the human race has done from what nature originally provided would be both absurd and impractical. In ancient times, the Romans may have drained a swamp or terraced a hill. These are now as much a part of the natural advantage of the British Isles as though the work had been done by an earthquake or a glacier. After a certain lapse of time, the value of such permanent improvements would be considered as having lapsed into that of the land. Accordingly, they would be taxed as land.

But this could have no deterrent effect on such improvements. Such works are frequently undertaken on land leased for a certain number of years. The fact is, each generation builds and improves for itself, not for the remote future. Furthermore, each generation is heir not only to the natural powers of the earth, but to all that remains of the work of past generations.

Another objection may be that taxation and representation cannot safely be divorced. It may be desirable to combine political power with the consciousness of public burdens, but the present system certainly does not secure it. Indirect taxes are mostly raised from those who pay little or nothing consciously. In our large cities, elections are decided by things similar to what influenced the Roman masses, who cared about nothing but bread and circuses.

Substituting a single land tax for numerous others would hardly lessen the number of conscious taxpayers.

Instead, the division of land now held on speculation would greatly increase the number. It would equalize the distribution of wealth. Even the poorest would be raised above abject poverty, while overgrown fortunes would be cut down.

The dangerous classes politically are the very rich and very poor. A person gains interest in government from feeling part of the community and its prosperity.

But if the tax on land values is so beneficial, why does government resort to so many different ones? The answer is obvious! A tax on land values is the only tax that does not distribute itself—that is, it cannot be passed on to others. It falls only on landowners. There is no way they can shift the burden to anyone else. Hence, a large and powerful interest is opposed to taxing land values.

Businesses do not oppose taxes they can easily shift from their own shoulders. In fact, they frequently try to maintain them. So do other powerful interests who might profit from the higher prices such taxes bring about. A multitude of taxes have been imposed with a view toward private advantage, rather than raising revenue.

The ingenuity of politicians has been applied to devising taxes that drain the wages of labor and the earnings of capital like a vampire sucking the blood of its victim. Nearly all of these taxes are ultimately paid by that indefinable being, "the consumer." They come in such small amounts, and in such insidious ways, that we do not notice them.

The Civil War was the golden opportunity of these special interests. Taxes were piled on every possible thing—not so much to raise revenue as to enable particular classes to participate in the advantages of tax-gathering and tax-pocketing.

For this reason, those taxes costing people the least have been easier to abolish than those costing the most. License taxes are generally favored by those on whom they are imposed. They tend to keep others from entering the business. Large manufacturers are frequently grateful for taxes on goods for similar reasons. This was seen in the opposition of distillers to the reduction of the whisky tax. Duties on imports tend to give certain producers special advantages.

In all such cases, special interests capable of concerted action favor those taxes. But a solid and powerful interest bitterly opposes taxing land values. Nonetheless, once the truth I am trying to make clear is understood by the masses, a union of political forces strong enough to carry it into practice will become possible.

Chapter 35

The Effect on Production

THE ADVANTAGES OF A SINGLE TAX on land become increasingly clear the more they are considered. Abolishing other taxes would be like removing an immense weight from a powerful spring. These taxes now hamper every type of exchange and every form of industry. Remove these burdens and production would proceed at an unimaginable pace. This, in its turn, would further increase land values, and create an even bigger surplus for common purposes.

The present method of taxation acts like artificial mountains and deserts. It costs more to get goods through a custom house than it does to carry them around the world. It penalizes industry and skill.

Suppose I work hard to build a good house, while you are content to live in a hovel. The taxman makes me pay a penalty every year for my effort by taxing me more. If I save while you squander, I am taxed while you are exempt. If I build something useful, I must pay for my industry as if I had done an injury to the state. If I offer a service to the public, I am taxed as though it were a public nuisance.

We say we want capital, but if I accumulate it I am charged as though it were a privilege.

The full burden of these taxes on production is realized only by those who have attempted to follow our system of taxation through its ramifications. As I noted, the heaviest part of taxation falls in increased prices. Abolishing these taxes would lift the whole enormous weight of taxation from productive industry. All would be free to make or save, to buy or sell, without being fined by taxes.

The state currently tells producers: "The more you add to the general wealth, the more you will be taxed." Instead, the state should say: "Be as industrious, thrifty, and enterprising as you choose. Keep your full reward. You won't be fined for adding to the community's wealth."

The whole community will gain by this—for there is a natural reward to the community as well. We cannot keep the good we do, any more than the harm. Every productive enterprise yields collateral advantages, in addition to what it returns to those who undertake it. Building a house, factory, ship, or railroad benefits others besides those who get the direct profits.

Let the individual producer keep all the direct benefits of exertion. Let the worker have the full reward of labor. Give the capitalist the full return on capital. The more labor and capital produce, the larger the common wealth in which all share.

This general gain is expressed in a definite and concrete form through the value of land, or its rent. The state may take from this fund, while leaving labor and capital their full reward. And with increased production, this fund would increase commensurately.

Shifting the burden of taxation, from production and

exchange to land value (or rent), would not merely give new stimulus to the production of wealth—it would open new opportunities. Under this system, no one would hold land without using it. So land now withheld from use would be thrown open to improvement.

The selling price of land would fall, and land speculation would receive its death blow. Land monopolization would no longer pay. Millions of acres, where others are now shut out by high prices, would be abandoned or sold at trivial prices.

This is true not only on the frontier, but in cities as well. The simple device of placing all taxes on the value of land would, in effect, put land up for auction to whoever would pay the highest rent to the state. The demand for land determines its value. If taxes took almost all that value, anyone holding land without using it would have to pay nearly what it would be worth to anyone else who wanted to use it.

This would apply not just to agricultural land, but to all land. Mineral land would be thrown open, too. In the heart of the city, no one could afford to keep land from its most profitable use. On the outskirts, no one could demand more for land than what its current potential use would warrant.

Everywhere land had attained a value, taxation would drive improvement. It would not act as a fine upon improvement, as it does now. Whoever planted an orchard, sowed a field, built a house, or erected a factory—no matter how costly—would pay no more in taxes than if the land were kept idle. The owner of a vacant city lot would pay for the privilege of keeping other people off. It would cost as much to keep a row of tumble-down shanties as a grand hotel or great warehouse.

Currently, everywhere labor is most productive, a bonus must be paid before labor can be exerted. This would be eliminated. Farmers would not have to mortgage their labor for years to obtain land to cultivate. City homeowners would not have to lay out as much for small lots as for the houses built on them. A company building a factory would not have to spend a great part of its capital for a site. Plus, all the other taxes now levied on machinery and improvements would be removed.

Consider the effect of such a change on the labor market. Competition would no longer be one-sided. Workers now compete with each other, cutting wages down to bare subsistence. Instead, employers would have to compete for labor. Wages would rise to the fair earnings of labor.

The greatest of all competitors would have entered into the labor market—one whose demand cannot be satisfied until all desire is satisfied: the demand of labor itself. Employers would have to bid not only against other employers—all feeling the stimulus of greater trade and increased profits—but against the ability of laborers to become their own employers. For natural opportunities would now be opened to them by a tax preventing monopolization.

Natural opportunities would be free to labor. Capital and improvements would be exempt from tax. Exchange would be unhampered. Recurring depressions would cease. Every wheel of production would be set in motion. Demand would keep pace with supply, and supply with demand. Trade would grow in every direction, and wealth increase on every hand.

Chapter 36

The Effect on The Distribution of Wealth

THE ADVANTAGES of a tax on land values—great as they already appear—cannot be fully appreciated until we consider the effect on the distribution of wealth.

All civilized countries have an unequal distribution of wealth that grows steadily worse. The cause, we have found, is that ownership of land provides greater and greater power to appropriate the wealth produced by labor and capital as material progress goes on. We can counteract this tendency by removing all taxes on labor and capital—and putting them on rent. If we went so far as to take all the rent in taxes, the cause of inequality would be totally destroyed.

Wealth produced in every community would be divided into two parts. One part would be distributed to individual producers—as wages and interest—according to what each had contributed to production. The other part—land rent collected as taxes—would go to the community as a whole. It would be distributed as public benefits to all members of that community. And justly so. Wages and interest represent the result of individual effort. Land rent represents the increased power that the community, as a whole, provides to the individual.

Rent, under this system, would promote equality, instead of causing inequality as it does now. To fully understand this effect, let's review some principles we have already determined.

Wages and interest are set by the margin of production—what can be made on land with no rent. Labor and capital keep only what is left *after* rent and taxes. Collecting rent through taxes would virtually abolish private ownership in land, because it would destroy speculative monopolization and reduce the price of land. This would increase wages and interest, by opening opportunities that are now monopolized. A new equilibrium would be established, with wages and interest much higher.

Productivity increases with population, with laborsaving invention, with improved methods of exchange. These benefits could no longer be monopolized. Any increase in rent arising from these advances would benefit the whole community. All would be richer, not just one class.

Further, if it were possible to calculate the full cost of poverty, it would be appalling. New York City alone spends over seven million dollars a year on charity. Yet spending by government, private charities, and individuals combined is merely the smallest item in the account. Consider the following items: the lost earnings of wasted labor; the social cost of reckless and idle habits; the appalling statistics on mortality, especially infant mortality, among the poor; the proliferation of liquor stores and bars as poverty deepens; the thieves, prostitutes, beggars, and tramps bred by poverty; and the cost of guarding society against them.

These are just part of the full burden that unjust distribution of wealth places on the aggregate society. The ignorance and vice produced by inequality show themselves in the stupidity and corruption of government, and the waste of public funds.

Appropriating rent for public purposes would not merely stop waste and relieve society of these enormous losses. Wages would rise and new avenues of employment would appear. Furthermore, it is well-known that labor is most productive where wages are highest. Higher wages increase self-respect, hope, and energy. This is true the world over. Mind, not muscle, is the greatest agent of production. The physical power evolved in the human frame is one of the weakest forces of nature. With human intelligence, matter becomes plastic to human will.

Who can say what level the wealth-producing capacity of labor might reach, if producers receive their fair share of its advantages? American invention and the American aptitude for laborsaving processes are the result of higher wages. Had our producers been condemned to the low reward of the Egyptian fellah or Chinese coolie, we would be drawing water by hand and transporting goods on our shoulders.

Increasing the reward of labor and capital would stimulate invention even further. The harmful effects of laborsaving machinery on workers would disappear. Currently, many people regard automation as a curse, not a blessing. By removing these defects, every new power would improve the condition of all.

The simple plan of taxation I propose would equalize the distribution of wealth, preventing waste and increasing productivity.

I shall not deny this may lessen the intensity with which wealth is pursued. It seems to me that in a society where no one fears poverty, no one would struggle and strain for great wealth, as people do now. Certainly the spectacle of people slaving away for the sake of dying rich is unnatural and absurd. In a society where fear of want had been removed, we would view those who acquire more than they can use as we now look on someone who wears a dozen hats.

Though we may lose this incentive, we can surely spare it. Whatever its function may have been in an earlier stage of development, it is not needed now. The dangers threatening our civilization do not come from weakness in production. They come from the unequal distribution of wealth.

Chapter 37
The Effect on Individuals and Classes

WE WOULD CONFISCATE RENT by placing taxes only on land. On first hearing this, landholders are likely to be alarmed; small farmers and homeowners will be told this would rob them of their hard-earned property. But a moment's reflection will show something different.

Everyone whose interest as worker and/or capitalist exceeds their interest as landowner will gain. Even large landholders ultimately will benefit, for production will increase much more than the loss to private land ownership. The whole community will share in these gains and in a healthier social condition.

It is obvious that those who live by wages, of head or hand, will benefit greatly: laborers, clerks, mechanics, and professionals. So will those who live partly by wages and partly by earnings of capital: merchants, manufacturers, and traders; from the peddler to the steamship owner. Furthermore, we may include all those whose income comes from investments other than land.

Consider a merchant or professional with a house and lot. She will not be harmed by our change, but will gain. The selling price of the lot will diminish*—but its

---

* The rent of land is capitalized into a selling price. As the community approaches collecting 100% of the rent, the selling price of land will approach zero.

usefulness will not. It will serve her purposes as well as ever. The value of other lots diminish in the same ratio, so she retains the same security of having a lot as she had before. If she needs a larger lot, or if her children need lots, she will reap the advantage. She is no more a loser than if she bought a pair of boots that later sell for less. The boots are just as useful, and the next pair will be cheaper.

Furthermore, though taxes on land will be higher, she will be free from taxes on the house and improvements, on furniture and personal property, and on all she and her family eat, drink, and wear. Meanwhile her earnings will increase greatly because of higher wages, constant employment, and greater trade. Her only loss would be if she wants to sell her lot without getting another. This is a small loss compared with a great gain.

The same is true of the farmer. I am not speaking of "farmers" who never touch a plow; I mean working farmers. Of everyone above mere laborers, they have the most to gain from placing all taxes on land values. This may seem contradictory until we fully understand the proposition.

Farmers generally sense they don't get as good a living as their hard work ought to earn them. However, they may not be able to trace the cause. The fact is, taxation, as now levied, falls on them with exceptional severity. All their improvements are taxed: houses, barns, fences, crops, and stock. Their personal property cannot be concealed or undervalued as easily as the more valuable kinds concentrated in cities. Not only are they taxed on personal property and improvements, which the owners of unused land escape; even worse, their land is generally taxed at a higher rate than land held on speculation—simply because it *is* improved.

A single tax on land values would fall hardest not on agricultural districts, where land is comparatively cheap, but on towns and cities, where prices are high. Taxes, being levied on the value of bare land, would fall as heavily on unimproved as improved land. Acre for acre, the improved and cultivated farm—with its buildings, fences, orchards, crops, and stock—would be taxed no more than unused land of equal quality. Thus, speculation would be reduced.

Destroying speculative land values would tend to diffuse population where it is too dense, and concentrate it where it is too sparse. City tenements would give way to homes with gardens. People in the country would share more of the economies and social life of the city.

Working farmers are not just landowners—they are laborers and capitalists, as well. They earn their living by their labor and their capital. To varying degrees, this is true of all landholders. While some may not be laborers, it would be hard to find one who is not a capitalist. Indeed, the general rule is: the larger the landowner, the greater the capitalist. This is so true that the two are often confused in common thought. Putting all taxes on land would largely reduce all great fortunes, but it would hardly leave the rich penniless.

Not only would wealth increase enormously—it would be equally distributed. This does not mean each individual would get the same amount. That would not be equal distribution, since different individuals have different powers and different desires. Rather, wealth would be distributed in accordance to how much each contributed. This would vary with the industry, skill, knowledge, or prudence of each individual.

Wealth would no longer concentrate in those who do not produce, taken from those who do. The idle rich would no longer lounge in luxury, while those who actually produce settle for the barest necessities. Any inequalities that continued to exist would be of natural causes. They would not be artificial inequalities, produced by denial of natural law. The great cause of inequality—monopoly of land—would be gone.

Chapter 38

Changes in Society

WE PROPOSE to readjust the very foundation of society. Space does not permit an elaborate discussion of all the changes this would bring about. Once general principles are applied, the details will be easily adjusted. Still, some of the main features merit mention.

Most notably, government could be vastly simplified. We could eliminate an immense and complicated network of governmental machinery needed to collect taxes, prevent and punish evasion, and check revenue from many different sources.

A similar saving would occur in the administration of justice. Much of the business of civil courts arises from disputes over ownership of land. If all occupants were, essentially, rent-paying tenants of the state, such cases would cease. With poverty ended, morality would grow stronger, reducing other business of these courts.

Wages would rise and everyone would be able to make an easy and comfortable living. This would immediately reduce, and soon eliminate, thieves, swindlers, and other criminals who arise from the unequal distribution of wealth. This would lighten the administration of criminal law, with all its paraphernalia of police, prisons, and penitentiaries. We should eliminate not only many judges, bailiffs, clerks, and jailers, but also the great host of lawyers now maintained at the expense of those who actually produce wealth. They would cease to be a drain on the vital force and attention of society. Talent now wasted in legal subtleties would be turned to higher pursuits.

The legislative, judicial, and executive functions of government would be vastly simplified. Public debts and standing armies historically were products of the change from feudal to allodial (i.e., private) land tenures. Once we revert to the idea that land is the common right of the people of a country, I do not think these would remain for long. Public debts could readily be paid off by a tax that would not lessen the wages of labor nor check production. As intelligence and independence grow among the masses, standing armies would soon disappear.

Society would approach the ideal of Jeffersonian democracy; repressive government would be abolished. Yet, at the same time and in the same degree, it would become possible to realize the goals of socialism without coercion. With many of its present operations simplified or eliminated, government could assume other functions that now demand recognition. Surplus revenue from land taxation would grow as material progress increased its speed, tending to increase rent. Government would change its character and become the administrator of a great cooperative society. It would merely be the agency by which common property was administered for common benefit.

Does this seem impracticable? Consider the vast changes in social life if labor kept its full reward. It would banish want and the fear of want. Everyone would have freedom to develop in natural harmony.

We are apt to assume that greed is the strongest human motive and that fear of punishment is required to keep people honest. It seems selfish interests are always stronger than common interests. Nothing could be further from the truth.

Don't these behaviors arise because of want? Poverty is the relentless hell waiting beneath civilized society. Poverty is not just deprivation; it is shame and degradation. It is only natural that people should make every effort to escape from this hell. People often do mean, greedy, grasping things in the effort to save their families, their children, from want.

In this struggle, one of the strongest motives of human action—the desire for approval—is sometimes distorted into the most abnormal forms. The hunger for the respect, admiration, or sympathy of our fellows is instinctive and universal. It is seen everywhere. It is as powerful among the most primitive savages as it is among the most highly cultivated members of polished society. It triumphs over comfort, over pain, even over fear of death. It dictates both the most trivial and the most important actions.

People admire what they desire. The sting of want—or fear of want—makes people admire riches above all else. To become wealthy is to become respected, admired, and influential.

Get money! Honestly, if you can—but at any rate get money. This is the lesson society daily and hourly exhorts. People instinctively admire virtue and truth. But poverty makes them admire riches even more. It is well to be honest and just, but those who get a million dollars by fraud and injustice have more admiration and influence than those who refuse it. They are on the list of "substantial citizens," sought and flattered by men and women. They may be patrons of arts, friends of the refined. Their alms may feed the poor, help the struggling, and brighten desolate places. Noble institutions commemorate their names.

Long after they have accumulated enough wealth to satisfy every desire, they go on working, scheming, and striving to add more riches. They are driven by the desire "to be something." This is not from tyrannical habit, but from the subtler satisfactions riches give: power and influence, being looked up to and respected. Their wealth not only raises them above want, but makes them people of distinction in the community. This is what makes the rich so afraid to part with money, and so anxious to get more.

The change I have proposed would destroy the conditions that distort these impulses. It would transmute forces that now disintegrate society into forces to unite it. Give labor its full earnings and expanded opportunity. Take, for the benefit of the whole community, that which the growth of the community creates. Then poverty would vanish.

Production would be set free. People would worry about finding employment no more than they worry about finding air to breathe. The enormous increase of wealth would give even the poorest ample comfort. The march of science and invention would benefit all.

With fear of poverty gone, the admiration of riches would decay. People would seek the respect and approval of their fellows in ways other than the acquisition and display of wealth. The skill, attention, and integrity now used for private gain would be brought to the management of public affairs and the administration of common funds.

The prize of the ancient Olympic games was a simple wreath of wild olive. Yet it called forth the most strenuous effort. For a simple bit of ribbon, people have performed services no money could buy.

Any philosophy based on selfishness as the master motive of human action is shortsighted. It is blind to the facts. If you want to move people to action, to what do you appeal? Not to their pockets, but to their patriotism; not to selfishness, but to sympathy. We will all give everything to preserve our lives. That is self-interest. But to higher impulses, people will give even their lives.

Call it religion, patriotism, sympathy, love of humanity, or love of God. Call it what you will. There is a force that overcomes selfishness and drives it out. It is a force beside which all others are weak. Anywhere people have ever lived, it has shown its power. Today, as ever, the world is filled with it. The person who has never seen or never felt it is to be pitied.

This force of forces now goes to waste, or it assumes perverted forms. We may use it, if we but choose. All we have to do is give it freedom and scope. We are made for cooperation, like rows of upper and lower teeth. One thing alone prevents harmonious social development: the wrong that produces inequality.

Some suppose that only impracticable dreamers could envision a society where greed is banished, prisons stand empty, individual interest is subordinated to general interest, and no one would seek to rob or to oppress neighbors. Practical, levelheaded people, who pride themselves on seeing facts as they are, have a hearty contempt for such dreamers. But those practical people, though they write books and hold chairs at universities, do not think.

Among the company of well-bred men and women dining together there is no struggle for food, no attempt to get more than one's neighbor, no attempt to gorge or steal. On the contrary, each is anxious to help a neighbor before helping himself or herself, offering the best to others. Should anyone show the slightest inclination to act the pig or pilferer, the hoarder would face a swift and heavy penalty of social contempt and ostracism.

All this is so familiar that it seems the natural state of things. Yet it is no more natural to be greedy for wealth than to be greedy for food. People are greedy for food when they are not assured there will be a fair and equitable distribution, which would give each enough. When these conditions are assured, they stop being greedy.

In society as presently constituted, people are greedy for wealth because the conditions of distribution are so unjust. Instead of each being sure of enough, many are condemned to poverty. This is what causes the rat race and the scramble for wealth. An equitable distribution of wealth would exempt everyone from this fear. It would destroy greed for wealth, as greed for food is destroyed in polite society.

On crowded steamers, manners often differed between cabin and steerage, illustrating this principle of human nature. Both had enough food. However, steerage had no regulations to insure efficient service, so meals became a scramble. In cabin, on the contrary, each was assigned a place, and there was no fear of not getting enough to eat. There was no scrambling and no waste. The difference was not in the character of the people, but simply in the arrangements. A cabin passenger transferred to steerage would participate in the greedy rush; a steerage passenger transferred to cabin would become respectful and polite.

The same would occur in society in general if the

present unjust system were replaced with a fair distribution of wealth. In cultivated and refined society, coarser passions are not held in check by force or law, but by common opinion and mutual desire. If this is possible for part of a community, it is possible for a whole community.

Some say there would be no incentive to work without fear of poverty; people would simply become idlers. This is the old slaveholders' argument that labor must be driven with the lash. Nothing is further from the truth. Want might be banished, but desire would remain. Humans are more than animals: we are the unsatisfied animal. Each step we take kindles new desires.

Work itself is not repugnant to humans, only work that shows no results. To toil day after day and barely get the necessities of life, this is hard indeed. But released from this prison, people would work harder and better. Were the lives of great people, like Benjamin Franklin or Michelangelo, idle ones? The fact is, work that improves the condition of humanity is not done to earn a living. In a society where poverty was eliminated, such work would increase enormously.

The waste of mental power is the greatest of all the enormous wastes resulting from the present organization of society. How infinitesimal are the forces that contribute to the advancement of civilization compared to the forces that lie dormant! Considering the great mass of people, how few are thinkers, discoverers, inventors, organizers. Yet many such people are born—it is conditions that permit so few to develop. What would their talents have mattered, had Columbus gone into the clergy instead of going to sea, or Shakespeare been apprenticed to a chimney sweep, or Isaac Newton become a farmer?

But, it will be said, others would have risen instead. And this is true. It shows how prolific human nature is. The common worker is transformed into the queen bee when needed. When circumstances are favorable, a common person rises to the status of hero or leader, sage or saint. But for every one who attains full stature, how many are stunted and denied?

How little does heredity count compared with conditions. Place an English infant in the heart of China, and it will grow up the same as those who are native. The person would use the same speech, think the same thoughts, show the same tastes. Switch a countess with an infant in the slums. Would the blood of a hundred earls give you a refined and cultured woman?

To remove the fear of want, to give to all classes comfort and independence and opportunities for development—this would be like giving water to a desert. Consider the possibilities if society gave opportunity to all. Factory workers are now turned into machines; children grow up in squalor, vice, and ignorance. They need but the opportunity to bring forth powers of the highest order. Talents now hidden, virtues unsuspected, would come forth to make human life richer, fuller, happier.

In our present state, even the fortunate few at the top of the social pyramid must suffer from the want, ignorance, and degradation underneath. The change I propose would benefit everyone, even the largest landholder. Wouldn't the rich person's children be safer penniless in such a society, than with the largest fortune in this one? If such a society existed, it would be a bargain to gain entrance by giving up all possessions.

I have now traced our social weakness and disease to

their source. I have shown the remedy. I have covered every point, and met every objection. But the problems we have been considering, great as they are, pass into problems greater still. They go to the grandest problems with which the human mind can grapple. I am about to ask the reader to go with me further still, into higher fields.

The Law of Human Progress

Chapter 39

The Cause of Human Progress

IF OUR CONCLUSIONS ARE CORRECT, they will fall under a larger generalization. We may rephrase our question, then, from a broader perspective:

What is the law of human progress?

Whether humans gradually developed from animals is not the question here. Inference cannot proceed from the unknown to the known. However humans may have originated, we can know our species only as we find it now. There is no trace of humans in any lower state than that of primitive people still found today. No vestige remains of what bridged the chasm between humans and animals.

Between the lowest savage and the highest animal, there is an irreconcilable difference. It is not a difference of degree, but of kind. Many of the characteristics, actions, and emotions of humans are seen in lower animals. But no matter how low on the scale of humanity, no person has ever been found without the one characteristic of which animals show not the slightest trace. It is something clearly recognizable, yet almost undefinable. Something that gives humans the power of improvement—that makes us the progressive animal.

The beaver builds a dam, the bird a nest—but always on the same models. Human dwellings pass from rude huts to magnificent mansions. A dog can, to a certain extent, connect cause and effect, and learn some tricks. But this capacity has not increased in all the ages it has been domesticated. Today's dog is no smarter than the dogs of ancient savages.

We know of no animal that uses clothes, cooks food, makes tools or weapons, breeds other animals to eat, or has an articulate language. Humans lacking these skills have never been found. In fact, human physical ability is so inferior that there is virtually no place we could exist without those skills. Humans everywhere, and at all times we know of, have exhibited this faculty—to supplement what nature has done for us by what we do for ourselves.

But the degree varies greatly. Between the steamship and a canoe, there is an enormous difference. These variations cannot be attributed to differences in original capacity. The most advanced today were savages within historic times. We also see wide differences between peoples of the same stock. Neither can they be accounted for by differences in physical environment. In many cases, the cradles of learning are now occupied by barbarians. Yet great cities rise in a few years over the hunting grounds of wild tribes.

These differences are evidently connected with social development. Beyond perhaps the simplest rudiments, it becomes possible for humans to improve only as we live with other people. We improve as we learn to cooperate in society. All these improvements in human powers and conditions we summarize in the term "civilization."

But what is the law of this improvement? Which social arrangements favor it and which do not? Different communities have arrived at different stages of civilization. Can some common principle explain this?

The prevailing belief is that civilizations progress by development or evolution. That is, by the survival of the fittest and hereditary transmission of acquired qualities. This explanation of progress is, I think, very much like the view naturally taken by the wealthy regarding the unequal distribution of wealth. There is plenty of money to be made by those who have the will and ability, they say; ignorance, idleness, or wastefulness creates the difference between rich and poor.

So the common explanation of differences among civilizations is one of differences in capacity. The more civilized races are superior races. Common Englishmen felt they had a naturally superiority over frog-eating Frenchmen. American opinion attributed their country's success in invention and material comfort to "Yankee ingenuity."

In the beginning of this inquiry, we examined—and disproved—certain economic theories that supported common opinion. This view saw capitalists as paying wages, while competition reduced wages. Just as Malthusian theory supported existing prejudices, seeing progress as gradual race improvement harmonizes with common opinion. It gives coherence and a scientific formula to opinions already prevailing. Its phenomenal spread since Darwin* has not been so much conquest as assimilation.

---

* Charles Darwin (1809-1882), British naturalist. He published *The Origin of Species* in 1859.

So this view now dominates thought: The struggle for existence, in proportion to its intensity, spurs people to new efforts and inventions. The capacity for improvement is established by hereditary transmission, and spread as the most improved (i.e., best adapted) individuals survive to propagate. Similarly, the best adapted tribe, nation, or race survives in the struggle between social groups. This theory is now used to explain the differences in the relative progress of societies, as well as the differences between humans and animals. These phenomena are now explained as confidently and as widely by this theory as, a short while ago, they were explained by special creation and divine intervention.

The practical effect of this theory is a sort of hopeful fatalism: progress is the result of slow, steady, remorseless forces. War, slavery, tyranny, superstition, famine, and poverty are the impelling causes that drive humans on. They work by eliminating poor types and extending the higher. Advances are fixed by hereditary transmission. The current individual is the result of changes perpetuated through a long series of past individuals. Social organization then takes its form from the individuals of which it is composed. Philosophers may teach that this does not lessen the duty of trying to reform abuses. But as generally understood, the result is fatalism. Why bother, since change can only occur through slow development of man's nature?

Yet we have reached a point where progress seems to be natural to us. We look forward confidently to greater achievements. Some even believe people may someday travel to distant planets. This theory of progression seems so natural to us amid an advancing civilization.

But, without soaring to the stars, if we simply look around the world, we are confronted with an undeniable fact—stagnant civilizations.

The majority of the human race today has no idea of progress. They look to the past as the time of human perfection. We may explain the difference between savage and civilized, saying savages are still so poorly developed that their progress is hardly apparent. But how shall we account for civilizations that progressed so far—and then stopped?

Today's Western civilization is not more advanced than India and China due to a longer period of development. We are not, as it were, adults of nature while they are children. They were civilized when we were savages. They had great cities, powerful governments, art, literature, and commerce when Europeans were living in huts and skin tents.

Yet while we progressed from this savage state to modern civilization, they stood still. If progress is the result of inevitable laws that propel people forward, how shall we account for this? These arrested civilizations stopped when they were superior in many respects to sixteenth century Europe. Moreover, both received the infusion of new ideas from conquering races with different customs and thought.

But it is not simply that current theory fails to account for these arrested civilizations. It is not merely that people have gone so far on the path of progress and then stopped. It is that people have gone so far—and then gone back. It is not merely an isolated case that thus confronts the theory — *it is the universal rule.*

Every civilization the world has ever seen has had its period of vigorous growth; of arrest and stagnation; then, decline and fall. True, our own civilization is more advanced and moves quicker than any preceding civilization. But so was Roman civilization in its day. That proves nothing about its permanence unless it is better in whatever caused the ultimate failure of its predecessors.

In truth, nothing could be further from explaining the facts of universal history than this theory that civilization is the result of natural selection. It is inconsistent with the fact that civilization has arisen at different times, and in different places, and has progressed at different rates. If improvements were fixed in man's nature, there might be occasional interruption, but in general, progress would be continuous. Advance would lead to advance, and civilization would develop into higher civilization. It is not merely the general rule, but the universal rule, that the reverse is true. The earth is the tomb of the dead empires.

In every case, the more advanced civilization, supposedly modified by heredity, has been succeeded by a fresh race coming from a lower level. The barbarians of one epoch have been the civilized people of the next. It has always been the case that, under the influences of civilization, people at first improve—and later degenerate. Every civilization that has been overwhelmed by barbarians has really perished from internal decay.

The moment this universal fact is recognized, it eliminates the theory of progress by hereditary transmission. Looking over the history of the world, advance does not coincide with heredity for any length of time. In any particular line, regression always seems to follow advance.

Can we say there is a national or race life, as there is an individual life? Does every social group have, as it were, a certain amount of energy to expend before it decays? Analogies are the most dangerous mode of thought. They may connect similarities, yet disguise or cover up the truth. The aggregate force of a group is the sum of its individual components. A community cannot lose vital power unless the vital powers of its components are lessened. As long as members are constantly reproduced with all the fresh vigor of childhood, a community cannot grow old by loss of its powers as a person does.

Yet within this analogy lurks an obvious truth. The obstacles that finally bring progress to a halt are actually raised by the course of progress itself. The conditions that have destroyed all previous civilizations have been conditions produced by the growth of civilization itself.

Chapter 40

Differences in Civilizations

To DISCOVER the law of human progress, we must first determine the essential nature of the differences between civilizations. Such great disparities cannot be explained by innate differences in the individuals who compose these communities. True, there are natural differences and hereditary transmission of particular traits. But these are nothing compared to social influences.

What is more ingrained than language? Nothing persists longer, nor shows nationality quicker. It is our medium of thought. Yet we are not born with a predisposition to any language. Although our ancestors have spoken one language for generations, children hearing a different tongue from birth will learn that just as easily.

Manners and customs of nation or class are also matters of education and habit, not hereditary transmission. White infants captured and raised by Indians demonstrate this: They become thorough Indians. That the reverse is not as true of Indians brought up by whites is due to the fact that they are never treated precisely the same as white children.

I once heard a highly intelligent Negro gentleman, Bishop Hillery, remark: "Our children, when they are young, are fully as bright as white children, and learn as readily. But as soon as they get old enough to appreciate their status—to realize that they are looked upon as belonging to an inferior race, and can never hope to be anything more than cooks, waiters, or something of that sort—they lose their ambition and cease to keep up."

Conditions and surroundings profoundly modify human character. Paupers will raise paupers, even if the children are not their own. Frequent contact with criminals may make criminals out of the children of virtuous parents. Those who learn to rely on charity inevitably lose the self-respect and independence necessary for self-reliance when the struggle is hard. Thus it is well known that charity often increases the demand for more charity.

In any large community, diverse classes and groups show the same kind of differences as we see between different civilizations: differences in knowledge, belief, customs, tastes, and speech. But these differences are certainly not innate. No baby is born a Methodist or Catholic, nor with a particular dialect or accent. These differences are derived from association in these groups.

This body of traditions, beliefs, customs, laws, habits and associations arises in every community and surrounds every individual. This, not hereditary transmission, makes the English different from the French, the American from the Chinese, and the civilized from the primitive. Heredity may develop or alter qualities—but much more so the physical than the mental characteristics.

Even in our wildest state, human life is infinitely more complex than animal life, for we are affected by an infinitely greater number of influences. Amid these, the relative influence of heredity diminishes. The physical differences between races are hardly greater than between black and white horses. If this is true of our physical structure, it must be reflected even more in our mental constitution. All our physical parts we bring with us into the world, but the mind develops afterward. We cannot tell whether the mind of a newborn infant is to be English or Chinese, or even the mind of a civilized person or the mind of a savage. That depends entirely on the social environment in which it is placed.

Suppose infants of highly civilized parents were taken to an uninhabited country and somehow kept alive until adulthood. They would be the most helpless savages imaginable. They would need to discover fire, to invent the simplest tools, and to construct a language. Just as children learn to walk, they would have to stumble their way to the simplest knowledge the lowest culture now possesses.

No doubt, they could do all these things in time. These possibilities are latent in the human mind, as the power of walking is latent in the human frame. But I do not believe they would do them better or worse, or quicker or slower, than children of barbarians under the same conditions. What could mankind attain if each generation were separated from the next by an interval of time, like seventeen-year locusts? Only one such interval would see the decline of mankind—not simply to savagery, but to a condition compared with which savagery, as we know it, would seem civilized. Conversely, if savage infants were placed in civilized homes, can we suppose that they would show any difference growing up? (We must assume in this experiment that they would be raised the same as other children.) The great lesson thus learned is that "human nature is human nature all the world over."

There is a people, found in all parts of the world, who illustrate which traits are transmitted by heredity and which are transmitted by association. The Jews have maintained the purity of their blood more scrupulously, and for a far longer time, than any European race. Yet the only characteristic that can be attributed to this is physical appearance. (And this is far less than conventionally supposed, as anyone who takes the trouble can see.) Although they have constantly married among themselves, the Jews have everywhere been modified by their surroundings. English, Russian, Polish, German, and Oriental Jews differ from each other, in many respects, as much as do the other people of those countries.

Yet they have much in common and have preserved their character no matter where they are. The reason is clear. The Hebrew religion has always preserved the distinctiveness of the Hebrew race. Certainly religion is not transmitted by heredity, but by association.

The Chinese have a very set character. Yet in California they easily adopt American methods of working, trading, and using machinery. They have no lack of flexibility or natural capacity. That they do not change in other respects is due to the Chinese environment that still persists and surrounds them. Coming from China, they plan to return. While here, they live in a little China of their own, as the English in India maintain a little England. We naturally seek to associate with those who share our peculiarities. Thus language, religion and custom tend to persist anywhere individuals are not absolutely isolated.

Modern civilization stands far above those who have preceded us, and far above our less advanced contemporaries. But not because we are any taller. We stand atop a pyramid. The centuries have built a structure to support us.

Let me repeat: I do not mean that all people possess the

same mental capacity, any more than I mean they are physically alike. I do not deny the influence of heredity in transmitting mental characteristics in the same way, and possibly to the same degree, as physical attributes. But the differences between communities in different places and at different times—what we call differences in civilizations—are not differences that reside in individuals, but differences that belong to their societies. That is, they result from the conditions individuals are exposed to in society.

Each society, small or great, weaves itself a web of knowledge, beliefs, customs, language, tastes, institutions, and laws. (More precisely, we should say webs. For each community is made up of smaller societies, which overlap and intertwine each other.) Into this, the individual is received at birth and continues till death. This is the matrix in which mind unfolds, and from which it takes its stamp. This is how customs, religions, prejudices, tastes, and languages develop and are perpetuated. This is how skill is transmitted and knowledge is stored. The discoveries of one time are made the common stock and stepping stone of the next.

Though this is often an obstacle to progress, it is also what makes progress possible. It enables a schoolboy in our time to learn more about the universe in a few hours than the ancient astronomers knew after a lifetime. It places an ordinary scientist today far above the level reached by the giant mind of Aristotle. This is to a civilization what memory is to an individual. Our wonderful arts, our far-reaching science, our marvelous inventions—they have come about through this.

Human progress goes on as the advances of one generation become the common property of the next—and the starting point for new ones.

Chapter 41

The Law of Human Progress

WHAT, THEN, IS THE LAW OF HUMAN PROGRESS? This law not only describes how civilization advances—it must also account for arrested, decayed, and destroyed civilizations. Since mankind presumably started with the same capacities at the same time, it must explain the great disparity in social development that now exists. It must account for regression, as well as progression; for different rates of progress; and for the bursts and starts and halts. In short, it must tell us what the essential conditions of progress are—and which social arrangements advance it and which retard it.

It is not difficult to discover such a law. If we simply look, we can see it. I do not pretend to give it scientific precision, but merely to point it out.

Desires inherent in human nature are the incentives to progress: to satisfy our physical, intellectual, and emotional wants. Short of infinity, they can never be satisfied—for they grow as they are fed.

Mind is the instrument by which humanity advances. Through it, each advance is retained and made higher ground for further advances. The narrow span of human life allows each individual to go only a short distance. Each generation does little by itself. Yet succeeding generations add to the gains of their ancestors, and gradually elevate humanity.

Mental power is, therefore, the motor of progress. Civilizations advance in proportion to the mental power expended in progression—that is, mental power devoted to the extension of knowledge, the improvement of methods, and the betterment of social conditions. There is a limit to the amount of work that can be done with the mind, just as there a limit to the work that can be done with the body. Therefore, the mental power that can be devoted to progress is only what is left over after what is required for other, non-progressive purposes.

These non-progressive purposes, which consume mental power, can be classified in two categories: maintenance and conflict. Maintenance includes not only supporting existence, but also keeping up social conditions and holding advances already gained. Conflict includes not only war or preparation for war; it encompasses all mental power expended seeking gratification at the expense of others, and resisting such aggression.

If we compare society to a boat, we see its progress is not based on the total exertion of the crew. Rather, it depends only on exertion devoted to propelling it. The total is reduced by any force expended on bailing, or fighting among themselves, or pulling in different directions.

A person living alone would need all of his or her powers just to maintain existence. Mental power is set free for higher uses only when human beings associate in communities. Improvement becomes possible when people come together in peaceful association. This permits the division of labor—and all the economies that come from cooperation. The wider and the closer the association, the greater the possibilities of improvement. Therefore, association is the first essential of progress.

Mental power is wasted in conflict to the extent moral law is ignored—for moral law gives each person equality of rights. The terms equality or justice signify the same thing here: the recognition of moral law. So equality, or justice, is the second essential of progress.

Association frees mental power for improvement. Equality keeps this power from dissipating in fruitless struggles. We thus arrive at our law:

Association in equality is the law of human progress.

Here, at last, is the law that can explain all diversities, all advances, all halts, and all retrogressions. People progress by cooperating with each other to increase the mental power that may be devoted to improvement. However, as conflict is provoked, or as inequality (of power or condition) develops, this tendency is lessened, checked, and finally reversed. The rate of development will depend on the resistance it meets. Obstacles may be external and internal. In earlier stages of civilization, external forces tend to be greater. Internal obstacles grow more important in later stages.

Humans are social animals. We do not need to be caught and tamed to persuade us to live with others. A family relationship is necessary due to our utter helplessness at birth and our long period of immaturity. We observe that the family is wider, and in its extensions stronger, among simpler peoples. The first societies are families. They expand into tribes, still holding a mutual blood relationship. Even when they have become great nations, they claim a common descent.

The first limit, or resistance, to association comes from

conditions of physical nature. These vary greatly with location, and must produce corresponding differences in social progress. Climate, soil, and physical features will largely determine population growth and the cohesion of society in the early stages. Association brings only minor improvement at first, especially under difficult conditions, or where mountains, deserts, or sea isolate people. On the rich plains of warm climates, people can exist with much less effort. More mental power can be devoted to improvement. Hence, civilization naturally first arose in the great valleys and table lands where we find its earliest monuments.

Diversity in natural conditions produces diversity in social development. Differences arise in language, custom, tradition, religion. Prejudice and animosity arise. Warfare becomes a chronic and seemingly natural relation of societies to each other. Power is depleted in attack or defense, in mutual slaughter and destruction of wealth, or in warlike preparations. Protective tariffs and standing armies among the civilized world today bear witness to how long these hostilities persist.

When small, separated communities exist in a state of chronic warfare, a conquering tribe or nation may unite these smaller communities into a larger one, in which internal peace is preserved. So conquest can promote association, by liberating mental power from the demands of constant war.

But conquest is not the only civilizing force. While diversities of climate, soil, and geography at first separate mankind, they also act to encourage exchange. Commerce also promotes civilization. It is in itself a form of association or cooperation. It not only operates directly—it also builds up interests opposed to war. It dispels ignorance, which is the fertile mother of prejudice and hate.

And likewise religion. Though it has sometimes divided people and led to war, at other times it has promoted association. Common worship has often furnished the basis of union. Modern European civilization arose from the triumph of Christianity over the barbarians. If the Church had not existed when the Roman Empire fell, Europe would have lacked any bond of association, and might have fallen to a primitive condition.

Looking over history, we see civilization springing up wherever people are brought into association—and disappearing as this association is broken up. As people have been brought into closer and closer association and cooperation, progress has gone on with greater and greater force.

But we shall never understand the course of civilization, and its varied phenomena, without considering the internal resistances or counter forces that arise in the very heart of advancing society. Only they can explain how a civilization, once adequately started, could be destroyed by barbarians—or stop by itself.

Mental power, the motor of social progress, is set free by association—or perhaps "integration" may be a more accurate term. In this process, society becomes more complex. Individuals become more dependent upon each other. Occupations and functions are specialized.

Instead of each person attempting to supply all wants in isolation, the various trades and industries are separated. One person acquires skill in one thing, and another in something else. The body of knowledge becomes larger than any one person can grasp. So it is separated into different parts, which different individuals pursue. Government acquires special functions for preserving order, administering justice, and waging war. Even religious ceremonies pass to people specially devoted to that purpose. Each member is then vitally dependent on the others.

This process of integration, and the specialization of functions and powers, is vulnerable to inequality. I do not mean that inequality is a necessary result of social growth. Rather, it is the constant tendency of social growth—if it is not accompanied by certain changes in social organization. These changes must secure equality under the new conditions that growth produces.

To put it plainly, the force that halts progress evolves along with progress. How does this operate? Let us recall two qualities of human nature: One is the power of habit; the other is the possibility of mental and moral decay. Because of our tendency to continue doing things the same way, customs, laws, and methods persist long after they have lost their original usefulness. Decay allows the growth of institutions and ways of thinking from which people's normal judgments would instinctively revolt.

The growth and development of society makes each person more dependent on the whole. It lessens the influence of individuals, even over their own conditions, compared with the influence of society. But even further, association gives rise to a collective power. This power is different than the sum of individual powers. Groups exhibit actions and impulses that individuals would not under the same circumstances. By analogy, as simple animals become complex, a power of the integrated whole arises above that of the parts.

We observed the same phenomenon in our inquiry into the nature and growth of rent. Where population is sparse, land has no value. To the degree that people congregate, land value land appears and rises. This is something clearly distinguishable from value produced by individual effort. It is a value that springs from association. It increases as association grows greater, and disappears as association is broken up.

The same thing is true of power. As society grows, habit tends to continue previous social arrangements. Collective power, as it arises, lodges in the hands of a portion of the community. This unequal distribution of wealth and power, which grows as society advances, tends to produce greater inequality. Then the idea of justice is blurred by habitual toleration of injustice.

The war chief of a band of savages is merely one of their number; they only follow him as their bravest. When large bodies act together, personal selection becomes more difficult. A blinder obedience is necessary and can be enforced. As collective power grows, the ruler's power to reward or punish increases. From the necessities of war on a large scale, absolute power arises. The masses are then mere slaves of the king's caprice.

And so of the specialization of function. When society has grown to a certain point, a regular military force can be specialized. It is no longer necessary to summon every producer away from work in case of attack. This produces a manifest gain in productive power. But this inevitably leads to the concentration of power in the hands of a military class or their chiefs.

Similarly, the preservation of internal order, the administration of justice, the construction and care of public works, and, notably, the practice of religion, all tend to pass to special classes. And it is their nature to magnify their function and extend their power.

But the greatest cause of inequality is the natural monopoly given by possession of land. The initial understanding of people always seems to be that land is common property. This is recognized at first by simple methods, such as cultivating land in common or dividing it annually. These approaches are only compatible with low stages of development.

The idea of property arises naturally regarding things of human production. This idea is easily transferred to land. When population is sparse, ownership of land merely ensures that the due reward of labor goes to the one who uses and improves it. As population becomes dense, rent appears. This institution ultimately operates to strip the producer of wages earned.

War and conquest tend to concentrate political power and lead to the institution of slavery. They also naturally result in the appropriation of land. A dominant class, who concentrate power in their own hands, will soon concentrate ownership of land. They take large portions of conquered land, while the former inhabitants are forced to farm it as tenants or serfs. Some public domain or common lands remain for awhile in the natural course of development. But these are readily acquired by the powerful, as we see by modern examples. Once inequality is established, ownership of land tends to concentrate as development goes on.

We can now explain all the phenomena of petrifaction and retrogression from the fact that inequality of wealth and power develops as social development occurs. This finally counteracts the force by which improvements are made and society advances. I will simply set forth this general fact here, because the particular sequence of events will vary under different conditions.

These two principles—association and equality—can be seen at work in the rise and spread, and then the decline and fall, of the Roman Empire. Rome arose from the association of independent farmers and free citizens of Italy. It gained fresh strength from conquests, which brought hostile nations into common relations. Yet the tendency to inequality hindered progress from the start, and it only increased with conquest. Inequality dried up the strength and destroyed the vigor of the Roman world. Rome rotted, declined, and fell. Long before Vandal or Goth broke through the legions, Rome was dead at the heart.

Great estates—"latifundia"—ruined Italy. The barbarism that overwhelmed Rome came not from without, but from within. It was the inevitable product of a system that carved the provinces into estates for senatorial families. Serfs and slaves replaced independent farmers. Government became dictatorship, patriotism became subservience. Vices were openly displayed, literature sank, learning was forgotten. Fertile districts became wastelands, even without the ravages of war. Everywhere inequality produced decay: political, mental, moral, and material.

Modern civilization owes its superiority to the growth of equality along with association. Two great causes contributed to this. First, power was split into numerous smaller centers. The second factor was the influence of Christianity.

Europe saw the association of peoples who had acquired, through separation, distinctive social characteristics. This smaller organization prevented concentration of power and wealth in one center. Petty chiefs and feudal lords grasped local sovereignty and held each other in check. Teutonic ideas of equality were a transforming influence, as they worked their way through the fabric of disconnected societies. Although Europe was split into countless separated fragments, the idea of closer association existed in the recollections of a universal empire and in the claims of a universal church. It is true Christianity was distorted by percolating through a rotting civilization. Yet the essential idea of equality was never wholly destroyed.

In addition, two things of utmost importance to the budding civilization occurred—the first was the establishment of the papacy; the second was the celibacy of the clergy. The papacy prevented spiritual power from concentrating in the same lines as temporal power. Celibacy prevented the establishment of a priestly caste, during a time when power tended to hereditary form.

In spite of everything, the Church still promoted association and was a witness for the natural human equality. In common hands, the Church placed a sign before which the proudest knelt. Bishops became peers of the highest nobles. Church edicts ran across political boundaries. The Pope arbitrated between nations and was honored by kings.

The rise of European civilization is too vast a subject to give proper perspective in a few paragraphs. But all its main features, and all its details, illustrate one truth: Progress occurs to the extent that society tends toward closer association and greater equality. Civilization is cooperation. Union and liberty are its factors.

Modern civilization has gone so much higher than any before due to the great extension of association—not just in larger and denser communities, but in the increase of commerce, and the numerous exchanges knitting each community together, and linking them with others far apart; and also in the growth of international and municipal law, advances in security of property and person, strides in individual liberty, and movement towards democratic government. In short, our civilization has gone farther in recognizing equal rights to life, liberty, and the pursuit of happiness.

The spirit of fatalism pervading current literature finds it fashionable to speak of war and slavery as means of human progress. But war is the opposite of association. It can aid progress only when it prevents further war, or breaks down antisocial barriers.

As for slavery, I cannot see how it could ever have aided progress. Freedom is the synonym of equality, the stimulus and condition of progress. Slavery never did, and never could, aid improvement. Slavery necessarily involves a waste of human power. This is true whether the community consists of a single master and a single slave, or thousands of masters and millions of slaves. Slave labor is less productive than free labor. Masters waste power holding and watching their slaves. From first to last, slavery has hampered and prevented progress—as has every denial of equality.

Slavery was universal in the classical world. This is undoubtedly why mental activity there polished literature and refined art, but never hit on any of the great discoveries and inventions of modern civilization. Robbing workers of the fruits of their labor stifles the spirit of invention. It discourages the use of improvements, even when made. No slaveholding people were ever an inventive people. Their upper classes may become luxurious and polished, but never inventive.

The law of human progress, what is it but moral law? Political economy and social science can teach only the same simple truths that underlie every religion that has striven to formulate the spiritual yearnings of man. Civilizations advance as their social arrangements promote justice. They advance as they acknowledge equality of human rights. They advance as they insure liberty to each person, bounded only by the equal liberty of every other person. As they fail in these, advancing civilizations come to a halt and recede.

Chapter 42
How Modern Civilization May Decline

OUR CONCLUSIONS about the law of human progress agree completely with our previous conclusions about the laws of political economy. They also show that making land common property—by taxing its value—would give an enormous boost to civilization. Furthermore, unless we do so, we will regress.

Every previous civilization has been destroyed by the unequal distribution of wealth and power. I have traced this tendency to its cause—and provided a simple way to remove it. I will now show how, if this is not done, modern civilization will decline to barbarism, as all previous civilizations have.

History clearly shows these periods of decline, though they were not recognized at their start. When the first Emperor was changing Rome from brick to marble and extending the frontier, who would have said Rome was entering its decline? Yet such was the case.

Our civilization appears to be advancing faster than ever. Yet anyone who looks will see the same cause that doomed Rome is operating today—with increasing force. The more advanced the community, the greater the intensity. Wages and interest fall, while rents rise. The rich get richer, the poor grow helpless, the middle class is swept away.

It is worthwhile to explain the process, since many people cannot see how progress could turn into retreat. They think such a thing is impossible. Many scoff at any implication that we are not progressing in all respects. The conditions of social progress, we have found, are association and equality. The general tendency of modern development has indeed been toward political and legal equality. We have abolished slavery, revoked hereditary privileges, instituted representative government, and recognized religious freedom. High and low, weak and strong have more equal security in their person and property. There is freedom of movement and occupation, of speech and of the press.

The initial effect of political equality is a more equal distribution of wealth and power. While population is sparse, unequal distribution of wealth is due mainly to inequality of personal rights. The inequality resulting from private ownership of land shows itself only as material progress advances. Political equality does not, in itself, prevent inequality arising from private ownership of land. Furthermore, political equality—when coexisting with an increasing tendency toward unequal distribution of wealth—will ultimately beget either tyranny or anarchy.

A representative government may become a dictatorship without formally changing its constitution or abandoning popular elections. Forms are nothing when substance has gone. And the forms of popular government are those from which the substance of freedom may go most easily. For there despotism advances in the name of the people. Once that single source of power is secured, everything is secured. An aristocracy of wealth will never struggle while it can bribe a tyrant.

When the disparity of condition increases, democratic elections make it easy to seize the source of power. Many feel no connection with the conduct of government. Embittered by poverty, they are ready to sell their votes to the highest bidder or follow the most blatant demagogue. One class has become too rich to be stripped of its luxuries, no matter how public affairs are administered. Another class is so poor that promises of a few dollars will outweigh abstract considerations on election day. A few roll in wealth, while the many seethe with discontent at things they don't know how to remedy.

Where there is anything close to equal distribution of wealth, the more democratic government is, the better it will be. Where there is gross inequality in the distribution of wealth, the opposite is true. The more democratic government is, the worse it will be. To give the vote to people who must beg or steal or starve, to whom the chance to work is a favor—this is to invoke destruction. To put political power in hands embittered and degraded by poverty is to wreak havoc.

Hereditary succession (or even selection by lot) may, by accident, occasionally place the wise and just in power. But in a corrupt democracy, the tendency is always to give power to the worst. Honesty and patriotism are a handicap, while dishonesty brings success. The best sink to the bottom, the worst float to the top. The vile are ousted only by the viler.

National character gradually absorbs the qualities that win power. In the long panorama of history, we see over and over that this transforms free people into slaves. A corrupt democratic government must finally corrupt the people. And when the people become corrupt, there is no resurrection. Life is gone, only the carcass remains. It is left but for the plowshares of fate to bury it out of sight.

Unequal distribution of wealth inevitably transforms popular government into despotism. This is not a thing of the far future. It has already begun in the United States, and is proceeding rapidly before our very eyes. Men of the highest ability and character avoid politics. The technique of handlers and hacks counts more than the reputations of statesmen. The power of money is increasing, while voting is done recklessly. Political differences are no longer differences of principle. Political parties are passing into the control of what might be considered oligarchies and dictatorships.

Modern growth is typified by the great city. Here we find the greatest wealth and the deepest poverty. And here popular government has most clearly broken down. In all the great American cities of today, a ruling class is defined as clearly as in the most aristocratic countries. Its members have whole wards in their pockets, select slates for nominating conventions, and distribute offices as they bargain together. "They toil not, neither do they spin,"* yet they wear the finest of raiment and spend money lavishly. They are men of power, whose favor the ambitious must court, and whose vengeance they must avoid.

Who are these men? The wise, the learned, the good? No. They are gamblers, fighters, or worse. Men who have made a trade of controlling votes, and buying and selling offices and legislation. Through these men, rich corporations and powerful financial interests pack the Senate and the courts with their lackeys. In many places today, a

---

* Matthew 6:28

Washington, a Franklin, or a Jefferson could not even get into the state legislature. Their very character would be an insurmountable disqualification.

In theory we are intense democrats. Yet growing among us is a class who have all the power of the aristocracy—without any of their virtues. A few men control thousands of miles of railroad, millions of acres of land, and the livelihood of thousands. They name the governors as they name clerks, and choose senators as they choose attorneys. Their will with legislatures is as supreme as a French king's.

The development of industry and commerce—acting in a social organization where land is privately owned—threatens to force every worker to seek a master. (Just as the collapse of the Roman Empire compelled every freeman to seek a feudal lord.) Industry takes on a form where one is master, while many serve. If a person steals enough, the punishment will only amount to losing part of the theft. And if a thief steals a fortune, colleagues will greet the embezzler like a Viking returning from pillage.

The most ominous political sign in the United States today is the growing complacency with corruption. Many believe there is no honest person in public office; or worse, that if there were one, he or she would be a fool not to seize the opportunities. The people themselves are becoming corrupted. Our democratic government is running the course it must inevitably follow under conditions producing unequal distribution of wealth.

Where this will lead is clear. Contempt for law develops, and reform becomes hopeless. Volcanic forces festering among the masses will explode when some accident gives them vent. Where will the new barbarians come from? Go through the squalid ghettos of great cities and you can already see them gathering.*

Hinting that our civilization may be in decline seems like wild pessimism. A fundamental belief in progress remains. But this will always be the case when advance gradually passes into retrogression. In social development, as in everything else, motion tends to continue in a straight line. Where there has been previous advance, it is extremely difficult to recognize decline—even after it has begun.

Civilizations do not decline along the same paths they came up. Government will not take us back from democracy to monarchy and to feudalism. It will take us to dictatorship or anarchy. Religion will not go back to the faiths of our forefathers, but into new forms of superstition.

The regression of civilization, after a period of advance, may be so gradual that it attracts no attention at the time. Indeed, many mistake such a decline for advancement. As the arts decline, the change may be accompanied by—or rather caused by—a change of taste. Artists who quickly adopted the new styles are regarded—in their day—as superior. As art and literature become more lifeless, foolish, and stilted—conforming to changing taste—the new fashion would regard its increasing weakness as increasing strength and beauty. Really good writers would not find

---

*The British historian Thomas Macaulay (1800-1859) predicted that after all the decent land had been claimed in the United States, poverty would reach the levels it did in England. The nation would then destroy itself through its own democratic institutions. "The Huns and Vandals who ravaged the Roman empire came from without; your Huns and Vandals will have been engendered within your own country by your own institutions [because]... There is nothing to stop you. Your constitution is all sail and no anchor." (Letter to Henry S. Randall, biographer of Thomas Jefferson.)

readers; they would be regarded as dull. The prevailing taste becomes that of a less cultured class who regard what they like as the best of its kind.

Whether current trends in taste and opinion indicate regression is not the point. Many other things beyond dispute indicate our civilization has reached a critical point—unless a new start is made toward equality. Inequality is the necessary result of material progress wherever land is monopolized. Inequality cannot go much further without carrying us into a downward spiral so easy to start and so hard to stop.

Industrial depressions, which cause as much waste and suffering as war or famine, are like twinges and shocks preceding paralysis. The struggle to survive is increasing in intensity. We must strain every nerve to keep from being trodden underfoot in the scramble for wealth. This saps the energy to gain and maintain improvements. Diseases from related causes proliferate. In every civilized country, poverty, crime, insanity, and suicide are increasing.

When the tide turns, it does not happen all at once. When the sun passes noon, the heat of the day continues to increase. One can tell only by the way the shadows fall. But as sure as the tide must turn, as sure as the setting sun brings darkness, so sure is it that our civilization has begun to wane. Invention marches on, our cities expand. Yet civilization has begun to wane when, in proportion to population, we have more prisons, more welfare, more mental illness. Society does not die from top to bottom; it dies from bottom to top.

But the decline of civilization looms far more palpable than any statistics. There is a vague but general disappointment, an increased bitterness, a widespread feeling of unrest and brooding revolution. If this were accompanied by some definite idea of how to obtain relief, it might be a hopeful sign. But it is not. Though we have been searching a long, long time, our power of connecting cause to effect seems not a whit improved.

A vast change in religious ideas is sweeping the world that may have a momentous effect, which only the future can tell. This is not a change in the form of religion—it is the negation and destruction of the ideas from which religion springs. Christianity is not simply shedding superstitions; it is dying at the root. And nothing arises to take its place.

The fundamental ideas of an intelligent creator and an afterlife are quickly weakening in the general mind. Whether or not this may be an advance in itself is not the point. The important part religion has played in history shows the significance of the change now going on. Unless human nature has suddenly changed its deepest characteristics, as shown by the universal history of the human race, the mightiest actions and reactions are thus being prepared.

Previously, such stages of thought have always marked periods of transition. To a lesser degree, a similar state preceded the French Revolution. But the closest parallel to the wreck of religious ideas now going on is when ancient civilization began to pass from splendor to decline.

What change may come, no mortal can tell. But that some great change must come, thoughtful people are beginning to feel. The civilized world is trembling on the verge of a great movement. Either it must be a leap upward, to advances yet undreamed of—or it will be a plunge downward, carrying us back toward barbarism.

Chapter 43

The Central Truth

OUR ECONOMIC INQUIRY led us to a certain truth. The same truth explains the rise and fall of civilizations. Furthermore, it agrees with our deep-seated perceptions of relation and sequence, which we call moral perceptions.

The evils arising from the unequal and unjust distribution of wealth become more and more apparent as modern civilization goes on. They are not signs of progress, but tendencies that will bring progress to a halt. They will not cure themselves. Unless their cause is removed, they will expand until they sweep us back into barbarism—the path every previous civilization has taken.

But this truth also shows that these evils are not imposed by natural laws. They arise solely from social maladjustments that ignore natural laws. Poverty, with all the evils that flow from it, springs from a denial of justice. By allowing a few to monopolize opportunities nature freely offers to all, we have ignored the fundamental law of justice.

By sweeping away this injustice—and asserting the rights of all people to natural opportunities—we shall conform ourselves to this law. We shall remove the great cause of unnatural inequality in the distribution of wealth and power. We shall abolish poverty; tame the ruthless passions of greed; and dry up the springs of vice and misery.

We shall light the lamp of knowledge in dark places; give new vigor to invention and a fresh impulse to discovery; substitute political strength for political weakness; and make tyranny and anarchy impossible.

The reform I have proposed will make all other reforms easier. It agrees with all that is desirable—politically, socially, or morally. It is simply carrying out, in letter and spirit, the self-evident truths set forth in the Declaration of Independence: that all people are created equal; that they are endowed by their Creator with certain unalienable rights; that among these are life, liberty, and the pursuit of happiness.

These rights are denied when the equal right to land is denied—for people can only live by using land. Equal political rights will not compensate for denying equal rights to the gifts of nature. Without equal rights to land, political liberty is merely the right to compete for employment at starvation wages.

We honor liberty in name and form. We set up statues and sound her praises. But we have not fully trusted her. And as we grow, her demands grow. She will have no half service. For liberty means justice, and justice is the natural law.

Some think liberty's mission is accomplished when she has abolished hereditary privileges and given the vote. They think she has no further relation to the everyday affairs of life. They have not seen her real grandeur. To them, her poets seem dreamers, her martyrs but fools. Yet it is not for an abstraction that people have toiled and died. In every age, the witnesses of liberty have stood forth.

We speak as if liberty were one thing, and virtue, wealth, knowledge, invention, and independence were others. But liberty is the source, the mother, the necessary condition, of all these. She is to virtue what light is to color; to wealth what sunshine is to grain; to knowledge what eyes are to sight.

In the history of every nation we may read the same truth. It is the universal law, the lesson of the centuries. Our primary social organization is a denial of justice. Allowing one person to own the land—on which and from which others must live—makes them slaves. The degree, or proportion, of slavery increases as material progress goes on.

This subtle alchemy is extracting the fruits of their labor from the masses in every civilized country, in ways they do not realize. It institutes a harder and more hopeless slavery in place of the one that has been destroyed. It brings tyranny out of political freedom, and must soon transform democratic institutions into anarchy. This is what turns the blessings of material progress into a curse, what crowds human beings into squalid tenement houses, and fills the prisons and brothels. This is what plagues people with want and consumes them with greed.

Civilization so based cannot continue. The eternal laws of the universe forbid it. The ruins of dead empires so testify. Justice herself demands that we right this wrong.

It is blasphemy to attribute the suffering and brutality that comes from poverty to the inscrutable decrees of Providence. It is not the Almighty, but we who are responsible for the vice and misery that fester amid our civilization. The Creator showers us with gifts — more than enough for all. But like swine scrambling for food, we tread them in the mire while we tear each other apart.

Suppose at God's command, for every blade of grass that now grows, two should spring up. And crops increase a hundred-fold. Would poverty be reduced? No—any benefit that would accrue would be temporary. The miraculous new powers could be utilized only through land. And while land is private property, the classes that currently monopolize the bounty of the Creator would monopolize all the new bounty.

Landowners alone would benefit. Rents would increase, but wages would still tend to the starvation point.

This is not merely a deduction of political economy—it is a fact of experience. We have seen it with our own eyes, in our own times.

The effect of invention and improvement on the production of wealth has been precisely the same as an increase in the fertility of nature.

What has been the result? Simply that landowners took all the gain. The wonderful discoveries and inventions of our century have neither increased wages nor lightened toil. The effect has simply been to make the few richer—and the many more helpless!

Can the gifts of the Creator be misappropriated with impunity? Can labor be robbed of its earnings, while greed rolls in wealth? Is it right that many should want, while a few are glutted? Turn to history! On every page we read that such wrongs never go unpunished. The nemesis that follows injustice never falters nor sleeps.

Look around today. Can this continue? The pillars of state tremble, and the foundations of society shudder from forces pent-up beneath. Great new powers, born of progress, have entered the world. They will compel us to a higher plane, or else they will overwhelm us.

The world is pulsing with unrest. There is an irreconcilable conflict between democratic ideas and the aristocratic organization of society. We cannot permit people to vote, then force them to beg. We cannot go on educating them, then refusing them the right to earn a living. We cannot go on chattering about inalienable human rights, then deny the inalienable right to the bounty of the Creator.

While there is still time, we may turn to justice. If we do, the dangers that threaten us will disappear. With want destroyed and greed transformed, equality will take the place of jealousy and fear. Think of the powers now wasted, the fields of knowledge yet to be explored, the possibilities that the wondrous inventions of this century only hint at. Who can presume the heights to which our civilization may soar?

Chapter 44

Conclusion: The Individual Life

MY TASK IS DONE. Yet behind the problems of social life lies the problem of individual life. This thought brought me cheer while writing this book, and it may be of cheer to those who, in their heart of hearts, take up the struggle.

The truth I have tried to show will not find easy acceptance. If that were possible, it would have been accepted long ago, and never obscured. But it will find friends who will suffer and toil for it; and if need be, die for it. This is the power of truth. Ultimately, it will prevail. But in our own times or even when any memory of us remains, who shall say?

Want and misery, ignorance and brutality are caused by unjust social institutions. Those who try to right them find bitterness and disappointment. So it has been in the past; so is it now. The most bitter thought is that the effort is hopeless, the sacrifice futile. This fear sometimes comes to even the best and bravest. How few of those who sow the seed will see it grow.

The standard of truth and justice has been raised many times. Over and over, it has been trampled down, often in blood. If the forces opposed to truth were weak, why would error so long prevail?

But for those who see the truth and would follow it, success is not the only thing. Lies and injustice often provide that! Must not truth and justice have something to give that is their own, by proper right?

When I set out on this inquiry, I had no theory to support, no conclusions to prove. Simply seeing the squalor and misery of a great city appalled and tormented me so that it would not let me rest. I constantly wondered what caused it and how it could be cured. Out of this, something came to me that I did not expect to find; a faith that was dead has been revived.

If we analyze the ideas that have destroyed the hope of an afterlife, we shall not find their source in physical science. Rather, they stem from certain teachings of political and social science that have permeated thought in all directions. These have their root in three doctrines: First, that population is larger than we can provide for. Second, that poverty, vice, and misery are the result of natural laws—and are actually the means by which civilization advances. Third, that human progress occurs through slow genetic changes.

These doctrines, which have generally been accepted as truth, reduce the individual to insignificance. They destroy the idea that there can be any regard for individual existence in the ordering of the universe. Or that there can be any recognition of what we would call moral qualities.

It is difficult to reconcile the concept of human immortality with the idea that nature constantly wastes people by bringing them into being where there is no room for them. It is impossible to reconcile the idea of an intelligent and beneficent Creator with the belief that wretchedness and degradation, which are the lot of such a large proportion of humankind, result from divine decrees. Finally, the idea that the human species is the result of slow modifications perpetuated by heredity irresistibly suggests the idea that the object of human existence is the life of the species, not the individual.

Our investigation has shown that these doctrines are false. Population does not tend to outrun subsistence. Poverty and human suffering do not spring from natural laws; they come from the ignorance and selfishness of people. Human progress does not come from changes in the nature of mankind. On the contrary, human nature, generally speaking, has always been the same.

Political economy has been called the dismal science. As currently taught, it is indeed hopeless and despairing. Yet, in its proper symmetry, political economy is radiant with hope.

When understood correctly, the laws governing the production and distribution of wealth demonstrate that poverty and injustice are not inevitable. On the contrary, a social state is possible in which poverty would be unknown. Then, the higher qualities of human nature would have an opportunity for full development.

Social development is not governed by divine providence nor merciless fate, but by natural law. Human will is the great determining factor. In the aggregate, the human condition is what we make of it. Economic law and moral law are essentially the same. The intellect grasps this truth after toilsome effort—but the moral sense reaches it quickly by intuition.

Science shows us the universality of law. The same law operates in the smallest divisions and in the immeasurable distances of space. An astronomer follows a moving body until it disappears from the range of the telescope. But this is merely the visible part of its orbit. Beyond sight, the law still holds. Centuries later, the astronomer's calculations are proven correct.

If we trace the laws that govern life in human society, we find they are the same in the largest community as in the smallest. We find that what seem to be, at first sight, divergences and exceptions are merely manifestations of the same principles. And we find that everywhere we can trace it, social law runs into and conforms with moral law. In the life of a community, justice infallibly brings its reward, injustice its punishment. But we cannot see this in individual life.

Human progress is not the improvement of human nature. The advances of civilization are not accumulated in the constitution of individuals, but in the constitution of society. They are not fixed and permanent, but may be lost at any time.

What then is the meaning of life inevitably bounded by death? To me, it seems intelligible only as an avenue to another life. Its facts can be explained only by a theory that must be expressed in myth and symbol. The Prince of Light still battles the Powers of Darkness.

To anyone who will hear it, the clarions of battle call. Strong souls and high endeavor, the world needs them now. Though truth and right seem often overwhelmed, we may not see it all. Shall we say that what passes from our sight passes into oblivion? Even animals have senses we do not. Far, far beyond our grasp, eternal laws must hold their sway.

Who Was Henry George?

By Agnes George de Mille

A HUNDRED YEARS AGO a young unknown printer in San Francisco wrote a book he called *Progress and Poverty*. He wrote after his daily working hours, in the only leisure open to him for writing. He had no real training in political economy. Indeed he had stopped schooling in the seventh grade in his native Philadelphia, and shipped before the mast as a cabin boy, making a complete voyage around the world. Three years later, he was halfway through a second voyage as able seaman when he left the ship in San Francisco and went to work as a journeyman printer. After that he took whatever honest job came to hand. All he knew of economics were the basic rules of Adam Smith, David Ricardo, and other economists, and the new philosophies of Herbert Spencer and John Stuart Mill, much of which he gleaned from reading in public libraries and from his own painstakingly amassed library. Marx was yet to be translated into English.

George was endowed for his job. He was curious and he was alertly attentive to all that went on around him. He had that rarest of all attributes in the scholar and historian—that gift without which all education is useless. He had mother wit. He read what he needed to read, and he understood what he read. And he was fortunate; he lived and worked in a rapidly developing society. George had the unique opportunity of studying the formation of a civilization—the change of an encampment into a thriving metropolis. He saw a city of tents and mud change into a fine town of paved streets and decent housing, with tramways and buses. And as he saw the beginning of wealth, he noted the first appearance of pauperism. He saw degradation forming as he saw the advent of leisure and affluence, and he felt compelled to discover why they arose concurrently.

The result of his inquiry, *Progress and Poverty,* is written simply, but so beautifully that it has been compared to the very greatest works of the English language. But George was totally unknown, and so no one would print his book. He and his friends, also printers, set the type themselves and ran off an author's edition which eventually found its way into the hands of a New York publisher, D. Appleton & Co. An English edition soon followed which aroused enormous interest. Alfred Russel Wallace, the English scientist and writer, pronounced it "the most remarkable and important book of the present century." It was not long before George was known internationally.

During his lifetime, he became the third most famous man in the United States, only surpassed in public acclaim by Thomas Edison and Mark Twain. George was translated into almost every language that knew print, and some of the greatest, most influential thinkers of his time paid tribute. Leo Tolstoy's appreciation stressed the logic of George's exposition: "The chief weapon against the teaching of Henry George was that which is always used against irrefutable and self-evident truths. This method, which is still being applied in relation to George, was that of hushing up .... People do not argue with the teaching of George, they simply do not know it." John Dewey fervently stressed the originality of George's work, stating that, "Henry George is one of a small number of definitely original social philosophers that the world has produced," and "It would require less than the fingers of the two hands to enumerate those who, from Plato down, rank with Henry George among the world's social philosophers." And Bernard Shaw, in a letter to my mother, Anna George, years later wrote, "Your father found me a literary dilettante and militant rationalist in religion, and a barren rascal at that. By turning my mind to economics he made a man of me...."

Inevitably he was reviled as well as idolized. The men who believed in what he advocated called themselves disciples, and they were in fact nothing less: working to the death, proclaiming, advocating, haranguing, and proselytizing the idea. But it was not implemented by blood, as was communism, and so was not forced on people's attention. Shortly after George's death, it dropped out of the political field. Once a badge of honor, the title, "Single Taxer," came into general disuse. Except in Australia and New Zealand, Taiwan and Hong Kong and scattered cities around the world, his plan of social action has been neglected while those of Marx, Keynes, Galbraith and Friedman have won great attention, and Marx's has been given partial implementation, for a time, at least, in large areas of the globe.

But nothing that has been tried satisfies. We, the people, are locked in a death grapple and nothing our leaders offer, or are willing to offer, mitigates our troubles. George said, "The people must think because the people alone can act."

We have reached the deplorable circumstance where in large measure a very powerful few are in possession of the earth's resources, the land and its riches and all the franchises and other privileges that yield a return. These positions are maintained virtually without taxation; they are immune to the demands made on others. The very poor, who have nothing, are the object of compulsory charity. And the rest—the workers, the middle-class, the backbone of the country—are made to support the lot by their labor.

We are taxed at every point of our lives, on everything we earn, on everything we save, on much that we inherit, on much that we buy at every stage of the manufacture and on the final purchase. The taxes are punishing, crippling, demoralizing. Also they are, to a great extent, unnecessary.

But our system, in which state and federal taxes are interlocked, is deeply entrenched and hard to correct. Moreover, it survives because it is based on bewilderment; it is maintained in a manner so bizarre and intricate that it is impossible for the ordinary citizen to know what he owes his government except with highly paid help. We support a large section of our government (the Internal Revenue Service) to prove that we are breaking our own laws. And we support a large profession (tax lawyers) to protect us from our own employees. College courses are given to explain the tax forms which would otherwise be quite unintelligible.

All this is galling and destructive, but it is still, in a measure, superficial. The great sinister fact, the one that we must live with, is that we are yielding up sovereignty. The nation is no longer comprised of the thirteen original states, nor of the thirty-seven younger sister states, but of the real powers: the cartels, the corporations. Owning the bulk of our productive resources, they are the issue of that concentration of ownership that George saw evolving, and warned against.

These multinationals are not American any more. Transcending nations, they serve not their country's interests, but their own. They manipulate our tax policies to help themselves. They determine our statecraft. They are autonomous. They do not need to coin money or raise armies. They use ours.

And in opposition rise up the great labor unions. In the meantime, the bureaucracy, both federal and local, supported by the deadly opposing factions, legislate themselves mounting power never originally intended for our government and exert a ubiquitous influence which can be, and often is, corrupt.

I do not wish to be misunderstood as falling into the trap of the socialists and communists who condemn all privately owned business, all factories, all machinery and organizations for producing wealth. There is nothing wrong with private corporations owning the means of producing wealth. Georgists believe in private enterprise, and in its virtues and incentives to produce at maximum efficiency. It is the insidious linking together of special privilege, the unjust outright private ownership of natural or public resources, monopolies, franchises, that produce unfair domination and autocracy.

The means of producing wealth differ at the root: some is thieved from the people and some is honestly earned. George differentiated; Marx did not. The consequences of our failure to discern lie at the heart of our trouble.

This clown civilization is ours. We chose this of our own free will, in our own free democracy, with all the means to legislate intelligently readily at hand. We chose this because it suited a few people to have us do so. They counted on our mental indolence and we freely and obediently conformed. We chose not to think.

Henry George was a lucid voice, direct and bold, that pointed out basic truths, that cut through the confusion which developed like rot. Each age has known such diseases and each age has gone down for lack of understanding. It is not valid to say that our times are more complex than ages past and therefore the solution must be more complex. The problems are, on the whole, the same. The fact that we now have electricity and computers does not in any way controvert the fact that we can succumb to the injustices that toppled Rome.

To avert such a calamity, to eliminate involuntary poverty and unemployment, and to enable each individual to attain his maximum potential, George wrote his extraordinary treatise a hundred years ago. His ideas stand: he who makes should have; he who saves should enjoy; what the community produces belongs to the community for communal uses; and God's earth, all of it, is the right of the people who inhabit the earth. In the words of Thomas Jefferson, "The earth belongs in usufruct to the living."

This is simple and this is unanswerable. The ramifications may not be simple but they do not alter the fundamental logic.

There never has been a time in our history when we have needed so sorely to hear good sense, to learn to define terms exactly, to draw reasonable conclusions. As George said, "The truth that I have tried to make clear will not find easy acceptance. If that could be, it would have been accepted long ago. If that could be, it would never have been obscured."

We are on the brink. It is possible to have another Dark Ages. But in George there is a voice of hope.

Agnes George de Mille was the granddaughter of Henry George. Famous in her own right as a choreographer and the founder of the Agnes de Mille Heritage Dance Theater, she received the Handel Medallion, New York's highest award for achievement in the arts. She was the author of thirteen books. This essay was published as the preface to the centenary edition of *Progress and Poverty* in 1979.

Index

The Robert Schalkenbach Foundation (RSF) was founded in 1925 to promote and develop the ideas of Henry George and to keep them in the public dialogue. George offered a response to the ideological polarization between collectivism and individualism, by presenting a social philosophy that reconciles the opposing features of capitalism and socialism.

RSF carries out its mission in several ways: 1) by publishing the works of Henry George and distributing the works of related authors, 2) by funding research to extend the ideas of Henry George in new contexts, and 3) by funding advocacy projects that apply his principles to specific situations.

RSF encourages those who are familiar with Henry George's ideas to approach the foundation through a one-page query letter about potential projects that might be of mutual interest. Please check our website for the most recent indication of the kinds of projects the foundation funds.

Robert Schalkenbach Foundation
90 John Street, Suite 501
New York NY 10038

Tel: 212-683-6424
Toll-free: 800-269-9555
Fax: 212-683-6454
www.schalkenbach.org
www.progressandpoverty.org
www.povertythinkagain.com
www.whyglobalpoverty.com

Books by Henry George

Published by the Robert Schalkenbach Foundation

Progress and Poverty — An Inquiry Into the Cause of Industrial Depressions and the Increase of Want with the Increase of Wealth... The Remedy
> Unabridged, 1992 (orig. 1879), 616 pp

Protection or Free Trade — An Examination of the Tariff Question, with Especial Regard to the Interests of Labor
> Unabridged, 1980 (orig. 1886), 335 pp
> Abridged, 2008 (orig. 1930), 172 pp.

Social Problems
> 1996 (orig. 1883), 310 pp

The Land Question — Viewpoint and Counter-viewpoint on the Need for Land Reform
> 2009 (orig. 1884), 328 pp

A Perplexed Philosopher — An Examination of Herbert Spencer's Utterances on the Land Question
> 1988 (orig. 1892), 276 pp

The Science of Political Economy
> Unabridged, 1992 (orig. 1898), 545 pp.
> Abridged, 2004, 284 pp.

Other works by Henry George and related authors are also distributed by the Foundation and/or published on its website. Free catalogue available on request, and online.
800-269-9555   www.schalkenbach.org

For Further Exploration

Tuition-free courses on the economics and social philosophy of Henry George are offered by:

Henry George School of Social Science, 121 East 30th Street, New York NY 10016. 212-889-8020
www.henrygeorgeschool.org

Henry George School of Philadelphia, 413 South 10th Street; Philadelphia, PA 19147. 215-922-4278
www.geocities.com/henrygeorgeschool

Henry George School of Chicago, 28 East Jackson #1004, Chicago IL 60604. 312-362-9302
www.hgchicago.org

Henry George School of Los Angeles, P.O.Box 55, Tujunga CA 94105. 818-352-4141
henrygeorgeschool@comcast.net

Henry George School of Northern California, 55 New Montgomery Street; San Francisco, CA 94105. 415-543-4294   www.henrygeorgesf.org

Correspondence courses (Internet or regular mail) based on the works of Henry George are offered by the Henry George Institute, 121 East 30th Street, New York, NY 10016   www.henrygeorge.org

A world-wide list of all Georgist organizations, with contact information, is available from the Council of Georgist Organizations, P. O. Box 57, Evanston IL 60204   www.progress.org/cgo